Using
MultiMate
Advantage™
2nd Edition

Kate Barnes

Que™ Corporation
Carmel, Indiana

Dedication

To Howard
my patient husband and business partner

Editors
Kathleen A. Johanningsmeier
Sandra Blackthorn

Acquisitions Editor
Pegg Kennedy

Technical Editors
Karla Ashmore
Dr. Melvin Prince

Production
Dan Armstrong
Jennifer Matthews
Cindy Phipps
Joe Ramon
Dennis Sheehan
Peter Tocco

Composed in Garamond and Que Digital
by Que Corporation

Cover designed by
Listenberger Design Associates

Screen reproductions in this book were created by means of the INSET program of Inset Systems, Inc.

Using MultiMate Advantage, 2nd Edition, is based on MultiMate Advantage II Version 1.0 and the earlier MultiMate Advantage Version 3.6, MultiMate Advantage Version 3.5, and MultiMate Professional Word Processor Series Versions 3.3.

About the Author

Kate Barnes

Kate Barnes is vice-president of Barnes Associates Software/Learning Systems, developers of software and self-instructional training materials.

Ms. Barnes received her B.A. with honors in Sociology and Education from the University of Iowa and her M.B.A. from the University of Phoenix.

For more than 12 years, Ms. Barnes has been involved in computer education. As the associate director of a large public agency, she established end-user training programs. Later, as a product developer for DELTAK, Inc., a subsidiary of Prentice-Hall, she developed self-instructional courses on computer-related topics. Ms. Barnes has designed and developed over 30 computer courses and contributes feature articles to computer magazines.

Table of Contents

3   Creating a Document 47

4 Editing a Document 63

5 The Cursor 69

8   Enhancing Document Appearance ... 113

11   Search and Replace 175

17   Key Procedures............................ 281

18   System and Document Defaults 289

Trademark Acknowledgments

Introduction

MultiMate Advantage II offers users the opportunity to insert graphics generated by other programs into MultiMate Advantage II documents; to integrate popular database program data into MultiMate Advantage II documents; to print line-by-line (like a typewriter) for small tasks such as addressing envelopes, typing short notes, or creating quick agendas; and to draw lines around blocks of text or create bar charts without a special graphics program. MultiMate Advantage II contains a thesaurus that reviews the definitions and alternate meanings of some 40,000 words and phrases, and special versions of MultiMate Advantage II will support the most popular Local Area Network systems.

MultiMate Advantage II's New Features

Here are the most striking new features of MultiMate Advantage II:

- Snake Column Mode, which permits you to wrap text from column to column in typical newspaper format

- Bound Column Mode, which allows you to create columns that vary in width and lie parallel to one another on your page

- Six-function math with percent and exponentiation

- Line and box drawing capabilities so that you can create a bar chart or highlight an important section of text by enclosing it within a box

- Automatic footnoting, endnoting, and section numbering

- Table of contents that can be generated from automatically numbered sections

- A thesaurus that you can use to check the definitions and alternate meanings of some 40,000 words, as well as the proper endings for plural words and verbs

- A link from the keyboard to the printer that makes it possible to type and print an envelope or a short message directly

- Pull-down menus and menu bypass

- The Undo Delete function

- Enhanced laser printer support

- Comments with comment suppression

- An expanded dictionary that includes both legal and medical terminology

- Additional file conversion formats

- Local Area Network support

- DOS access from within MultiMate Advantage II

Until now, learning to use MultiMate Advantage II's rich and varied available features could be time-consuming. Several manuals and reference guides that listed features, procedures, and helps were available, but a **single** clear and comprehensive guide for using the program was not available.

Using MultiMate Advantage fills the documentation void by introducing each MultiMate Advantage II feature in a straightforward fashion and supporting that introduction with actual application suggestions. The tips and tricks presented in *Using MultiMate Advantage* will help you learn **more** about MultiMate Advantage II **faster**.

About This Book

Chapter 1 discusses basic word-processing concepts, and it describes how MultiMate Advantage II resembles other programs and how it differs from other programs. If you have word-processing experience but are not familiar with MultiMate Advantage II, this comparison will help you understand MultiMate Advantage II's word-processing features and capabilities.

Chapter 2 describes how to install MultiMate Advantage II on both a floppy disk system and a hard disk system. The chapter offers hints on handling disks and provides instruction for using the menus and the keyboard to communicate with the MultiMate Advantage II program. Special notes for network users are included, and use of pull-down menus is covered.

Chapters 3 and 4 discuss creating and editing documents. Chapter topics include document parameters, naming documents for easy identification, and organizing documents for efficient use. The three screens that are used to create a document are introduced, as are the methods used to move quickly between menus. Creating and editing documents from the DOS prompt (Hot Start) are addressed.

Chapter 5 identifies the many options that are available for moving the cursor on the screen. These options range from cursor movements that are slow and precise to options that allow the cursor to leap from one section to another on a page—or even move one page at a time. The arrow keys, the backspace key, the tab key, other dedicated cursor-movement keys, word wrapping, and scrolling are explored.

Chapter 6 reviews the contents of the Status Line, demonstrates how the Format Line controls document appearance, explains why the Format Line is important, and suggests procedures for customizing the Format Line. Centering text and previewing what the printed document will look like are also covered.

Chapter 7 explores one of the most important word-processing capabilities: changing a document without retyping it. The chapter surveys inserting text; deleting short and long sections of text; highlighting text to be deleted, moved, or copied; and copying text into a document from a second document residing on either the same disk or another disk. Undoing deleted text and importing ASCII text are addressed.

Options that create more professional-looking documents are discussed in Chapter 8. Options such as automatic and manual underlining, symbols, hyphens, hard spaces, margins, print modes (from dark to light), print pitch, printer control, superscripts and subscripts, headers and footers, comments, and strikeout are included in this chapter.

In Chapter 9, pagination is explored. The topics included in this chapter are how to control the appearance of pages on your screen, how to end pages, how to create pages with any given number of lines, how to designate footnotes and endnotes, and how to include section numbers and table of contents designations.

Chapter 10 explains the procedures for saving and printing documents. Special notes for laser printer users are included. Chapter 11 covers the Search and Replace function and illustrates how it makes editing text easier.

Written for persons who use columns frequently in their work, Chapter 12 describes how to align numbers and text, using either the decimal point or the comma. Column insertion, deletion, move, and copy are covered, as well as Bound and Snake column options.

MultiMate Advantage II's horizontal and vertical column addition, subtraction, multiplication, division, percentage, and exponent capabilities are explained as the chapter illustrates features that provide MultiMate Advantage II with some of the power of spreadsheet software.

Chapter 13 describes disk operating system (DOS) procedures accessible from within MultiMate Advantage II. The chapter also explains how to print Document Summary screens, how to search them to identify documents with specific contents, and how to restore backed-up documents.

Chapters 14, 15, and 16 explain spell-checking, the thesaurus, and Merge Document. How to store frequently used keystroke sequences and how to create key procedures are discussed in Chapter 17.

Chapter 18 illustrates how system defaults, such as Format Lines and drive and document defaults, may be changed.

Chapter 19 points out how advanced utilities can be used to edit printer tables and key procedures, to convert documents for use with other programs, to change the color and shading of the screen, and to recover damaged documents.

Chapter 20 describes On-File™, a program for entering, sorting, and printing data. On-File offers you greater flexibility as you store and retrieve data. On-File converts data so that the data may be used with MultiMate Advantage II's Merge feature to create personalized form letters and documents.

In the appendixes, you will find a diagram of the MultiMate Advantage II keyboard and the menu map that is referred to throughout this book.

Using MultiMate Advantage II Version 1.0

Although this book is based on MultiMate Advantage II Version 1.0, you will find the information helpful with other versions of MultiMate. Other versions may display screens and prompts that differ from the figures presented in *Using MultiMate Advantage*, 2nd Edition.

1
MultiMate Advantage II

MultiMate Advantage II is professional word-processing software for IBM®
Personal Computers and IBM compatible computers. One of the most powerful and popular word-processing software packages available, MultiMate Advantage II continues to enjoy success because it is **easy to use**. In addition
to offering virtually all the features found on more expensive stand-alone word-
processing systems, Advantage II permits you to do more than just word
processing.

MultiMate Advantage II on the Personal Computer

MultiMate Advantage II uses a personal computer system that contains four
hardware components: a *keyboard*, a *monitor*, a *system unit (CPU)*, and a
printer.

The Keyboard

First-time users often fear that simply pressing the wrong key will cause the
computer to "blow up." The fear is unfounded. If you are a first-time MultiMate
Advantage II user and **if** you do happen to press the wrong key, a message
will appear on the monitor, describing the error that you have made. You
then have the opportunity to "undo" the error, using the message as a guide.

The Monitor

Similar in appearance to a television screen, the *monitor* is a screen on which
you view the *documents* you create and edit.

The System Unit

The system unit contains the computer's "brain," the *central processing unit (CPU)*, which controls your computer's functions and provides processing power and *memory*. Your computer may require *floppy disks* in its *disk drive(s)*, or it may use a *hard disk* that is permanently installed in the system. The MultiMate Advantage II program, as well as the documents you create, is stored in memory.

The Printer

The two most common printers are the *dot-matrix* printer, which prints characters composed of a series of dots, and the *letter-quality* printer, which uses a printing element called a *daisywheel* to print typewriter-like letters. Without a printer, you can create and edit documents, but you cannot generate a *hard copy* (paper copy) of your work.

How MultiMate Advantage II Works

It is wise to remember that the computer program is not an intelligent being—it is simply a tool designed to make your work easier. Used properly, MultiMate Advantage II will accept your directions and produce the results you want.

You can use MultiMate Advantage II to create anything you would normally create on a typewriter: reports, interoffice correspondence, form letters, business proposals, manuscripts, memos, and mailing lists. Word processing resembles typing in some ways, but, with word processing, you can simplify your writing and editing tasks to a degree not possible with conventional typewriters.

MultiMate Advantage II organizes your work into *documents* consisting of pages, just as you organize the letters and reports you prepare on the typewriter. MultiMate Advantage II can be compared to a conventional filing system because the computer *stores* your documents for later use. However, the computer stores your documents on magnetic disks rather than on paper in a file cabinet. One 5 1/4-inch disk can contain over one hundred pages of information. When you're ready to work on your memo or report, you simply *recall* that document from storage, and it is displayed on the screen.

By creating documents on the screen rather than on paper, you can make changes and corrections before printing the document. You'll never again have to retype a page or an entire document to make simple revisions; you can even make major corrections, like moving a whole paragraph to another page, with one or two keystrokes.

As you type a letter or report on a typewriter, you must be aware of the right margin, and, when you near the end of a line, you must decide whether to fit in the last word, hyphenate the word, or start the next line with that word. Then, when you reach the end of the line, you have to press the Return key to move to the following line.

Word processing eliminates these time-consuming steps with word wrapping. Word wrapping allows you to set the line length and type without pausing to press a Return key. When you reach the end of the line, the cursor automatically wraps around to the next line at the left margin. And, when you reach the end of a page, you do not have to stop and insert paper; you simply continue typing, allowing MultiMate Advantage II to do the work for you.

Most of us have experienced the situation in which the letter or report we've spent so long typing is complete . . . except for one "small" change. Without a word processor, a small change can involve hours of retyping.

MultiMate Advantage II allows you to make changes in your work by simply inserting, deleting, or typing over existing text. As changes are made, MultiMate Advantage II automatically *reformats* the margins, and you can then reprint the document. If you need to make changes throughout a document (replacing Ajax, Inc., with Ajax Company, for instance) your system will search for Ajax, Inc., and replace it with Ajax Company—automatically.

After you've finished working on a page of your document, MultiMate Advantage II automatically *saves* that page, a feature that minimizes the chance that your entire document will be "lost" if the power goes out or some other mishap occurs.

With MultiMate Advantage II, you can choose from several functions—separating pages, combining pages, and automatically repaginating—to reorganize the pages before you print your document.

When you use a typewriter, you are actually printing the "final" document as you type each character. With MultiMate Advantage II, printing the document is a separate operation. First, you create the document by typing in the text and making editing changes. As you create the document, you'll tell the computer to *save* (store) the entire document in memory. Then, when you are satisfied with the final version of your document, you'll give the computer instructions that will cause the printer to print the document.

How Is MultiMate Advantage II Different?

All word processors help you write, store, and print documents. But MultiMate Advantage II is **easy to use**—and that makes MultiMate Advantage II different from some other word-processing systems.

To create and edit documents on many word-processing systems, you must first memorize a complicated series of keystrokes. MultiMate Advantage II simplifies the process with *function keys* and *dedicated keys* performing editing functions, such as inserting characters, deleting characters and words, and creating page breaks. With MultiMate Advantage II, you can accomplish most traditional word-processing tasks by pressing only one or two keys.

MultiMate Advantage II's easy-to-read menu screens assist you as you create, edit, and print your documents. The menus are there to help you, but they won't "get in your way" as you become more experienced.

Prompts are another MultiMate Advantage II support feature. As you create and edit your documents, messages are displayed automatically on the screen. These messages may tell you what the system is doing or what to *enter* (type) so that the system can complete your work. For instance, when you tell the computer to move text from one page of your document to another, the prompt MOVE WHAT? appears on the screen. When you finish defining the text to be moved, MultiMate Advantage II prompts TO WHERE? Prompts help you keep track of what function your computer is *executing* (carrying out)—they act as your personal "reminders" of your next step.

Spell-checking, document merging, library creation, file conversion, data handling, and mathematical functions are just a few of the advanced capabilities that are standard features of MultiMate Advantage II. These capabilities either are not available on most other word processors or must be purchased at an additional cost.

MultiMate Advantage II's spell-checking feature challenges the spelling of all the words in your documents and identifies every word that does not appear in its dictionary. You can then correct the misspelled words yourself (if you are sure of the correct spelling) or ask the computer to produce a list of correct spellings before you make changes.

A nice feature of the MultiMate Advantage II dictionary is that you can make it more complete and helpful by adding words that are frequently used in your profession or words that are particularly troublesome for you.

The document merging feature permits you to create individualized form letters and to combine mailing lists. MultiMate Advantage II also allows you to create *libraries*, each containing such information as an address, a legal phrase, or a salutation that you include in letters and reports over and over. To create the library, you enter the data (the address, phrase, or sentences) once and program a specific key. (You'll find out how to do it in Chapters 15 and 17.) Now, when you need to include that library information in your document, you are able to recall it with one or two keystrokes instead of retyping it again and again.

The following are special MultiMate Advantage II features:

- The math function

- File-conversion capabilities for WANG®, IBM DisplayWriter™, Xerox™, DECmate II™, and other software

- On-File data manipulation features not available in other word processors

- MultiMate Advantage II versions that support the most popular Local Area Networks so that MultiMate Advantage II information may be shared among a network of users

In addition to all of the features we have discussed, Ashton-Tate® provides full support with technical personnel available by telephone, a free electronic bulletin board, a listing of user groups throughout the country, and training materials and resources. There is a charge for these services.

MultiMate Advantage II's History

MultiMate was designed and developed for Connecticut Mutual Life Insurance Company, a large financial institution. The company was interested in a WANG-like word-processing system for IBM Personal Computers that would provide greater interface flexibility. They needed a system that would allow their employees to insert standard material with a single keystroke and merge mailing list information with form letters.

The company contracted with W. H. Jones and Associates to create the package; with that contract, a new software company was born. W. H. Jones founded SoftWord Systems, Inc., to market Word Mate (MultiMate's original name) nationally. As the popularity of MultiMate software grew, SoftWord Systems, Inc., realized that the product name was more widely known than the company name.

Because of the recognition accorded their product, SoftWord Systems, Inc., changed its name to Multimate International and expanded the line of software to include MultiMate On-File and GraphLink. Ashton-Tate acquired Multimate International, and the Advantage II system has continued to expand in feature and function.

2
Getting Started

Before you can begin using MultiMate Advantage II, you must install it on your computer. You'll need the following:

- An IBM Personal Computer, an IBM PS/2 computer, or an IBM compatible computer with at least two double-sided disk drives or one double-sided disk drive and a hard disk. A hard disk is recommended.

- PC DOS or MS-DOS, Version 2.0 or later

- A minimum of 384K memory

- At least 11 blank, double-sided, 5 1/4-inch diskettes, or 6 blank, double-sided, 3 1/2-inch diskettes

- The MultiMate word-processing disks

- MultiMate Advantage II documentation

Remember, the IBM Personal Computer or IBM compatible computer must be able to use *double-sided* disks. Also, keep in mind that the minimum memory requirements previously specified are for IBM Personal Computer products; some IBM compatibles may require more memory. If you are using an IBM compatible, verify its memory requirements with your computer dealer.

The 3 1/2-inch disks have greater capacity than 5 1/4-inch disks; therefore, one 3 1/2-inch MultiMate Advantage II disk may contain the same information as two 5 1/4-inch disks. Consequently, the disks are labeled differently.

The 5 1/4-inch disks are labeled as follows:

Boot Disk
System Disk
On-File Utility
On-File Boot/System
Dictionary/Speller Disk
Thesaurus Disk
Printer Tables Disk

11

Utilities
Beginning
Conversions 1
Conversions 2

The 3 1/2-inch disks are labeled as follows:

Boot/System Disk
On-File Boot/System and Utility Disk
Dictionary/Speller and Thesaurus Disk
Printer Tables and Utilities Disk
Beginning
Conversions 1 and 2

Installation instructions also differ between the 5 1/4- and the 3 1/2-inch diskettes. As you install MultiMate, be sure to follow the appropriate instructions for the size of disks you are using.

Using Disks

Whether you use 5 1/4-inch or 3 1/2-inch diskettes, you should handle them carefully. Either kind of disk can be damaged by exposure to magnetic fields or to extreme heat or cold. The 5 1/4-inch diskettes are especially vulnerable to damage because they are not as well-protected as 3 1/2-inch diskettes.

Disks are magnetic, so placing them near a magnetic field can damage them. Paper-clip containers, copyholders, memo boards, and other small office tools often contain magnets. X rays also can disturb a disk's magnetic field. If you take your disks with you while traveling by air, pass them by hand through the security check rather than risk having them damaged by security equipment.

Another potential hazard is concentrated fluorescent light; as a rule, it's best not to store disks within one foot of fluorescent light fixtures. And because temperature extremes can damage disks, you must be careful that your disks aren't left lying in direct sunlight, forgotten in your car in freezing weather, or stored near a heat source. Generally, temperatures that range between 50 and 125 degrees Fahrenheit are safe for disks.

If you use 5 1/4-inch diskettes, *handle them with care*. Simply touching the recording surface of a disk can destroy the information stored on that disk. The disk's jacket protects most of this surface, but some of the recording surface is still visible through the oval holes. Be sure to handle disks by the edges nearest the label.

To change labels on 5 1/4-inch diskettes, place the new label over the old one. Don't try to remove the old label. You should write on the label before placing it on the disk, but, if you must write on the label after you affix it to the disk, use a felt-tip pen (**never** a pencil or ballpoint pen).

Never bend or staple the disk's protective jacket.

If you tuck your disks inside the pages of a book, you may damage the recording surfaces of the disks. Placing objects on top of your disks can cause scratches on them. Dropping food or beverages on your disks may render them useless. Even cigarette smoke particles can cause disk damage.

When you are not using your disks, put them in the paper envelopes designed to protect them from dust and store them upright in a hardcover box to prevent them from being crushed or bent.

To be certain that you are inserting your 5 1/4-inch disk into the disk drive properly, look at figure 2.1.

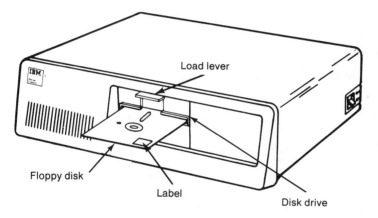

Fig. 2.1. Inserting a 5 1/4-inch diskette.

1. Check to see that the load lever is in the open position.

2. Hold the disk with the label end toward you and facing up.

3. Place the disk into the drive and carefully push the disk toward the rear of the disk drive. Never force the disk into the drive.

4. Close the disk drive door by pushing down on the load lever until it clicks shut. If the disk drive door won't close easily, remove the disk and start over.

To make sure you are inserting your 3 1/2-inch disk properly, look at figure 2.2.

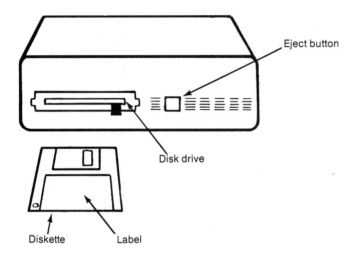

Fig. 2.2. Inserting a 3 1/2-inch diskette.

1. Hold the diskette so that the label is facing up and is toward your body.

2. Push the diskette into the drive until the diskette stops.

Installing MultiMate Advantage II Using Dual Floppy Drives

If you have dual floppy drives (and no hard disk), use the following process to install MultiMate Advantage II. If your computer has a hard disk, skip this section and read the section called *Installing MultiMate Advantage II Using a Hard Disk.*

Before you install MultiMate Advantage II, you must load DOS and run the ID program.

Loading DOS

Follow these steps to load DOS into your system's memory:

1. Insert your DOS disk into drive A (the left drive).

2. Turn the computer **ON**.

3. Type the **date** (see table 2.1).

4. Press **Return**.

Table 2.1
Date Entry

Date	Becomes
May 26, 1988	05-26-88
October 30, 1987	10-30-87
February 2, 1988	02-02-88

5. Type the **time** (see table 2.2).

Table 2.2
Time Entry

Time	Becomes
5:00 p.m.	17:00
8:15 a.m.	08:15
1:45 p.m.	13:45

6. Press **Return**.

After the DOS prompt A> appears on your screen,

7. Insert the MultiMate Advantage II 5 1/4-inch Boot diskette or the 3 1/2-inch Boot/System diskette into drive A.

   (Before you begin, make certain the diskette is not write-protected. If an adhesive tab covers the notch on the edge of your 5 1/4-inch disk, remove it. If the small, square opening at the corner of the 3 1/2-inch disk is open, move the slider so that the hole is covered.)

Running the ID Program

Before you can run MultiMate Advantage II, you must run a program that identifies you (or your company) as the owner of your copy of MultiMate Advantage II. Follow these steps and make sure you follow the appropriate instructions for 5 1/4-inch or 3 1/2-inch disks.

1. After the A> prompt, type **id**

2. Press **Return**.

3. The ID screen appears.

4. Enter your company's name, your serial number as it appears on the MultiMate Advantage II Boot diskette label, and your name.

5. Press **F10**.

6. When the information is entered correctly, this message appears:

   `Is the information you entered correct? (Y/N)`

7. If the information is correct, press **Y**.

   If any information is not acceptable, a message will appear. Carefully reenter the information and proceed.

8. When the ID process is complete, this message appears:

   `ID program complete--press any key`

9. Press **any key** to return to DOS.

Copying the Boot Diskette

Now you need to make a copy of the MultiMate Advantage II Boot diskette. Begin by preparing a blank diskette:

1. Remove the Boot (or Boot/System) diskette from drive A and insert the DOS diskette again.

2. Type **format b:**

Whether you type in uppercase or lowercase is unimportant; the computer recognizes both forms. However, you must be sure that every letter and space you type is exactly as you see it in the previous command.

3. Press **Return**.

This message is displayed on your screen:

   `Insert new diskette for drive B`
   `and strike ENTER when ready`

4. Label a disk. Use *MultiMate Advantage II Boot Working Disk* for a 5 1/4-inch disk or *MultiMate Advantage II Boot/System Working Disk* for a 3 1/2-inch disk.

5. Insert the disk into drive B.

6. Press **Enter**.

After a short wait (about a minute), you should see this message on your screen:

```
Formatting...Format complete
     XXXXXX bytes total disk space
     XXXXXX bytes available on disk
     XXXXXX bytes used by system
Format another (Y/N)?
```

7. Press **N**.

8. Press **Return**.

9. Remove the DOS disk from drive A and again insert the Multimate Advantage II Boot (or Boot/System) diskette.

10. Type **copy a:*.* b:**

11. Press **Return**.

Creating or Modifying a CONFIG.SYS File

Before using MultiMate Advantage II, you must create or modify the CONFIG.SYS file on your DOS diskette.

1. Remove the Boot (or Boot/System) diskette from drive A and insert the DOS diskette.

2. Type **dir config.sys**

3. Press **Return**.

If your screen displays the message

```
File not found
```

1. Type **copy con config.sys**

2. Press **Return**.

3. Type **files=20**

4. Press **Return**.

5. Press **Ctrl-Z**.

6. Press **Return**.

Your screen will display this message:

```
1 file(s) copied
```

7. Hold down **Ctrl-Alt** and press **Del** to reboot the system.

If the system does find a CONFIG.SYS file after you type *dir config.sys*,

    1. Type **type config.sys**

    2. Press **Return**.

Several lines will appear on your screen. Look for this line:

    `Files=20`

If the value is 20 or greater, you are ready to move on. If the value is less than 20,

    1. Type **copy con config.sys**

    2. Press **Return**.

Reenter each line that was displayed after you entered *type config.sys* except the *Files=nn* line and press Return at the end of each line. For the *Files=nn* line,

    1. Type **Files=20**

    2. Press **Return**.

After you have typed all the lines,

    1. Press **Ctrl-Z**.

    2. Press **Return**.

This message will appear on your screen:

    `1 Files(s) copied`

    3. Press **Ctrl-Alt-Del** to reboot the system.

Creating the System Working Disk

If you are installing 3 1/2-inch diskettes, skip to the next section. If you are installing 5 1/4-inch disks, follow these steps to create a working copy of the System disk.

    1. Insert into drive A the disk labeled System diskette.

    2. Next, label a new disk *System Working Disk*.

    3. Insert the newly labeled disk into drive B.

After the A> prompt appears,

    4. Type **diskcopy a: b:**

    5. Press **Return**.

6. Press **any key**. (The source and target disks are already inserted.)

Copying Printer Files

To be certain that your printer files are copied to the System disk, look in Appendix D of the *MultiMate Advantage II Reference Manual* to identify the PAT, SAT, and/or CWT files that you'll need to work with your printer.

Once you have identified the files,

1. Remove the System (or Boot/System) diskette from drive A and insert the Printer Tables diskette.

2. Type **printer**

3. Press **Return**.

4. The Printer Installation screen appears, and the name of each printer supported appears.

5. Enter **b:**

6. Press **F9**.

7. Mark with your cursor the name of the printer you want to use.

Press *PgUp* or *PgDn* to move between printer screens. Use the arrow keys to move between printer names. Or you may type the first letter of the printer name.

8. When the cursor is on the printer of choice, press **Return**.

9. Continue to highlight the names of all printers you will use.

10. Press **F10**.

11. When the message Press any key appears, press **any key**.

12. Press **Esc** to return to DOS.

Creating the Remaining Working Disks

1. Insert the 5 1/4-inch Dictionary/Speller diskette or the 3 1/2-inch Dictionary/Speller and Thesaurus disk into drive A.

2. Label a disk *Speller/Dictionary Working Disk* or *Speller/ Dictionary and Thesaurus Working Disk* and insert it into drive B.

After the A> prompt appears,

    3. Type **diskcopy a: b:**

    4. Press **Return**.

Repeat steps 1 through 4 to create the remaining working copies of the original diskettes. Here are the remaining 5 1/4-inch disks to be copied:

    On-File Utility
    On-File Boot/System
    Thesaurus Disk
    Utilities
    Conversions 1
    Conversions 2

Here are the remaining 3 1/2-inch disks to be copied:

    On-File Boot/System and Utility Disk
    Printer Tables and Utilities Disk
    Conversions 1 and 2

Setting Up a Virtual Disk

Because MultiMate Advantage II is a page-oriented word-processing system, it writes to the disk every time you change pages. Depending on your computer, this process can take up to eight seconds every time you move from one page to another.

To help you move more quickly between pages (as well as to help you perform other functions more quickly), you may want to take advantage of the DOS VDISK.SYS device command available with DOS 3.0. To use the VDISK.SYS command with MultiMate Advantage II, you must have 128K more RAM memory than the 384K required by MultiMate Advantage II.

VDISK stands for "virtual disk." A virtual disk is nothing more than RAM memory that has been set aside as an extra drive for you to work from. You can use the virtual disk to create a *drive C* in RAM memory.

You can create other virtual drives as well. To do this, you need only to alter the CONFIG.SYS file that you created, which contains the *Files=20* statement.

Here is the procedure:

    1. Insert the DOS disk into drive A.

    2. Type **copy con: a:config.sys**

    3. Press **Return**.

4. Type **files=20**

5. Press **Return**.

6. Type **device** = **vdisk.sys**

7. Press **Return**.

8. Press **Ctrl-Z**.

This message appears on the screen:

```
^Z

1 File(s) copied
```

You have created a CONFIG.SYS file that will automatically set aside default values of 64K RAM memory for a virtual drive C, using the default values of 128 sectors with the capability of creating 64 files.

For MultiMate Advantage II to recognize drive C, you will need to alter the drive defaults. Boot MultiMate Advantage II and then follow these steps:

1. Type **7** (System and Document Defaults from the MultiMate Advantage II Main Menu).

2. Type **2** (Edit Drive Defaults).

3. Type **F** under the letter C at the Installed Drive Table field.

4. Press **F10**.

You may now use the virtual drive C just as you would drive B. You may use the DOS commands to copy to and from drive C. You may also use MultiMate Advantage II commands to copy documents to and from drive C.

Because the virtual drive C resides in RAM memory, the contents of it are lost if you reboot the system, turn off the computer, or lose power.

You must remember to use the DOS COPY command to copy files from drive C to drive B. For example, suppose that your file name is *filename.doc*. After the DOS prompt A>, type

copy c:filename.doc b:

To copy your files, you may also use the MultiMate Advantage II copy command described in Chapter 13.

For dual floppy disk system users, VDISK makes MultiMate Advantage II perform at top efficiency. Functions that previously took up to eight seconds to execute now do so without delay.

Installing MultiMate Advantage II Using a Hard Disk

To install MultiMate Advantage II on a hard disk system such as the IBM PC XT or AT, you must do the following:

- Run the ID Program.
- Install DOS (the Disk Operating System) on the hard disk, if DOS is not already installed.
- Create a *path* to DOS.
- Create a MultiMate Advantage II *subdirectory*.
- Copy MultiMate Advantage II.
- *Configure* the system.

If your computer uses a hard disk, use the following process to install MultiMate Advantage II.

Loading DOS

Begin by starting your computer. If DOS already is installed on the computer, start the machine in the usual manner. If DOS is not already installed, follow these steps:

1. Place the DOS diskette into drive A (the left drive).
2. Turn the computer **ON**.
3. If necessary, type in the **date** and **time** and press **Return** after each.

Running the ID Program

Before you can run MultiMate Advantage II, you must run a program that identifies you (or your company) as the owner of your copy of MultiMate Advantage II. Follow these steps and make sure you follow the appropriate instructions for 5 1/4-inch or 3 1/2-inch disks.

1. Place the 5 1/4-inch MultiMate Advantage II Boot diskette (or the 3 1/2-inch Boot/System diskette) into drive A.

   (Before you begin, make certain the diskette is not write-protected. If an adhesive tab covers the notch on the edge of your 5 1/4-inch disk, remove it. If the small, square opening at the corner of the 3 1/2-inch disk is open, move the slider so that the hole is covered.)

2. Type **a:** and press **Return**.

3. After the A⟩, type **id**

4. Press **Return**.

5. The ID screen appears.

6. Enter your company's name, the serial number that appears on the MultiMate Advantage II Boot diskette label, and your name.

7. Press **F10**.

8. When the information is entered correctly, this message appears:

   Is the information you entered correct? (Y/N)

9. If the information is correct, press **Y**.

If any information is not acceptable, a message will appear. Carefully reenter the information and proceed.

10. When the ID process is complete, this message appears:

    ID program complete--press any key

11. Press **any key** to return to DOS.

Using Directories

To use MultiMate Advantage II on a hard disk system, you must understand directories. A *directory* is a list of the files stored on a disk. All directories are organized under a *root* or main directory that lists files and the names of other directories. These "other" directories are called *subdirectories*. Sub-directories can contain even more directories. Figure 2.3 illustrates what the directory structure looks like.

The directory structure permits you to organize your disk just as you would organize a cabinet full of files. By placing groups of related files in their own directories, you can move to a specific directory to search for a file without looking through a number of files randomly. As an example, you might store in a subdirectory called *MEMO* all the memos you create, and sales letters might be stored in a subdirectory called *SALES*.

The root directory holds a maximum of 112 files. You should place DOS in its own directory and give MultiMate Advantage II its own subdirectory as well.

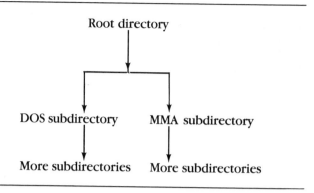

Fig. 2.3. Tree-structured directory.

Copying the Disk Operating System (DOS)

If DOS is already installed on your hard disk, skip to the section *Creating a MultiMate Advantage II Subdirectory*. If DOS is not installed, follow the instructions in this section and the next section to place a copy of DOS in its own subdirectory on the hard disk.

First, make certain that you are in the root directory and that the DOS prompt C> appears on your screen.

If you aren't sure that you are in the root directory,

1. Type **cd**

2. Press **Return**.

To create a DOS subdirectory,

1. Type **md\dos**

2. Press **Return**.

The *MD (Make Directory)* command creates a subdirectory called DOS.

Enter the subdirectory:

1. Type **cd\dos**

2. Press **Return**.

You are now in the DOS subdirectory.

To copy the DOS files to the subdirectory you've created on the hard disk,

1. Insert your DOS disk into drive A.

2. Type **copy a:*.* c:**

3. Press **Return**.

As the system copies files, the screen displays the names of the copied files. When the copying process is complete, the DOS prompt C> reappears on the screen.

Now move back to the root directory so that you can create a subdirectory for MultiMate Advantage II.

1. Type **cd**

2. Press **Return**.

Creating a Path to the Disk Operating System

These instructions explain how to create a path to the DOS subdirectory. This path enables you to use DOS with your MultiMate Advantage II directory.

After the C> prompt appears,

1. Type **cd**

2. Press **Return**.

Be sure that you type the *backslash* (\) rather than the *forward slash* (/) in this next line:

3. Type **path c:\dos**

4. Press **Return**.

5. Type **copy con: autoexec.bat**

6. Press **Return**.

7. Type in the word **date**.

8. Press **Return**.

9. Type in the word **time**.

10. Press **Return**.

11. Type **path c:\dos**

12. Press **Return**.

13. Press **Ctrl-Z**.

This message appears on your screen:

^Z

14. Press **Return**.

This message is displayed on your screen:

1 File(s) copied
C>

Creating a MultiMate Advantage II Subdirectory

Remember, to use MultiMate Advantage II, you must first install DOS on your hard disk. If DOS has not been installed on your hard disk, follow the procedure outlined in the section called *Copying the Disk Operating System*. If DOS has been installed on your hard disk but MultiMate Advantage II has not, you must create a new subdirectory and copy MultiMate Advantage II to it.

To return to the root directory,

1. Type **cd**

2. Press **Return**.

To make the subdirectory named *MMA* for MultiMate Advantage II,

1. Type **md\mma**

2. Press **Return**.

To enter the MultiMate Advantage II subdirectory,

1. Type **cd\mma**

2. Press **Return**.

The *CD (Change Directory)* command takes you to the *MMA* subdirectory.

To copy the MultiMate Advantage II file diskette Boot to the *MMA* subdirectory on your hard disk,

1. Insert the Boot diskette.

2. Type **copy a:*.* c:**

3. Press **Return**.

As the system copies MultiMate Advantage II files, the screen displays the file names. When the copying process is complete, the C> prompt appears. Remove the Boot (or Boot/System) diskette. If you are installing MultiMate from 5 1/4-inch disks, repeat steps 1 through 3 to copy each of these disks:

System Disk
Dictionary/Speller Disk
Thesaurus Disk
Utilities
Conversions 1
Conversions 2
On-File Utility
On-File Boot/System

If you are installing MultiMate from 3 1/2-inch disks, repeat steps 1 through 3 to copy each of these disks:

Boot/System Disk
On-File Boot/System and Utility Disk
Dictionary/Speller and Thesaurus Disk
Printer Tables and Utilities Disk
Conversions 1 and 2

Copying Printer Files

To be certain that your printer files are copied to the System disk, look in Appendix D of the Reference Manual to identify the PAT, SAT, and/or CWT files you'll need to work with your printer. Once you have identified the files,

1. Insert the Printer Tables diskette into drive A.

2. Type **a:**

3. Press **Return**.

4. Type **printer**

5. Press **Return**.

6. The Printer Installation screen appears, and the name of each printer supported appears.

7. Enter **c:\mm**

8. Press **F9**.

9. Mark the name of the printer you want to use with your cursor.

Press *PgUp* or *PgDn* to move between printer screens. Use the arrow keys to move between printer names. Or you may type the first letter of the printer name.

10. When the cursor is on the printer of choice, press **Return**.

11. Continue to highlight the names of all printers you will use.

12. Press **F10**.

13. When the message Press any key appears, press **any key**.

14. Press **Esc** to return to DOS.

You may create subdirectories within your MultiMate Advantage II directory. For example, you can store notes in a subdirectory called NOTES. The NOTES subdirectory can be created like this:

1. Type **cd\mma**

2. Press **Return**.

(You are now in the MultiMate Advantage II directory *MMA*.)

1. Type **md notes**

2. Press **Return**.

You have created the subdirectory NOTES, which can be accessed while you use MultiMate Advantage II. To return to the MultiMate Advantage II directory,

1. Type **cd\mma**

2. Press **Return**.

Configuring Your System

If you are using DOS Version 2.0 or greater, you must place a CONFIG.SYS file in the root directory.

1. Type **cd**

2. Press **Return**.

3. Type **dir config.sys**

4. Press **Return**.

If your screen displays the message

File not found

1. Type **copy con config.sys**

2. Press **Return**.

3. Type **files=20**

4. Press **Return**.

5. Press **Ctrl-Z**.

6. Press **Return**.

Your screen will display this message:

```
1 file(s) copied
```

7. Press **Ctrl-Alt-Del** to reboot the system.

If the system *does* find a CONFIG.SYS file after you type *dir config.sys*,

1. Type **type config.sys**

2. Press **Return**.

Several lines will appear on your screen. Look for this line:

```
Files=20
```

If the value is 20 or greater, you are ready to move on. If the value is less than 20,

1. Type **copy con config.sys**

2. Press **Return**.

Reenter each line that was displayed after you entered *type config.sys* except the *Files=nn* line and press Return at the end of each line. For the *Files=nn* line,

1. Type **Files=20**

2. Press **Return**.

After you have typed all of the lines,

1. Press **Ctrl-Z**.

2. Press **Return**.

This message will appear on your screen:

```
1 File(s) copied
```

3. Press **Ctrl-Alt-Del** to reboot the system.

Modifying Drive Defaults

MultiMate Advantage II is set up to have the following drive defaults:

Drive C   System drive   The drive on which the system program
is stored

Drive C   Document drive   The drive on which your documents are
stored

Drive C   Library drive   The drive on which your library
documents are stored

Drive C   Dictionary drive   The drive on which your dictionary is
stored

If you have installed MultiMate Advantage II for use without a hard disk, you must modify these drive defaults to look like those in figure 2.4. For instructions on how to do this, see Chapter 18.

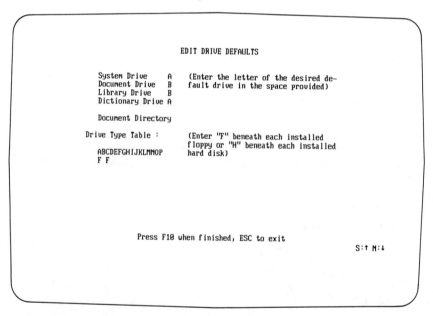

Fig. 2.4. Floppy disk drive defaults.

For the examples throughout this book, an assumption is that drive C stores the MultiMate Advantage II program files. If your system does not have a hard disk, or if you do not store MultiMate Advantage II and your documents on drive C, then you must substitute the letter of the drive you use for the c: in the examples.

Formatting Document Disks

Before you can use MultiMate Advantage II, you must format the disks that will hold the documents you create. If you have a dual floppy disk system, your documents are saved on the disk in drive B. If you have a hard disk system, the documents you create are stored on the hard disk; however, even with a hard disk system, you'll need formatted document disks so that you can make backup copies of your work.

The disks you select for formatting may be disks that never have been used or disks that contain outdated information. The formatting procedure erases any documents on the disk and prepares it to receive and store the data you write to it. Formatting tells the computer where to place information on the disk and sets up directions for finding the information during retrieval.

Use the procedure described in the following sections to format your document disks.

Formatting Document Disks on a Dual Floppy Disk Drive System

If you have two floppy drives, use these instructions to format document disks; if you have a hard disk, skip to the next set of instructions. Format several disks at one time, and you'll avoid running out of readily available storage space.

With the DOS diskette in drive A, and after the A> prompt appears, proceed as follows (be sure to type the commands exactly as they appear here):

1. Type **format b:**

The screen displays this message:

```
Insert new disk for drive B:
and strike any key when ready
```

2. Insert a disk into drive B.

3. Press **any key**.

For about one minute, the screen will display this message:

```
Formatting...
```

Then, these lines appear:

```
Formatting...Format complete
       XXXXX bytes total disk space
       XXXXX bytes available on disk
Format another (Y/N)?
```

Type *Y* (Yes) to format another disk or *N* (No) if you have completed formatting your disks.

    4. Press **Return**.

Formatting Document Disks on a Hard Disk System

Use this procedure to format document disks on a hard disk system.

When the C> prompt appears,

    1. Type **format a:**

    2. Press **Return**.

The screen displays this message:

```
Insert new disk for drive A:
and strike any key when ready
```

    3. Insert a disk into drive A.

    4. Press **any key**.

For about one minute, your screen displays this message:

```
Formatting...
```

Then, these lines appear:

```
Formatting...Format complete
       XXXXXX bytes total disk space
       XXXXXX bytes available on disk
Format another (Y/N)?
```

Type *Y* to format another disk or *N* if you are done formatting, and press Return. When formatting your disks, be certain that you indicate **a:** after the format command in step 1. Specifying *drive A* assures you that you don't format or erase *drive C* (your hard disk drive) in error.

Using MultiMate on a Local Area Network

If you are not a Local Area Network supervisor, skip this section and read the next section, which is called *Booting MultiMate Advantage II on a Dual Floppy Disk System*.

A Local Area Network (LAN) allows you to store one copy of MultiMate Advantage II that network users can access by a *network server* (see fig. 2.5).

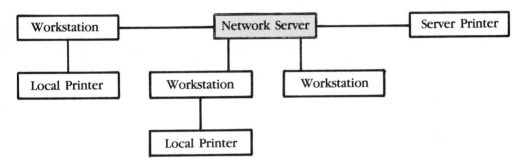

Fig. 2.5. Typical Local Area Network arrangement.

The network system supervisor typically places MultiMate Advantage II in a common storage area on the network server and sets up individual user dictionaries.

Before assigning shared directories and resources to users, the system supervisor should consult with users to determine which common and shared dictionaries they need, as well as which resources they need for access to files, key procedures, libraries, and printers.

LANs require the special Local Area Network version of MultiMate Advantage II. The "stand-alone" version of MultiMate Advantage II will not work in a network environment. And as you might expect, the LAN version of MultiMate Advantage II will not work on a single-user system.

Your LAN requires a version of MultiMate Advantage II designed specifically for *your* network system. MultiMate Advantage II LAN packages are not interchangeable, and installation procedures vary between network brands.

You must follow the installation procedures included in your network software package. Generally, installation involves these basic steps:

1. Write the MultiMate Advantage II system files to a subdirectory on the network server hard disk.

2. Set up the MultiMate Advantage II drive default, the printer default, and the system defaults.

    On the Modify System Defaults screen, type *N* in response to the screen prompt Keep Documents Closed for Safety. Doing so allows only one user to access a file at a time. If a second user tries to access the file, this error message may appear:

    ```
    Network Error:  file in use during OPEN File=d:
    filename.doc Abort,  Retry, Ignore?
    ```

    Your LAN manual tells you how to respond to this message.

    Choose *Y* if you want multiple users to be able to access individual files at the same time. You may want to test multiple access to make certain that your network handles multiple access without error.

3. Create a directory and *logon file* for each user. Shared directories should be created as needed.

4. Write the user files and custom dictionaries to the appropriate directories. You may copy *upsysd.sys* to the drives to permit users to change system defaults.

5. Show each user how to log on and how to access MultiMate Advantage II. Give each user a list of the drives he or she may use and explain how those drives should be used. Provide users with information specific to the particular LAN system in use.

The functions *up* and *mm* work the same on the LAN system as on a stand-alone system with a few special printing considerations. Chapter 10 provides information about printing. Hot Print and Typewriter Mode work only with a workstation's local printer. The Print Parameters For Document screen includes this network printer option:

```
P(arallel)/S(erial)/L(ist)/A(uxiliary)/F(ile)/N(etwork)
```

P, S, L, and *A* send the print to a local printer attached to a workstation. *F* creates an ASCII file. *N* sends the print to the network server printer. The Printer Queue Control screen includes a Network File Status:

```
File Status: Printing  Network  Hold  Errors will Blink
```

When the document is sent to the network's printer queue, the document file name appears underscored on the Printer Queue Control screen. Once the document is in the network printer queue, it can be removed from the queue but not *placed on hold, moved in the queue*, or *restarted*. If you place a document on hold when it is partially in the network printer queue, the pages sent will print, and the entire document will be placed on hold.

You may want to include a banner (see fig. 2.6) printed at the beginning of each document to identify the user name, file name, directory path, print station, and time and date of the printout. From the Modify System Defaults screen, enter *Y* in response to the prompt Banner Page For Network Print?

```
********************************************************
* User Name:   Kay             Directory:   SYS:SUPER  *
* File Name:   TEST.DOC        Station:     3          *
* September 26, 1989           12:12:34 pm             *
********************************************************
*       K    K          A  A          Y         Y      *
*       K   K           A   A           Y       Y       *
*       K  K           A     A           Y     Y        *
*       KK            A       A           Y Y Y         *
*       K  K         AAAAAAAAAAA            Y           *
*       K   K        A         A            Y           *
*       K    K       A         A            Y           *
********************************************************
*   TTTTT EEEEE   SSS    TTTTT      DDDD   OOO   CCC    *
*     T   E      S   S     T        D   D O   O C   C   *
*     T   E      S         T        D   D O   O C       *
*     T   EEEE    SSS      T        D   D O   O C       *
*     T   E          S     T   ...  D   D O   O C       *
*     T   E      S   S     T   ...  D   D O   O C   C   *
*     T   EEEEE   SSS      T   ...  DDDD   OOO   CCC    *
********************************************************
```

Fig. 2.6. LAN banner.

If a user tries to enter a function where access is not permitted (changing defaults without *wpsysd.sys* written to the dictionary, for example), this message appears on the screen:

    Sorry. You do not have access to this function

Booting MultiMate Advantage II on a Dual Floppy Disk System

Once your MultiMate word-processing system is installed, you can begin using it. The following instructions explain how to boot the system. If you use a hard disk system, skip this section and go to the next.

1. Insert your DOS disk into drive A.

2. Turn the power switch **ON**.

The system checks itself with a power-up memory test (that takes a few seconds); then it loads DOS into memory and executes it.

3. Enter the **date** and **time** if necessary.

When the A> system prompt appears,

4. Put the *Boot Working Diskette* into drive A.

5. Type **mm**

6. Press **Return**.

The MultiMate Advantage II boot-up menu appears, instructing you to press the space bar. Next, the MultiMate Advantage II Main Menu appears. It is illustrated in figure 2.7.

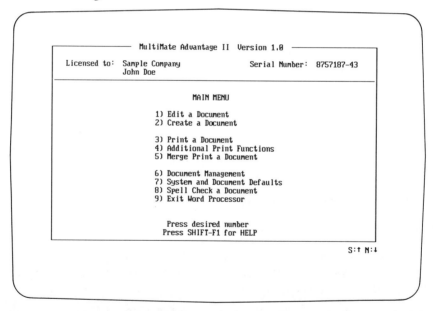

Fig. 2.7. MultiMate Advantage II Main Menu.

Booting MultiMate Advantage II on a Hard Disk System

The MultiMate Advantage II boot-up menu is a superset of the MultiMate Advantage II Professional Word Processor Main Menu. The boot-up menu allows you to access Word Processor, On-File, Advanced Utilities and Conversions, On-File Utility Programs, DOS, and your other programs.

To display the MultiMate Advantage II boot-up menu, follow this procedure. Be certain that you are in the MultiMate Advantage II subdirectory by typing *cd\mm* and Return, if necessary.

At the C> prompt,

1. Type **mm**

2. Press **Return**.

The MultiMate Advantage II boot-up menu appears (see fig. 2.8).

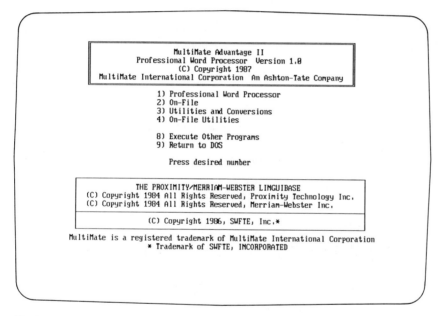

```
                    MultiMate Advantage II
              Professional Word Processor  Version 1.0
                        (C) Copyright 1987
      MultiMate International Corporation  An Ashton-Tate Company

                  1) Professional Word Processor
                  2) On-File
                  3) Utilities and Conversions
                  4) On-File Utilities

                  8) Execute Other Programs
                  9) Return to DOS

                     Press desired number


                THE PROXIMITY/MERRIAM-WEBSTER LINGUIBASE
      (C) Copyright 1984 All Rights Reserved, Proximity Technology Inc.
      (C) Copyright 1984 All Rights Reserved, Merriam-Webster Inc.

                  (C) Copyright 1986, SWFTE, Inc.*

      MultiMate is a registered trademark of MultiMate International Corporation
                   * Trademark of SWFTE, INCORPORATED
```

Fig. 2.8. MultiMate Advantage II boot-up menu.

To access the MultiMate Advantage II Professional Word Processor Main Menu,

3. Type **1**

Note: When making your selections, you must be certain that the program you select is available. If you select 1, 2, 3, or 4, and the system cannot find the program, the screen in figure 2.9 appears.

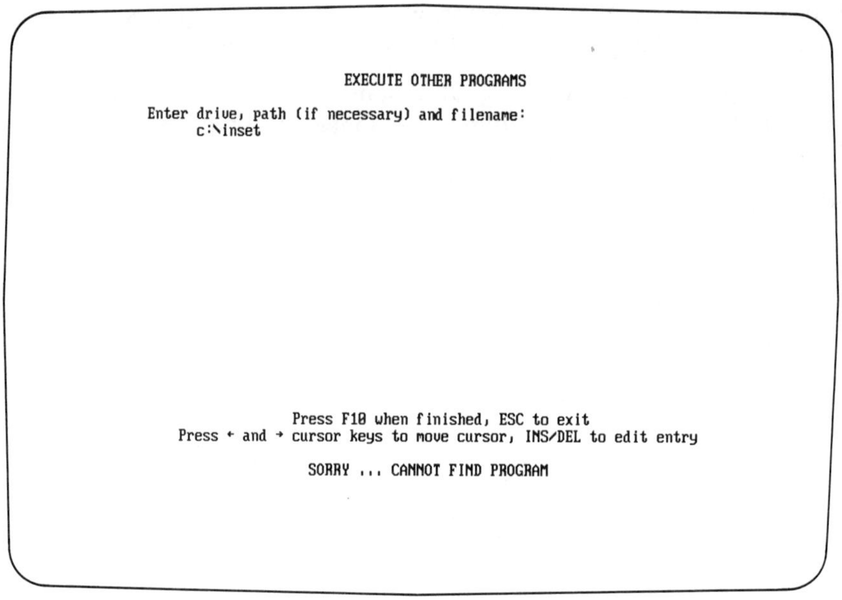

```
                    EXECUTE OTHER PROGRAMS
      Enter drive, path (if necessary) and filename:
            c:\inset






              Press F10 when finished, ESC to exit
      Press ← and → cursor keys to move cursor, INS/DEL to edit entry

              SORRY ... CANNOT FIND PROGRAM
```

Fig. 2.9. Prompt screen that is displayed when the selected program cannot be found.

To give your computer further instructions about how to find the program,

1. Type in the **drive designation** followed by a **colon** and a **backslash**.

   Example: C:\

2. Type in the **path (subdirectory name) designation** and a **backslash**.

   Example: dos\

3. Enter the **program name**.

   Example: basica

Your typed instructions to the system should look like this example:

   C:\dos\basica

4. Press **Return**.

If you're accessing a program on drive A,

1. Type **A:yourprogramname**

2. Insert the appropriate disk into drive A.

3. Press **Return**.

Using the MultiMate Advantage II Main Menu

The MultiMate Advantage II Main Menu lists the options available to you. To access the option of your choice, make sure your cursor appears after the DESIRED FUNCTION: prompt. Then, type the number of the option you want.

This is a list of the options and their functions:

- *Edit a Document*

  Allows you to make corrections or changes in a document already created and saved on a document storage disk.

- *Create a Document*

  Permits you to develop a new document.

- *Print a Document*

  Offers you the opportunity to select various ways to print existing documents.

- *Additional Print Functions*

  Allows you to check the status of documents that are printing, to print defaults, and to use your printer in Typewriter Mode.

- *Merge Print a Document*

  Enables you to merge two documents during printing.

- *Document Management*

  Assists you in moving, copying, deleting, or renaming documents. Also, restores backed-up documents and handles summary screens.

- *System and Document Defaults*

  Allows you to change standard format values already set in MultiMate Advantage II and to control the disk drives.

- *Spell Check a Document*

  Enables you to check and correct spelling in part or all of a document.

- *Exit Word Processor*

Permits you to exit from MultiMate Advantage II and return to
DOS or the Advantage II Copyright Screen. Once in DOS, you
can use DOS commands, go to other programs, or turn off your
system.

Using the Help Function

Help is a valuable MultiMate Advantage II support option. If you don't know
what a function (Move or Delete, for instance) is or how that function can
be used, you can access Help for a description of that function and a list of
that function's procedure steps. You can access Help while you view the Main
Menu, while you edit a document, or while you consider system utilities.

To access Help,

1. Press **Shift-F1**.

2. Then, depending on your need, choose from a variety of Help
   screens by following the directions on the screen.

Figure 2.10 illustrates a portion of the Help Menu.

```
DOCUMENT: JUNK                    ‖PAGE:   1‖LINE:   1‖COL:   1‖

The following is a list of all functions and the key(s) to press for help:

FUNCTION        KEY(S)   FUNCTION        KEY(S)   FUNCTION        KEY(S)
--------------- -------  --------------- -------  --------------- -------

ADD. PRINT FUNC..Alt 4   ALT KEYBOARD.....Alt K   AUTO HYPHENATION.Ctrl F2
AUTO PAGE NUMBER.#        AUTO UNDERLINE...Alt -   AUTO UND (ALPHA).Alt =
BACK SPACE.......<<--     BOLD PRINT.......Alt Z   CENTER...........F3
CHAR DELETE......- (Kypd) CHAR INSERT......+ (Kypd) CLEAR PLACEMARKS.Alt Y
COLUMN MODE......Shift F3 COLUMN TYPES.....Ctrl Ret COMMENTS.........Ctrl [
COPY.............F8       CREATE DOCUMENT..Alt 2   CURSOR DOWN......↓
CURSOR UP........↑        DECIMAL TAB......Shift F4 DELETE...........Del
DOC MANAGEMENT...Alt 6    DOCUMENT REORG...Ctrl F2  DOS ACCESS.......Ctrl 2
DOUBLE UNDERLINE.Ctrl _   DRAFT PRINT......Alt D    EDIT A DOCUMENT..Alt 1
END..............End      ENDNOTES.........Ctrl ]   END OF PAGE......Ctrl End
ENHANCED PRINT...Alt N    EXIT WORD PROCES.Alt 9    EXTERNAL COPY....Shift F8
FOOTER...........Alt F    FOOTNOTES........Alt U    FORMAT CHANGE....F9
FORMAT CURRENT...Shift F9 FORMAT PAGE......Alt F9   FORMAT SYSTEM....Ctrl F9
GO TO (Page).....F1       GO TO PLACE MARK.Ctrl F1  HARD SPACE.......Alt S
HEADER...........Alt H    HOME.............Home     HORIZONTAL MATH..Ctrl F3
HOT PRINT........H        HYPHEN (Soft)....Shift F7 IMPRT ASCII FILE.Ctrl 6
INDENT...........F4       INSERT...........Ins      KEY PROC-BUILD...Ctrl F5
     Press ESC to exit, RETURN to go to previous menu, SPACEBAR to scroll  S:↑ N:↓
```

Fig. 2.10. Help Menu listing.

For assistance with a function, you can press any function key or key combinations from the Help Menu screen.

If you want help with a particular function, simply press that function key or keystroke combination. A Help screen will appear to explain the use of the keystroke. Press *Esc* to return to what you were doing before you accessed Help.

You may access Help instructions in the middle of a function. After pressing the keys to perform the function, press *Shift-F1*. Help instructions will appear on the lower part of the screen. Use the space bar to scroll through the instructions or press *Esc* to exit. You may access Help during such functions as Copy, Delete, Insert, Move, Search, and Format.

Using Menus To Communicate

To recap, you use the MultiMate Advantage II Main Menu to access Help or to display additional menus that contain options which may be selected.

Picture this menu structure as a branching family tree: the MultiMate Advantage II Main Menu is the "head" menu that points to subordinate menus, which contain additional options. A menu map is in Appendix B, and it illustrates the relationship among MultiMate Advantage II menus.

As you begin to use MultiMate Advantage II, you may want to use the pull-down menus to select functions to perform. To use a pull-down menu,

    1. Press **Alt-L**.

A pull-down menu like the one shown in figure 2.11 appears. Each of the seven available pull-down menus is listed across the top of the screen. The Cut & Paste pull-down menu is shown.

    2. Use the **right**- and **left-arrow** keys to select one of the seven pull-down menus; a light bar marks your selection on the menu.

    3. Press the **up**- and **down-arrow** keys or the first letter of a selection to choose the function you want.

A description of the selection highlighted by the light bar appears on the bottom of the screen.

    4. Press **F10** to choose the selection that is highlighted.

Table 2.3 lists the seven pull-down menus and the options on each. Using the pull-down menus takes more key presses than the MultiMate Advantage II shortcut key combinations. The shortcut key combinations are used

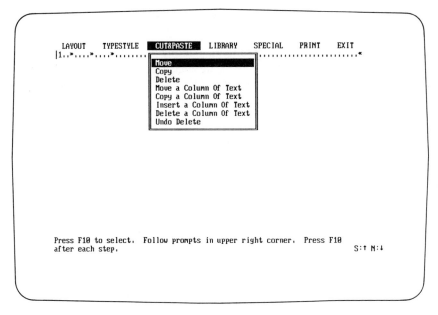

Fig. 2.11. Pull-down menu.

throughout this book. If you will use the pull-down menus, you may want to
keep table 2.3 handy to help identify which functions may also be performed
with pull-down menus.

Table 2.3
Pull-Down Menus

LAYOUT	*TYPESTYLE*
Insert Current Format Line	Superscript
Insert Copy of Current Format Line	
	Subscript
Insert Copy of Page Format Line	Draft
Insert Copy of System Format Line	
	Enhanced
Decimal Align	Bold
Center	Shadow
Indent	Underline Text
Page Break	Underline Alpha
Page Combine	Underline Double
Document Reorganization	
Preview	

CUT & PASTE
Move
Copy
Delete
Move a Column of Text
Copy a Column of Text
Insert a Column of Text
Delete a Column of Text
Undo Delete

SPECIAL
Sort
Import ASCII Files
Line & Box Drawing
Footnotes
Thesaurus
Spell Check Entire Document
Spell Check Portion of
    Document
Spell Edit Flagged Word

LIBRARY
Attach
Copy Text to a Library
Insert Library Entry Into
    Document

PRINT
Current Document
Current Page

EXIT
Save Text
Save Text/Exit
Exit Without Saving Text
Edit Another Document
Create a New Document
Exit Word Processor

DOS Access

Using the Keyboard To Communicate

MultiMate Advantage II communicates with you through its menu system. You can communicate with MultiMate Advantage II using your keyboard. Familiarizing yourself with the location of the keys on the keyboard and becoming comfortable with how those keys are used is important.

In Appendix A, you will find keyboard diagrams for the IBM PC and the Enhanced Keyboard. Refer to the keyboard diagram provided by the manufacturer of your computer to determine how the keystrokes that are discussed in this book may be made applicable to your computer.

Figure 2.12 illustrates the three groups of keys found on the keyboard of the IBM Personal Computer. Figure 2.13 shows the IBM Enhanced Keyboard.

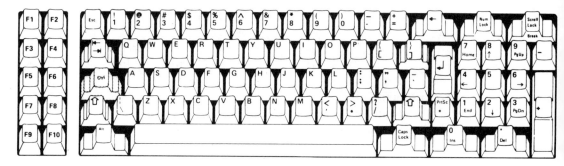

Fig. 2.12. IBM PC keyboard.

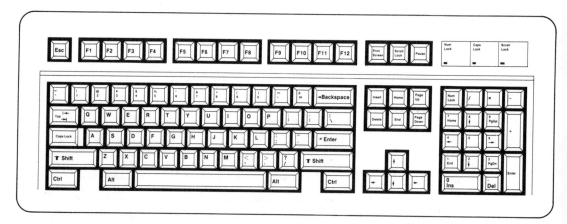

Fig. 2.13. IBM Enhanced Keyboard.

- The *Alphanumeric keys* are located in the center of the keyboard. These keys are the familiar "typewriter" keys. You'll use them to type the text and figures in your documents. You'll also combine some of them with the *Alt* key to perform special functions.

- The *Numeric/cursor keypad* is located on the right side of the IBM PC keyboard. The keys move the cursor. If you press the *Num Lock key*, these keys can be used as number keys. The IBM Enhanced Keyboard has separate cursor-movement keys as well. (Caution: never use the numeric keys to enter a number for a function or an option selection. Always use the numbers above the typewriter keys for this purpose.)

- The *Function keys* are located on the left side of the IBM PC keyboard and across the top of the Enhanced Keyboard. These keys are numbered F1 through F10. Use them alone or with other keys to perform functions.

The keyboard diagram in Appendix A illustrates the functions performed by the keys on the keyboard. The MultiMate Advantage II software package includes labels that you can place on your keys to help you remember which keys carry out a particular function. As you look at the labels, notice the color and location of the function name (above or below the character on the key). The color and location identify the key combination you must press to perform each function.

1. To perform the functions labeled at the *top* of the 10 function keys (F1 through F10), hold down the **Shift key** and press the desired **function key**.

   Example: **Shift-F2** combines pages.

2. To perform the functions labeled *under* the numbers on the function keys, press only the **function keys**.

   Example: Pressing only **F2** creates a page break.

3. To perform the functions labeled on the *top front* of the function or numeric keys, hold down the **Ctrl key** and press the **function key**.

   Example: **Ctrl-F2** repaginates documents.

4. To perform the functions labeled on the *bottom front* of the function or numeric keys, press **Alt** and the **desired key**.

   Example: Pressing **Alt-F2** controls page length.

For some MultiMate Advantage II users, the keyboard diagram is the most important aid in using the software. A number of keystroke options are available (because MultiMate Advantage II is able to perform a number of tasks), but you'll quickly become familiar with those you use most often.

3
Creating a Document

The first thing you will do after installing MultiMate Advantage II on your system is create a document. That document can be a report, a memo, an agenda, a form letter—almost any kind of written material.

A Word About Documents

All documents are made up of pages of text—pages that can be combined or divided in a number of ways.

With MultiMate Advantage II, you'll use a series of three screens to create your documents. However, before you begin, you should be aware of the limitations that the program places on both the length of the document page and the number of pages in each document.

If you plan to create an especially long document (a year-end sales report or a training manual, for instance), you will need to divide it into several documents. For example, this book was written using MultiMate Advantage II. The text for each chapter was entered as an individual document to control the size of the document.

Guidelines for Document Length and Size

- Maximum page length - 199 lines
- Maximum characters per page - 6,000 characters
- Maximum pages per document - 250 pages
- Maximum document size - 128K

As you can see in the chart on the following page, decreasing either the number of lines per page or the number of characters per page increases the number of pages in the document.

Number of characters on a page	1 to 510	2500	6,000 max.char. per page
Number of possible document pages	250 max.pgs.per document	50	21

A standard document can reach approximately 128K at 50 pages. Remember, if you exceed either the maximum number of characters per page or the maximum number of pages per document, an error can occur, and you may lose work you've done on the document.

The number of pages you can save on a disk depends on the size of the documents and the disk's storage capacity. MultiMate Advantage II tracks and reports available disk space.

Do not suppose that one screenful of information equals one printed page. Most monitors display 25 lines at a time. An 8 1/2-by-11-inch sheet of paper has 66 lines. You generally use about 50 of those 66 lines, depending on how many lines you reserve for the top and bottom margins. Those 50 lines, single-spaced, occupy about two screens.

Margins

Your monitor does not show the left and right margins that govern how your document is printed. With MultiMate Advantage II, *line length* replaces the concept of right and left margins.

Instead of setting margin width, you decide how long you want your line to be—that is, how many characters will appear on each line. When you are ready to print your document, you tell MultiMate Advantage II where to place the left margin; the system uses the line length you specified to calculate the right margin.

File Handling

It is appropriate to think of your documents simply as files that you create, edit, and print. However, MultiMate Advantage II files are more powerful than the traditional, office paper file.

With MultiMate Advantage II, you create the document and instruct your system to record its name and file it. When you must access the document for editing or printing, you instruct the system to retrieve the document either by its name or by the information identifiers you have filed the document under.

MultiMate Advantage II permits you to file a document under many different identifiers (simultaneously); therefore, you can search for all the names of files containing letters to the same addressee, or you can search for a specific letter in the file. The document's name and the filing information can be changed at any time. You can print the entire document or just one page of it. And, you can "clean house," discarding those documents you no longer need.

Using the Create a Document Screen

You will use three preliminary screens to describe the document to the system before you *enter* (type in) document text. The descriptions that you enter on the preliminary screens help you locate your document for editing or printing.

Option *2* on the Main Menu takes you to the first of three screens—the Create a Document screen. You will use this screen to name your document (see fig. 3.1).

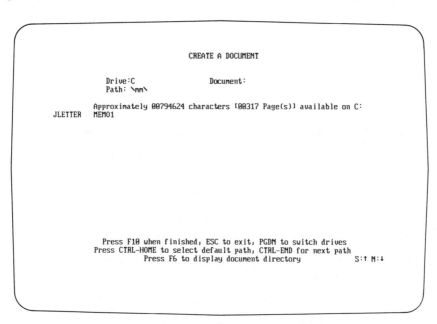

```
                           CREATE A DOCUMENT


                   Drive:C                    Document:
                   Path: \mm\

                   Approximately 00794624 characters [00317 Page(s)] available on C:
         JLETTER   MEMO1







                   Press F10 when finished, ESC to exit, PGDN to switch drives
                   Press CTRL-HOME to select default path, CTRL-END for next path
                         Press F6 to display document directory          S:↑ M:↓
```

Fig. 3.1. Create a Document screen.

The second line of the screen tells you on which disk drive that document is located. You can change the drive designation. For example, on a dual floppy disk drive system, your MultiMate Advantage II program files will use up most of the available space on the disk in drive A. For that reason, it's a good idea to create and store your documents on drive B. Most hard disk systems have expanded storage capabilities, so, on a hard disk system, both the MultiMate Advantage II program files and the documents you create will probably reside on drive C (the hard disk).

To change the designated drive, type either *A*, *B*, or *C* over the displayed character. Another way to change the drive designation is to press *PgDn*. The drive-designation letter on the screen changes.

If your drive is not "ready," MultiMate Advantage II lets you know. For example, suppose that you switch from drive C to drive A, and the door on drive A is open. MultiMate Advantage II prints a message on the screen asking you to close the drive door or insert a disk.

If you are using a hard disk and have created one or more subdirectories for *MMA* on drive C, you can move among those subdirectories by pressing *Ctrl-End*. (This moves the cursor to the next subdirectory on the drive.)

The subdirectory name will appear on the screen. For example, if you have a subdirectory named *LETTER*, the subdirectory name will appear in this message line:

```
Approximately 00782336 characters [00312 Page(s)] available on Drive C: LETTER
```

To move to the default directory, press *Ctrl-Home*.

The line on your screen will look similar to this line:

```
Approximately 00782336 characters [00312 Page(s)] available on Drive C:
```

Or, you may type in the subdirectory path in the field named *Path:*

Naming Your Document

When the screen displays the correct drive, proceed to the next field to name your document. Use these guidelines as you name your documents:

- You can use up to 20 characters to name your document; however, the first eight characters must be unique.

- The characters can be numbers or letters.

- The characters can be either uppercase or lowercase or a combination of both.

- When the document name is displayed in the document listing, all of the letters will be uppercase.

- The hyphen is the only form of punctuation you can use in naming your document. Do not use spaces.

Table 3.1 provides examples of valid and invalid MultiMate Advantage II document names.

Table 3.1
Valid and Invalid MultiMate Advantage II Names

Valid Names	Invalid Names	Invalid because
Example2	Example 2	Spaces not allowed
123-TEST	Test#123	Punctuation other than hyphen not allowed
SAMPLEOFNAME	THISISANEXAMPLEOFANAME	More than 20 characters

When MultiMate Advantage II displays the document name on your screen, only the first eight characters appear. Those eight characters *must not* be the same as the first eight characters of any of your other document names.

Check the directory in the center of the Create a Document screen to determine which eight-character names are being used on the drive. If you happen to enter a name that already exists, a prompt will appear on your screen, and you can enter another name.

You *must* name your document. If you do not, a beep sounds, and your system cues you to reenter a valid document name.

Remember that you will use the name you select to access that document in the future, so choose a name that clearly identifies the document. *Try to be as specific as possible*. Instead of assigning a year-end report the very general name *REPORT*, name it *YE-REPT*. The document name you choose does not have to be final; you can change it, as you will learn in a later chapter.

Checking Disk Capacity

The fourth line on the Create a Document screen indicates approximately how many characters and pages are left on the disk in the current drive. This information will be helpful as you arrange documents on your disk. Always check to be sure that the disk has space for what you estimate your document will require.

Using the Document Directory

Directly below the line that reports disk capacity is a list of documents stored on the drive you've selected. MultiMate Advantage II lists your documents in alphabetical order from left to right on the screen. Only the first 112 files fit in the directory window. To scroll the directory, you can press *Ctrl-PgUp* and *Ctrl-PgDn*. If you are creating the very first document (no other documents exist), this area will be blank.

Changing the drive designation permits you to see the directories on other drives. To change the drive, press *PgDn*.

As the directory changes, the letter of the drive changes. Each time you press *PgDn*, MultiMate Advantage II displays another drive directory (until the program reaches the last drive). Pressing *PgDn* begins the cycle, and the program displays the drive A directory again.

If you are using a hard disk and want to move to a subdirectory, press *Ctrl-End*. To return to the default directory, press *Ctrl-Home*.

Using the Key Status Symbols

Notice the symbols in the lower right corner of your screen:

S:↓ N:↓

The *S* arrow indicates the status of the *Caps Lock* key; the *N* shows the position of the *Num Lock* key (number lock). When you press Caps Lock, the arrow next to the *S* points up, which means that all the letters you type will appear in uppercase.

If you press Shift when the *S* arrow is pointing up, all the letters you type will appear in lowercase (until you release Shift). Pressing the Caps Lock key a second time releases it, so all letters appear in lowercase. If you press the Shift key now, your letters will appear in uppercase while this key is held down.

The Num Lock key controls the numeric keypad on the far right side of your keyboard. When you press Num Lock, the arrow next to the *N* points up, indicating that you can type only numbers on the numeric keypad. Pressing Num Lock a second time releases that key and permits you to use the four arrow keys again.

The Document Summary Screen

When you have finished entering information on the Create a Document screen and want to move on to the second screen, which is the Document Summary screen, press *F10*.

In only one instance do you disregard this screen; that instance is when the document you are creating is a *library*—a document that contains words or forms that you use often and do not want to type each time (see Chapter 15).

The Document Summary screen is used to create a record that contains the most pertinent information that your document contains. This record permits you to recall facts about your document without reading the full text (see fig. 3.2).

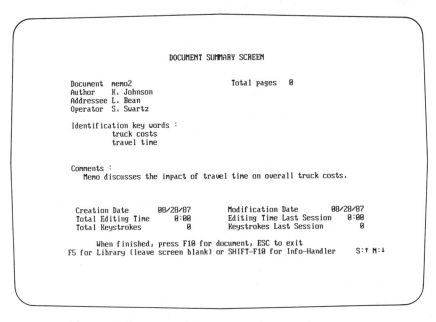

```
                        DOCUMENT SUMMARY SCREEN


        Document  memo2                    Total pages   0
        Author    K. Johnson
        Addressee L. Bean
        Operator  S. Swartz

        Identification key words :
                truck costs
                travel time


        Comments :
             Memo discusses the impact of travel time on overall truck costs.


        Creation Date      08/28/87      Modification Date       08/28/87
        Total Editing Time    0:00       Editing Time Last Session   0:00
        Total Keystrokes         0       Keystrokes Last Session        0

              When finished, press F10 for document, ESC to exit
        F5 for Library (leave screen blank) or SHIFT-F10 for Info-Handler    S:↑ N:↓
```

Fig. 3.2. Document Summary screen before a document is typed.

MultiMate Advantage II automatically fills in some fields such as the Document (name), Creation Date, Modification Date, Total Editing Time, Editing Time Last Session, Total Keystrokes, and Keystrokes Last Session fields. You fill in the remaining fields or leave them blank.

Later, you will learn how to use MultiMate Advantage II to search through all the Document Summary screens for information common to all your documents. For example, you can search for the names of all your files that contain documents addressed to Joe Jones. Or, you can search for the names of all your files that contain documents created in the month of June.

Document Name and Total Pages Fields

The first line on the Document Summary screen contains the *Document* (name) field, which already contains the name you assigned to the document on the Create a Document screen.

To the right of the Document field is the *Total Pages* field. If you are creating a new document, this field contains a zero. After you have typed in the document, the zero is replaced with the number of pages in your document.

Author, Addressee, and Operator Fields

You can use the next three lines to enable future searches for names of files that contain common information. Fill in information that will help you file and retrieve documents effectively. The *Author* is the person who writes the document, the *Addressee* is the person who receives the document, and the *Operator* is the person who types the document.

Remember to keep the spelling of names consistent from document to document. If Joe Jones is called J. Jones in one document, J.J. in another document, and Joe in a third, searching for "Joe Jones documents" in a single pass will be impossible.

Pick one version of each name entered in your documents and use that name consistently. If you are one of a number of users on a Local Area Network system, you may want to develop an office policy that standardizes name entry.

Identification Key Words Fields

The fields for the *Identification Key Words* occupy lines five through eight. You will probably use these fields to retrieve documents. For example, you could retrieve letters sent to truck owners (even if the letters have different addressees) by typing *truck owners* in the Identification Key Words field on the Document Summary screen for each document.

Comments Field

You use the four lines in the *Comments* field to describe the contents of the document. This field should contain information you do not want to include in the document itself—for example, a comment describing the letter written to a customer. The Comments information can help you select the appropriate document, without recalling and reading the document.

Creation and Modification Dates Fields

MultiMate Advantage II fills in the Creation Date and Modification Date fields. The *Creation Date* is the date you entered when you booted the system or the DOS programmed date. The *Modification Date* is the date you last edited or reviewed the document.

Editing Time Fields

The *Total Editing Time* shows the number of total hours and minutes (hh:mm) spent editing the document. The *Editing Time Last Session* shows the total hours and minutes spent in the most recent editing session. Use this information to identify how long document development takes.

Keystrokes Data Fields

MultiMate Advantage II also fills in the Keystrokes Last Session and Total Keystrokes fields. *Keystrokes Last Session* tells you how many keys you pressed (keystrokes) the last time you worked on the document. *Total Keystrokes* tells you how many keys you have pressed since the document was created. This information can be used to determine how efficiently you enter and edit text.

Field Content Editing

To change any of the information you have entered in a field,

    1. Move to that field using either the **tab key** or **Return**.

    2. Type the new information over the existing information.

When the fields display the correct information,

    3. Press **F10**.

(This moves the cursor to the next screen.)

The Modify Document Defaults Screen

Use the Modify Document Defaults screen (see fig. 3.3) to set certain MultiMate Advantage II characteristics for the document. After completing this screen, you can begin entering the text of your document.

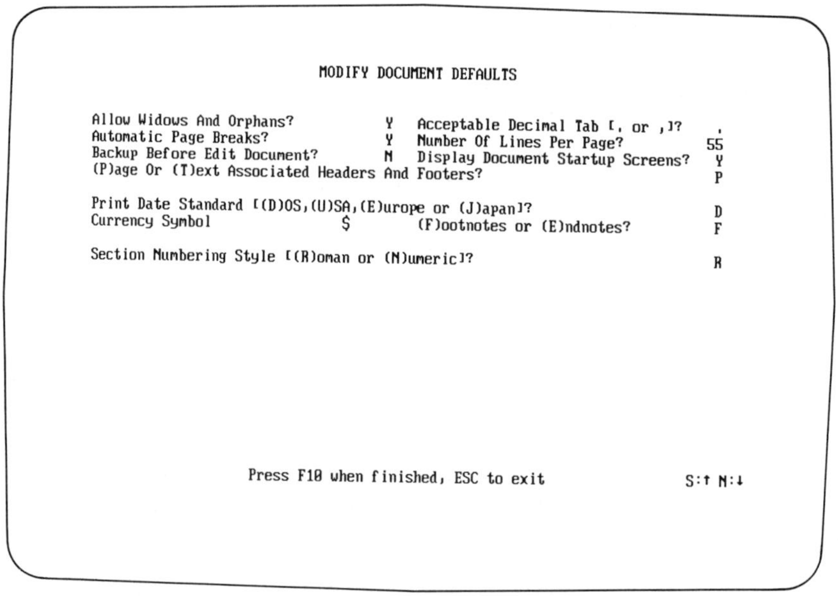

```
                        MODIFY DOCUMENT DEFAULTS

    Allow Widows And Orphans?          Y    Acceptable Decimal Tab [. or ,]?     .
    Automatic Page Breaks?             Y    Number Of Lines Per Page?           55
    Backup Before Edit Document?       N    Display Document Startup Screens?    Y
    (P)age Or (T)ext Associated Headers And Footers?                            P

    Print Date Standard [(D)OS,(U)SA,(E)urope or (J)apan]?                      D
    Currency Symbol              $          (F)ootnotes or (E)ndnotes?          F

    Section Numbering Style [(R)oman or (N)umeric]?                            R




                   Press F10 when finished, ESC to exit               S:↑ N:↓
```

Fig. 3.3. Modify Document Defaults screen.

Notice that MultiMate Advantage II has already filled in all the fields on this screen with *system defaults*—the standard values that MultiMate Advantage II "assumes" you want to use in setting up documents. (Later, you will learn how to change many of these defaults.)

If the fields on this screen contain the values you want to use,

1. Press **F10** to continue.

To change one or more of the fields,

1. Press **Return** or the **cursor-movement keys** to move the cursor to that field.

2. Type the new default value over the system default value.

Allow Widows and Orphans Field

The first field asks Al l ow Wi dows and Or phans? An *orphan* occurs when a paragraph begins on the last line of a page. A *widow* occurs when a page starts with the last line of a paragraph. Figure 3.4 illustrates a widow and an orphan.

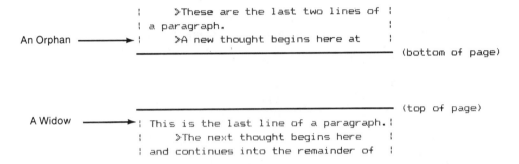

Fig. 3.4. Examples of a widow and an orphan.

The widows and orphans information you enter is used by the system when it repaginates your documents. The Repaginate function automatically renumbers and reformats your document based on the number of lines you want on a page.

If you want to allow widows and orphans during repagination, type *Y* (for yes) in the field. If you do not want to allow widows and orphans, type *N* (for no).

Automatic Page Breaks Field

The *Automatic Page Breaks* field works with the Number of Lines Per Page field.

If you desire automatic page breaks, type *Y*. A new page automatically starts when the number of lines typed equals the number specified in the Number of Lines Per Page field.

If you do not want automatic page breaks, type *N*. Your system will not start new pages automatically; however, a warning beep sounds, and the page number flashes when you reach the line number specified in the Number of Lines Per Page field. You can end the page manually or continue entering text. Remember to enter a page break before exceeding the maximum total line number (199).

Acceptable Decimal Tab Field

In the *Acceptable Decimal Tab* field, you must decide whether you want to use the American symbol (.) or the European symbol (,) in column calculations (see table 3.2). The symbol you select depends on the kinds of numbers you most often align in your document.

Table 3.2
Examples of Acceptable Decimal Tab Field Settings

American	European
37.2	37,2
3.14159	3,14159
101.0	101,0

Number of Lines Per Page Field

You can enter any number from 1 to 199 in the *Number of Lines Per Page* field. When you specify double-spacing, your system counts the extra space (the blank line) as a line. To print 25 double-spaced lines on a page, specify *50* in the Number of Lines Per Page field.

The Number of Lines Per Page field has room for three digits. If you specify a number with fewer digits than the default number, you must either delete the extra digit or type a zero over it.

For example, to change a default of 100 to 50,

   1. Type **050**

  Or

   1. Type **50**

   2. Delete the last 0 on the right.

If you answered *Y* in the Automatic Page Breaks field, each page ends on the line you've specified in the Number of Lines Per Page field, and the screen for the next page appears automatically. If you typed *N*, the line number flashes, and a beep sounds to remind you to enter a page break manually.

Making a Backup Copy

If you want your system to create a backup copy of your document before you edit it, type *Y*. The copy is stored on the same disk as the original document, and only the most recent backup is stored.

If you do not want your system to create and store a backup copy, type *N*.

Chapter 13 explains how to restore a backup copy so that you can use it.

Displaying Document Start-Up Screens

If you select *Y* in the field, you will be taken through the Document Summary screen when *editing* a document, and you will be taken through the Document Summary screen and the Modify Document Defaults screen when *creating* a document. If you enter *N* in the field, you will be taken directly from the Main Menu selection to the document. You will not be able to access the Document Summary screen or the Modify Document Defaults screen for the document.

If you enter *N*, you may not create a library or an Information Handling File.

(T)ext or (P)age Associated Headers and Footers

This option affects your text when your system automatically repaginates a document that contains headers and footers. A *header* is a heading that appears at the top of more than just one page of your document. A *footer* appears at the bottom of more than one page of your document. As an example, in this book, the book name and chapter names are headers, and the page numbers are footers.

If you type *P* (for Page) in the (T)ext or (P)age Associated Headers and Footers field, the headers and footers are counted in the total page count. The headers and footers remain on the page where they are entered.

If you press *T* (for Text), the headers and footers are not included in the page count—they stay with the related text. For more information about re-paginating with headers and footers, see Chapter 9.

Printing the Date Standard

In Chapter 8, you will learn how to use the *&DATE&* command to enter the date automatically in your documents. The date can appear in any of several formats, determined by the values U, E, J, or D. Table 3.3 illustrates the ways dates are printed.

Table 3.3
Formats in which Dates Can Be Printed

Entry	Standard	Printed Appearance	Example
D	Default/DOS	Month/Day/Year	05/25/88
U	U.S.	Month/Day/Year	05/25/88
E	European	Day/Month/Year	25/05/88
J	Japanese	Day-Month-Year	25:05:88

Currency Symbol

A dollar sign ($) is the default. You may enter any symbol you want. The symbol is used with the math functions in MultiMate Advantage II.

(F)ootnotes or (E)ndnotes

If you enter *F* for footnotes, each footnote is printed at the bottom of the page on which the note is found. If you enter *E* for endnotes, footnotes are printed after the endnote symbol (if entered) or at the end of the document.

Section Numbering Style

You can automatically number sections of your documents with this feature.

For Roman style (I., A., . . . (a)), type *R*.

For Numeric style (1., 1.1., . . . 1.1.1.1.1.1), type *N*.

See Chapter 9 for an extended discussion of section numbering.

Screen Completion

When you are ready to accept the information on the screen, press *F10*. Now you can begin typing your document.

After making changes on the Modify Document Defaults screen, you may decide to eliminate all the changes and retain the system defaults. If so, press *Esc*.

Your system will return you to the Main Menu, where you'll find the first menu you use to create a document.

Hot Start Document Creation

You may create a new document from the DOS prompt and skip these four screens: Main Menu, Create a Document, Document Summary, and Modify Document Defaults.

1. At the DOS prompt, enter **wp**, a **space**, and the **new document name**.

2. Press **Return**.

You are taken to the first page of the document.

4
Editing a Document

After you have created your document, you will probably want to reread it and make revisions by adding, deleting, or reorganizing text. To edit your document, you'll use both the Edit a Document screen and the Document Summary screen.

An *old document* is any document that you have already created (using the Create a Document option from the Main Menu) and stored either on a document disk or the hard disk. The document can be one that you completed only minutes ago or one that has been stored on the disk for months. It is an *existing* document.

The Edit a Document Screen

To begin editing your work, start at the MultiMate Advantage II Main Menu. To move to the Edit a Document screen from the Main Menu, press *1*.

The Edit a Document screen will be displayed on your monitor (see fig. 4.1).

The Drive and Document Name Fields

MultiMate Advantage II sets the Drive field at the system default value.

If you've just finished working on a MultiMate Advantage II document, the name of that document will appear in the Document name field. If that is the name of the document you intend to edit, skip the Document and Drive fields.

If it is not the name of the document you must edit, or if the Document name field is blank, enter the name of the document you plan to work on and the drive on which it is located. If you enter an invalid name, the screen will display an error message, telling you that the document does not exist. After the message disappears, type over the invalid name with the correct name.

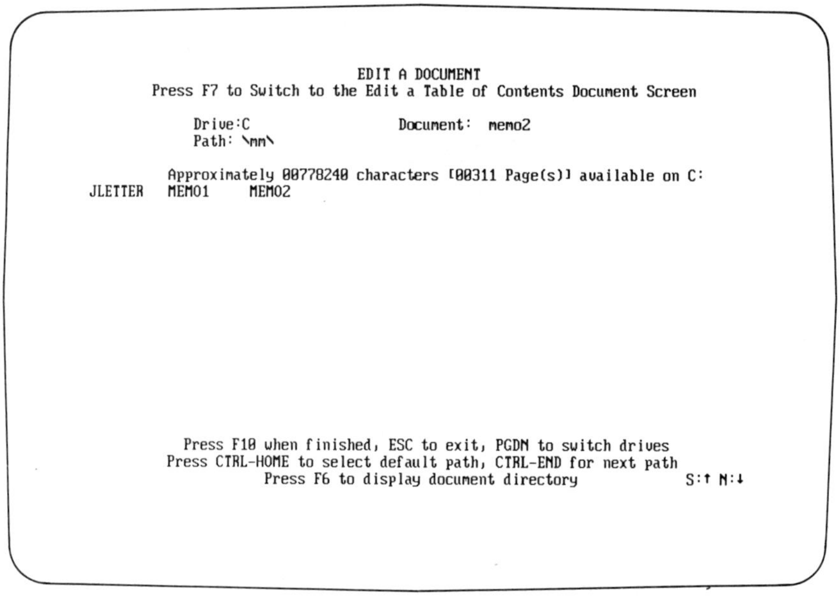

```
                              EDIT A DOCUMENT
               Press F7 to Switch to the Edit a Table of Contents Document Screen

               Drive:C                  Document:  memo2
               Path: \mm\

               Approximately 00778240 characters [00311 Page(s)] available on C:
      JLETTER   MEM01     MEM02








               Press F10 when finished, ESC to exit, PGDN to switch drives
               Press CTRL-HOME to select default path, CTRL-END for next path
                    Press F6 to display document directory          S:↑ N:↓
```

Fig. 4.1. Sample Edit a Document screen.

The Document Directory

If you have created several documents, you may need help remembering which documents reside on each drive. The Edit a Document screen, like the Create a Document screen, displays an alphabetical directory of all the documents on each drive.

To see a list of documents on drives other than the drive you are in now, press *PgDn*. The drive designation changes, and the system displays the directory for the designated drive.

You must have a disk in the drive being displayed, or your system will indicate that the drive is "not ready." If the "not ready" message appears on the screen,

1. Insert the disk.

2. Press **R** (to retry the operation).

If you insert the wrong disk, the screen will display an error message stating that the document cannot be found. If that happens,

1. Replace the disk with the correct disk.

2. Press **Return.**

Only the first eight characters of the name appear in the document directory on your screen, so a document name on the screen may look different from the name you typed when you created the document. You can type these first eight characters, or you can type the document's full name in the Document name field. The system accepts both options.

Do not change the drive if the document name appears on the screen. If you do not see the document name on the screen, you can change the drive by pressing *PgDn* until the document name and the corresponding drive appear.

If you are using a hard disk and want to move to a subdirectory, press *Ctrl-End*. To return to the default directory, press *Ctrl-Home*. Or, you may enter the path in the *Path:* field.

The Disk's Capacity

Before adding text to your document, check to be certain that the disk has enough room to store the text. The line above the document directory displays the approximate number of characters and pages *remaining* on the disk in the current drive. Exceeding disk capacity can result in an error and cause you to lose information.

When the correct drive and document name appear on the Edit a Document screen, press *F10* to move to the next screen.

The Document Summary Screen Revisited

You may recognize the Document Summary screen in figure 4.2. It is the screen that you entered information on when you created your document. The information you entered then is shown on the screen now. Use that information to make sure that the document you selected from the document directory on the Edit a Document screen is the one you want to edit. If the document is not the one you want to work on, press *Esc* to return to the Main Menu.

You can change some of the information you entered on the Document Summary screen, but, at this point, you cannot change the name of the document. (See Chapter 13 for instructions on how to change document names.) You can, however, change most of the other information simply by typing over it.

To move from field to field, press *Return* or *tab* or the *cursor arrow* keys. After you finish reviewing or making changes to the fields, press *F10* (to move to the first page of your document).

```
                          DOCUMENT SUMMARY SCREEN


          Document   memo2                    Total pages   1
          Author     K. Johnson
          Addressee  L. Bean
          Operator   S. Swartz

          Identification key words :
                     truck costs
                     travel time


          Comments :
              Memo discusses the impact of travel time on overall truck costs.


          Creation Date        08/28/87    Modification Date         08/28/87
          Total Editing Time      0:03     Editing Time Last Session   0:01
          Total Keystrokes         528     Keystrokes Last Session       1

                  Press F10 when finished, ESC to exit

                                                          S:↑ M:↓
```

Fig. 4.2. Sample Document Summary screen after a document is typed.

Be careful when making any changes to fields that you use as cross-references for file retrieval. For example, suppose that you change an addressee's name from Gary Brown to Brown, Gary. Later, you ask the system to search for all the documents listing the addressee Gary Brown; the program will ignore the document with Brown, Gary, as the addressee.

As you become familiar with MultiMate Advantage II screens, you will learn to move quickly through the opening screens to your document.

The Document Defaults

When you routinely edit a document, you do not see the Modify Document Defaults screen.

If you do decide to change any of the document defaults that were set when you created the document you're currently editing,

1. Save the document that you are editing.

2. Press **F10**.

(This returns you to the MultiMate Advantage II Main Menu.)

    3. Type **7**

    4. Select **Edit Document Defaults**.

The defaults will be changed when you create a new document, but documents already created will not be affected.

Chapter 18 for further discussion of this utility.

The End of an Edit Session

After you finish editing your document, press *F10* to save it and all the changes you made to it and to return to the Main Menu.

If you have edited a one-page document and want to end the edit session without saving the changes you made, press *Esc*. The system displays this prompt:

    Do you wish to escape without saving this page? (Y/N)

Press *Y* to return to the Main Menu. Any editing done during this particular session is lost. If you press *Esc* accidentally, press *N* to cancel the Esc function that was used. The screen continues to show your document.

As you move from one page to the next in your document, MultiMate Advantage II saves each page. The program does not save the last page of the document unless you do one of the following to end the editing session: press *F10* to save and exit to the Main Menu or press *Shift-F10* to save and remain in the document.

You may elect to save your document and continue working with other MultiMate Advantage II functions without returning to the Main Menu. Press *Alt* and the number key associated with a Main Menu selection. For example, if you want to save a document and immediately go to the screen to begin printing, press *Alt-3*.

Hot Start Document Editing

You may edit a new document from the DOS prompt. These screens are skipped: Main Menu, Edit a Document, and Document Summary.

    1. At the DOS prompt, enter **wp**, a **space**, and the **document name**.

    2. Press **Return**.

You are taken to the first page of the document.

5

The Cursor

The *cursor* is represented on your screen by a small, blinking rectangle that indicates where the next character will appear in your text. As you type, the cursor moves one space at a time from the left side of your screen to the right side of your screen.

Word Wrapping

If you've used a typewriter, you know that when you have typed to the right margin, a warning bell sounds. When this occurs, you must press the Return key to move the typehead to the left margin of the next line.

The MultiMate Advantage II *Word Wrapping* feature counts the characters entered and eliminates the manual "return" step. When the cursor reaches the end of a line, the cursor moves automatically to the left margin of the next line. In other words, you may type continuously without worrying about returning as you reach the right margin—MultiMate Advantage II automatically wraps your words around to begin at the left margin on the next line.

You need to press Return only at the end of a paragraph or at the end of a line that does not extend to the right margin. Your cursor then moves to the beginning of the next line.

Pressing Return at the left margin, before you type any text, marks the line as blank and moves the cursor down to the next line.

Cursor-Movement Keys

There will be times while you are creating or editing your document that you'll want to move the cursor to another location on the screen. Perhaps you've left out a word in a sentence, or perhaps you need to add several sentences to a paragraph.

MultiMate Advantage II provides you with many cursor-positioning functions that allow you—with only one or two keystrokes—to move the cursor quickly almost anywhere in the document. Table 5.1 lists the cursor-movement options available to you.

Table 5.1
Cursor-Movement Keys

Function	Key(s)
Backspace	←
Back Tab	**Shift-Tab**
Cursor Down	↓
Cursor Left	←
Cursor Right	→
Cursor Up	↑
End of Page	**Ctrl-End**
End of Screen	**End**
Enter a Space	**space bar**
Go to Page	**F1-Page#-Return**
Next Page	**Ctrl-PgDn**
Next Screen	**PgDn**
Next Word	**Ctrl-Right Arrow**
Previous Page	**Ctrl-PgUp**
Previous Screen	**PgUp**
Previous Word	**Ctrl-Left Arrow**
Scroll Left	**Alt-F3**
Scroll Right	**Alt-F4**
Tab	⊢ →|
Top of Page	**Ctrl-Home**
Top of Screen	**Home**

Cursor Arrow Keys

You use the keys on the *numeric/cursor keypad*, located on the right side of your keyboard (see fig. 5.1), to move the cursor one space at a time—up or down, left or right. The arrows printed on the keys indicate the direction in which the cursor will move. (If you are using the IBM Enhanced Keyboard, you will have dedicated arrow keys in addition to this numeric/cursor keyboard.)

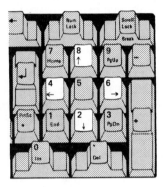

Fig. 5.1. Cursor arrow keys.

The *Num Lock* (number lock) key controls the use of the keys on the numeric/cursor keypad. This key is a toggle switch that is either on or off. To use the numbers designated on the top left corner of the keys in the numeric/cursor keypad, press *Num Lock*. Now, to use the arrow keys, press *Num Lock* again.

When Num Lock is in the unlocked position, the number lock indicator, *N* (on the lower right side of the screen), displays an arrow pointing downward. You then can use the keys on the numeric keypad to move the cursor.

Pressing the left-arrow key (←) once moves the cursor to the left one character space at a time; pressing the up-arrow key (↑) once moves the cursor up one line at a time, and so on.

If you hold down the key, the cursor continues to move in that direction. For example, if the cursor were located here █ in this sentence, and you pressed the right-arrow key (→) once, the cursor would move under the "i" in the word "in." If you continued holding down the right-arrow key, the cursor would continue to move right; when it reached the end of a line, it would wrap around and move to the next line.

You also can use the arrow keys to move the cursor from one page to another within your document. If you hold down the down-arrow key (↓), the cursor will move beyond the end of the page you are working on, and you'll find yourself on a new page.

If no next page exists, your system displays this prompt:

    THIS IS THE LAST PAGE

If you press the up-arrow key long enough, your cursor will move to the previous page. If no previous page exists, the system displays this prompt on the bottom line of the screen:

    THIS IS THE FIRST PAGE

If you have a few lines of text typed on your screen (an outline, for example) and you use the arrow keys to move the cursor vertically, the cursor may seem to hop around the screen. Actually, the cursor is moving to positions on the screen that either have contained a character or have been passed over with the space bar (space holders). As far as MultiMate Advantage II is concerned, only those areas of the screen that have not held the cursor are really blank.

As you use the arrow keys to move the cursor over existing text, the cursor does not enter areas that are blank but, instead, jumps between characters and space holders.

Imagine that this and the previous paragraph are on the screen, and the cursor is at the end of the previous paragraph. If you held down the right-arrow key, the cursor would move from the Return after the period ending the previous paragraph to the beginning of the blank line between paragraphs and then to the beginning of this paragraph. All blank areas in between would be skipped. The arrow keys can be used to move from field to field and across characters that you have entered on a system or menu screen.

The + and - keys on the numeric/cursor keypad can be used to insert and delete single character spaces.

To insert a space,

    1. Press +

To delete a space or character,

    1. Press -

Chapter 7 presents other ways to insert and delete text.

Space Bar for Cursor Movement

Using the arrow keys to move the cursor from place to place within your document doesn't change the document in any way. Only the cursor position changes.

If you elect to use the space bar to move the cursor, remember that the space bar erases every character that the cursor passes over. Each character is replaced with a space.

Home and End Screen Positions

Although the four arrow keys will move the cursor to any location in a document, they are not practical for covering long distances because they move slowly—one character at a time.

There are other keys on the numeric/cursor keypad that can be used to move the cursor more quickly.

To move the cursor quickly to the first character or space on the current screen, press *Home*. To move the cursor quickly to the last character on the current screen, press *End*.

Screen Scrolling

Your screen displays only 22 lines of text at a time. Imagine that the rest of your document (if it has more than 22 lines) is wound on a scroll inside your system. To view the rest of the document, you must unwind the scroll so that subsequent lines will be displayed on the screen. With MultiMate Advantage II, you'll use the scrolling-up or scrolling-down functions.

Let's assume that you want to move the cursor to the bottom of the page. (Remember, the screen can't display a full document page.) You could move the cursor by pressing the down-arrow key until the cursor reaches the end of the screen. If you have more than 22 lines of text in your document, you could continue to move the cursor, and the lines would continue to scroll up. However, because the cursor moves only one space at a time, scrolling the screen this way is very slow. MultiMate provides faster ways to scroll larger amounts of the screen at one time.

Scrolling the Page

The Home and End keys move your cursor to either the top or bottom of the screen. If, instead, you want to move the cursor to the beginning of the current page, press *Ctrl-Home*. The cursor moves to the first character or space at the top of the current page.

If you want to move to the end of the current page, press *Ctrl-End*. The cursor moves to the space immediately following the last character on the current page.

Scrolling 18 Lines at a Time

If you want to see the previous 18 lines of the document you are working on, press *PgUp*. MultiMate Advantage II shifts the current screen up 18 lines in your document.

To see the next 18 lines of your document, press *PgDn*. The current screen shifts down 18 lines.

Because you are scrolling 18 lines at a time, four lines from the screenful of text you most recently viewed appear either at the top or the bottom of the screen.

Scrolling Left and Right

To move the cursor automatically to the first character or character space at the left margin of the current line, press *Alt-F3*. To move the cursor automatically to the last character at the right margin of the current line, press *Alt-F4*.

A computer monitor usually displays 80 columns (positions for characters and symbols) at one time. If your right margin is set beyond column 80, and you scroll right, the text on the left side of your screen seems to disappear. In fact, you appear to be scrolling off the screen. The cursor still appears on the right end of the line, but you cannot see the leftmost characters. They are there; scroll left to see them.

Backspace Key

Located above the numeric/cursor keypad, to the left of the Num Lock key, is the backspace key. The *backspace* key moves the cursor left one space. If you hold down this key, the cursor continues to move left and eventually wraps around into the previous line. Normally, the backspace key erases words in your documents—a process called a *destructive backspace*.

If you do not want to use the backspace key to delete text in a document, you can set destructive backspace to *N* (for no) as a system default. (In Chapter 18, you will learn how to change the destructive backspace key.)

Tab Key

When you press the *tab* key (located next to the Q key), the cursor moves under a tab symbol (») on the Format Line at the top of the page. (Chapter 6 describes Format Lines and suggests ways in which you may alter tab symbols.)

Word-to-Word Movement

Whenever you want to move the cursor to the first character of the word that follows the cursor, use the *Next Word* function: hold down *Ctrl* and press the *right-arrow* key. MultiMate Advantage II automatically repositions the cursor under the first character in the next word.

Use the *Previous Word* function to move the cursor to the first character in the previous word: hold down *Ctrl* and press the *left-arrow* key. The system automatically repositions the cursor under the first character in the previous word.

Page-to-Page Movement

When you are working with multiple-page documents, you will use the Go to Page key often.

   1. Press **F1**.

This prompt appears at the bottom of the screen:

     GO TO PAGE? [ ]

   2. Type in the page number.

   3. Press **Return**.

MultiMate Advantage II quickly displays the page.

When you enter the page number, make sure that it is the same as the number on the *Status Line* at the top of the page you want to go to. You can assign any page numbers to the documents you print, so the printed-document page number and the Status-Line page number may differ.

The Go to Page feature is often used with the Delete, Copy, and Move functions. Before you can delete, copy, or move material, you must highlight it. (See Chapter 7.) You highlight a character on one page and highlight another character on a subsequent page; your system highlights all the characters between those two characters. This procedure speeds up a Delete, Copy, or Move function on a large block of text.

You may also use the Go to Page feature to move quickly to the beginning or end of your document.

To move the cursor to the first line of the last page of the document, press *F1-End*. To move the cursor to the first line of the document, press *F1-Home*.

Moving from the First or Last Space on a Page

To move to the bottom of the previous page,

> 1. Place the cursor on line 1, column 1, of the page.
>
> 2. Press **PgUp**.
>
> Or
>
> 1. Place the cursor on line 1, column 1, of the page.
>
> 2. Press the **up-arrow** key.

If no previous page exists, this message appears on the bottom line of your screen:

> THIS IS THE FIRST PAGE

To move to the following page,

> 1. Place the cursor on the last line and column of a page.
>
> 2. Press **PgDn**.
>
> Or
>
> 1. Place the cursor on the last line and column of a page.
>
> 2. Press the **down-arrow** key.

The system will prompt you if your document has no next page.

Using the Previous Page and Next Page Functions

If your cursor is not in the first or last character space on a page, and you want to move to the bottom line of the previous page, press *Ctrl-PgUp*.

To move to the top line of the following page, press *Ctrl-PgDn*.

If you are already on the last page, this message will appear:

    THIS IS THE LAST PAGE

Escape Key

If you begin a function and choose not to complete it, you can return the cursor to the position it held prior to beginning the function: press *Esc*.

For example, if you start to create a document and then decide not to continue, press *Esc* to cancel the function and return the cursor to the Main Menu.

These functions can be canceled by pressing *Esc* before the function is completed:

Copy	Page Length
Delete	Pull-Down Menus
External Copy	Repagination
Format	Replace
Insert	Search
Key Procedure	Spell Check
Library	Spell Edit
Merge Print	Thesaurus
Move	

6

Tabs, Margins, Line Spacing, Center, and Preview

Formatting your text on the screen is an important step in creating readable and attractive printed materials. The MultiMate Advantage II word processing package permits you to organize and reorganize your documents using such formatting options as centering, indenting (blocks of text or single lines of text), tabs, margins, and line spacing. All of these formatting functions help you create professional-looking documents.

The Status Line

As you create your documents, notice the line at the top of the screen. The line is called the Status Line. As the name suggests, the *Status Line* provides you with information about the document upon which you are working. (The Status Line does not appear in your printed document.)

Status Line ──────▶

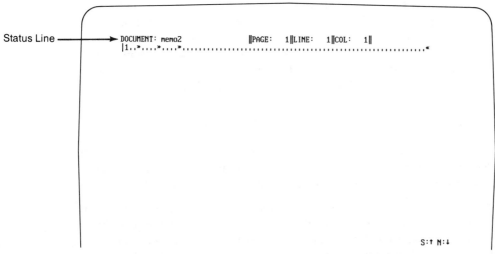

Fig. 6.1. A sample Status Line.

The DOCUMENT Field

The *DOCUMENT* field (at the far left of the Status Line) displays the name of the document that you are currently creating or editing. In figure 6.1, the document has been named *MEMO2*.

The PAGE Field

The *PAGE* field displays the document's page number. The PAGE field information is particularly helpful if you are writing a document that must fall within a range of pages. You can easily track how many pages you have completed by glancing at the number in the PAGE field. If you are typing a very long document, you can use the PAGE field information to calculate how many pages can be added before reaching the approximate 250-page limit.

The LINE Field

The *LINE* field indicates on which line (on the page) your cursor currently rests. You use this information to estimate how many lines are left on a page. Suppose that you are using an 8 1/2-by-11-inch sheet of paper (which holds up to 66 lines of regular-size text); you want top and bottom margins, and you want each page to have no more than 50 lines of printed text. As you develop the page, you can check the LINE field to determine how many additional lines will fit on the page.

You may remember that on the Modify Document Defaults screen, you completed the Number of Lines Per Page field and answered either *Y* or *N* to the Automatic Page Breaks question. If you answered *N*, the number in the LINE field flashes when your cursor moves below the maximum number of lines per page. The flashing prompt is intended to remind you to create a new page. If you responded *Y*, MultiMate Advantage II automatically creates a new page when your cursor passes the maximum line number for a page.

The COL Field

The last field in the Status Line, *COL* (for column), displays the number of the column in which your cursor currently rests. As you position your work on the screen, you'll use this information often.

If you are creating a chart or a list, you'll want the items to line up at a given column position. Occasionally, you'll want to verify the right-margin column number. If you use MultiMate Advantage II to print information on preprinted forms, you'll use both the column and line information to determine where the material must lie on the screen so that it will line up correctly on the form after it is printed. (If you do use forms, make sure to read the sections in this chapter called *Using a Positioning Ruler in Line Spacing* and *Using a Positioning Ruler To Set Margins.*)

The Status Line Prompts

A blank space appears on the far right side of the Status Line. That space is reserved for prompts. Specific keys evoke specific prompts. Some prompts ask questions (like the prompt INSERT WHAT? which appears as you center text). Other prompts keep you informed about what your system is doing as it carries out an operation (like the prompt FORMAT CHANGE, which appears when you've pressed the F9 key to tell your system to make a format change). When the operation is complete, the prompt disappears.

The Format Line

When you create a document, the default Format Line appears on Line 0, directly under the Status Line. The *Format Line* controls tab settings, line length, and line spacing. You can see the Format Line as you work in the first 23 lines of a document. As you move beyond the 23rd line, the Format Line scrolls up and disappears from view.

In MultiMate, you may work in Document or Page Mode. These options are discussed fully in Chapter 18. Briefly, *Document Mode* is the default and causes "pages" to scroll together and appear on the screen one after another. *Page Mode* breaks pages on your screen so only one page appears at a time.

Figure 6.2 shows the Format Line as it appears in Page Mode. Figure 6.3 shows the appearance of the Format Line in Document Mode. When the line is edited, it appears in the Page Mode. For readability, we will use the Page Mode throughout this text. What you use is a matter of preference.

In the Format Line in figure 6.2, the line spacing is set at 1 so that the printer will print single-spaced text. Tab settings appear at columns 5, 10, and 15. The right margin is set at column 65. Line 0 always contains a Format Line. You can insert, change, and delete Format Lines within your text. You'll learn how to edit the Format Line later in this chapter. As you learn how to edit the Format Line, you may want to refer to the keyboard diagram in Appendix A.

Format Line ———→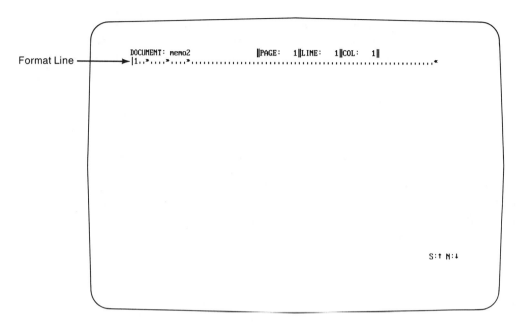

Fig. 6.2. A sample Format Line for Page Mode.

Format Line ———→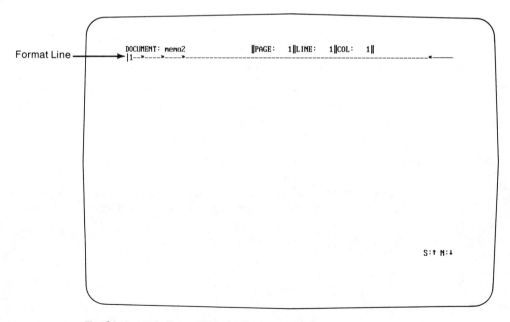

Fig. 6.3. A sample Format Line for Document Mode.

Changing a Format Line

To change an existing Format Line,

>   1. Press **F9**.

Wherever your cursor is in the document, the cursor moves to the Format Line; then the line can be edited. The cursor can move freely within the Format Line.

In the upper right corner of the screen, MultiMate Advantage II displays the prompt FORMAT CHANGE; this tells you that the program is ready for you to enter changes.

>   2. Make changes in the Format Line.

>   3. Press **F9**.

The system makes your changes, and the cursor returns to the position it held prior to the Format Line edit.

For example, you may change the right margin from column 65 to column 40 by pressing Return at column 40. When you press F9 to move out of the Format Line (step 3), MultiMate Advantage II reformats the text according to the new margin.

MultiMate does not immediately save your Format Line changes or, for that matter, any changes made to the document. Only when you use one of the conventional document-save methods—such as pressing the F10 key or moving to a new page—does the program save the newly modified Format Line.

If you press F9 to edit a Format Line and then decide that you want to keep the original Format Line, press *Esc*. Pressing this key restores the original Format Line and returns your cursor to the location it held prior to the F9 keystroke.

Inserting Format Lines in Text

There are three key combinations to insert Format Lines in your text. You can use this capability if a document must be double-spaced for several pages, then single-spaced for part of the document, and then double-spaced again. Inserting Format Lines in text is helpful when a chart requires tab settings that differ from the tab settings in the rest of the document.

Inserted Format Lines neither print in your document nor take up a line in the document. Format Lines appear on your screen only to help you organize the material on the screen.

Three options exist for inserting Format Lines: Alt-F9, Shift-F9, and Ctrl-F9.

Alt-F9

Press *Alt-F9* to insert the same Format Line (as the one that appears at the top of the page) into your document. If you have inserted several other Format Lines between the top of the document and the current position of your cursor, press *Alt-F9* to insert a Format Line like the one at the top of the document (Line 0).

Shift-F9

To insert the current (or most recent) Format Line used, press *Shift-F9*. You may have inserted several Format Lines on a page and then changed them. Pressing Shift-F9 inserts the current Format Line directly above the spot where you are inserting the new Format Line.

Ctrl-F9

Press *Ctrl-F9* to insert the document default Format Line. (In Chapter 18, you will learn how to change many MultiMate Advantage II defaults, including the Format Line.) If you change the Format Line on Line 0 of page 1 and then want to use the default Format Line at a later point, press *Ctrl-F9*.

Figure 6.4 presents sample Format Lines. Suppose that the cursor is at the bottom of the screen; if you press *Alt-F9*, Format Line C appears at the cursor location. If you press *Shift-F9*, Format Line A appears at the cursor location. Format Line B appears at the cursor location if you press *Ctrl-F9*.

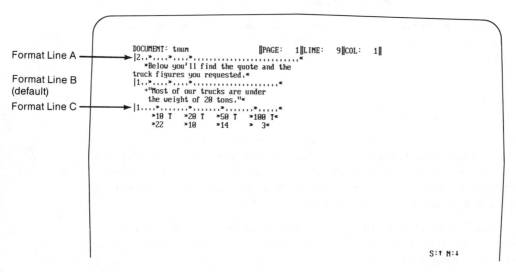

Fig. 6.4. Sample Format Lines.

Deleting a Format Line

You cannot delete the Format Line at the top of the page (Line 0), but you can delete those Format Lines you've inserted in your document.

To delete a Format Line (see fig. 6.5),

1. Select the Format Line you want to delete.

2. Place the cursor on the character below this Format Line.

3. Press **Del**.

4. Press **F9**.

5. Press **Del** or **F10**.

MultiMate Advantage II deletes the Format Line.

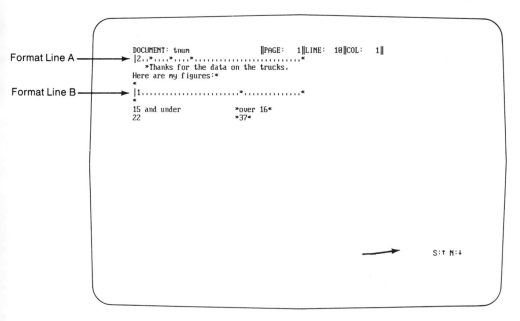

Fig. 6.5. Deleting a Format Line.

You cannot delete a Return symbol directly above a Format Line—an unusual MultiMate Advantage II quirk. For example, you could not delete the Return symbol in the line above Format Line B in figure 6.5.

Line Spacing

On the screen, characters always appear single-spaced, one line after the other. But, what you see on the screen is not necessarily how your document will appear after it's printed.

The line-spacing setting takes effect only when you ask the system to print your document or when you view the document in Preview Mode. Remember, the Format Line controls the line spacing in your documents. The number at the far left of the Format Line indicates how MultiMate Advantage II spaces the text. For example, a document with a Format Line space setting of *2* appears single-spaced on the screen, but it previews and prints double-spaced.

All the examples you have seen so far in this chapter used *1* (for single-spacing) or *2* (for double-spacing), but a total of *eight* line-spacing options are available (see table 6.1).

A 50-line, double-spaced document contains 25 lines of text. The Status Line's LINE field counts two each time the cursor moves from one line to the next. A 50-line, single-spaced document contains 50 lines of text. The Status Line's LINE field counts one each time the cursor moves from one line to the next.

Table 6.1
Line-Spacing Options

Number	Spacing Represented
1	Single Space
2	Double Space
3	Triple Space
0	Zero Space
H	Half Space
Q	Quarter Space
+	One and One-Half Space
=	Two and One-Half Space

Single Line Spacing

If the number *1* appears at the far left side of the Format Line, your document is single-spaced and prints as it appears on the screen—one line after another.

Double Line Spacing

If the number *2* appears at the far left of the Format Line, your document appears to be single-spaced on the screen but, in fact, previews and prints with a blank line between each line of text. The Status Line reflects double-spacing by counting two as you move the cursor from one line to the next.

Triple Line Spacing

If the number *3* appears at the left of the Format Line, your document previews and prints with two blank lines between each line of text. The text on your screen will appear as single-spaced text, but the Status Line counts three each time you move from one line to the next.

Zero Line Spacing

If the number *0* appears at the left of the Format Line, one line will print over the previous line. (You cannot preview this effect.) You certainly would not want to use an entire page of zero line spacing, but it does have some effective uses.

For example, legislators may need to show portions of written text that have been removed from legislative bills. To effect a comparison of the text, zero line spacing might be selected to indicate which words have been stricken without actually deleting them from the original printed text. Seeing both versions at once permits a comparison of the texts and an evaluation of the changes.

If you use zero line spacing (be certain to enter the number 0, **not** the letter O, in the far left position of the Format Line), the text that appears on the screen in figure 6.6 will print like the example shown in figure 6.7.

Notice that the Return key was pressed after the single-spaced Format Line. Without this Return, the words "without notice" would print on top of the previous line.

Another way to achieve this effect is to use the MultiMate Advantage II *Strikeout* function, explained in Chapter 8.

Half Line Spacing

To use half line spacing, type *H* or *h* at the far left of the Format Line. Half spacing places your lines very close together—half the space of single-spacing.

```
DOCUMENT: tnum                    ‖PAGE:   1‖LINE:   4‖COL:   1‖
|1..».....».....».................................................«
No alcohol will be consumed in city parks between the«
|8..».....».....».................................................«
illegal hours of 8 a.m. to 9 a.m. and 4 p.m. to 6 p.m.«
                    /////////////////////«
|1..».....».....».................................................«
«
without notice.«






                                                    S:↑ N:↓
```

Fig. 6.6. Example of zero line spacing on-screen.

```
No alcohol will be consumed in city parks between the
illegal hours of 8/a/m//to/9/a/m//and/4 p.m. to 6 p.m.
without notice.
```

Fig. 6.7. Example of zero line spacing in print.

Quarter Line Spacing

Quarter-spaced lines almost touch. To use quarter spacing, type *Q* or *q* at the far left of the Format Line. Some printers do not support quarter line spacing; others do support it, but they don't produce acceptable results. Test your printer before using this option extensively.

One and One-Half Line Spacing

One and one-half line spacing inserts one and one-half lines between each printed line of your document. To specify one and one-half line spacing, hold down the *Shift* key and press the + key.

Two and One-Half Line Spacing

Two and one-half line spacing causes two and one-half lines to appear between every line of text in your document. Press = in the Format Line to specify this type of spacing.

Altering Line Spacing

To alter the line spacing (from single-spacing to double-spacing, for example),

1. Position the cursor on the Format Line.

2. Press **F9** to access the Format Line.

3. Move the cursor back one space using the **left-arrow key**.

4. Type in the new line space value.

5. Press **F9** to move the cursor from the Format Line.

If you type a line space value that doesn't appear in table 6.1, the system will display this message:

```
INVALID KEY FOR FORMAT MODE
```

Not all printers will print all of the options listed in table 6.1, so check your printer instructions to see which options are supported.

Using a Positioning Ruler in Line Spacing

Because the document you type on the screen can look different after it is printed, arranging the text on the screen can be difficult. A *positioning ruler* can be purchased at a stationery store; it will help you format text by permitting you to position the text on the screen, to calculate horizontal column spacing, to determine vertical line spacing, to avoid misaligned text, and to set margins.

The positioning ruler is used with both the paper you will be printing on and with the LINE field information on the Status Line.

Assume that you want to print the title page for a report. Based on the Status Line information, you know that the title is on line 10, and your name and address begin on line 45. To see what this arrangement looks like on the printed page, you could print the page, edit the document, print a new page, and perhaps edit and print again—a time-consuming process.

A quicker way to accomplish your goal is to use the "lines of text" marks on the positioning ruler to determine the proper placement of the information

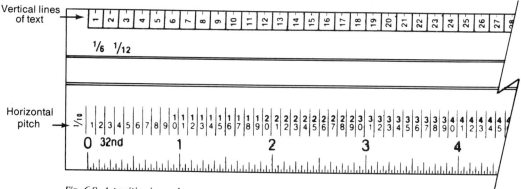

Fig. 6.8. A positioning ruler.

on the paper you will be using. When you lay the positioning ruler vertically on an 8 1/2-by-11-inch sheet of paper, you see that the title should be on line 25 and that your name and address should start on line 53. Now you can position the text on the screen, and, if you are careful, you will need to print the page only once.

Tab Key

The tab key can be used to indent the first line of a paragraph and to space characters for charts or lists. When you press *tab*, this symbol appears on your screen: . The symbol doesn't appear in your printed document. It is a screen symbol telling you that the tab key was pressed. To delete a tab, simply delete the tab symbol, and the remaining characters move to the left.

Where the cursor rests after you press the tab key is determined by the tab settings in the Format Line. The tab setting indicators in the Format Line look the same as the tab symbol itself. Those Format Line tab symbols represent tab settings that can be changed depending on your document format needs.

To change the tab settings in the Format Line, press *F9* to position the cursor on the Format Line.

You can also insert a Format Line (as described earlier in this chapter) to change tab settings. The cursor always enters to the left of the Format Line. After the cursor has moved to the Format Line, use the keys illustrated in table 6.2 to modify tab settings.

If you want to use the first tab setting but change the second, use either the right-arrow or left-arrow key to move over a tab setting without disturbing it.

Table 6.2
Keys Used To Edit the Format Line

Key	Procedure
Cursor arrows	Move the cursor over existing tab settings or into the line spacing number on the left.
Space bar	Remove tab settings.
Tab	Set a new tab setting.
Ins (insert)	Insert dots (affecting Format Line length).
Del (delete)	Delete dots (affecting Format Line length).
Home	Move to the left of the Format Line.
End	Move to the right of the Format Line.
Return	Mark the end of the Format Line.

To delete a tab setting, use the space bar. To enter a new tab setting (while in the Format Line), press *tab*.

To extend the Format Line, press *Ins*. To shorten the Format Line, press *Del*.

To set the length of the Format Line at the cursor position, press *Return*. To move quickly between the beginning of the Format Line and the end of the Format Line, press *Home-End*.

After you have completed all modifications, press *F9* to exit from the Format Line.

Use tabs to create your tables, and you'll simplify later table editing chores. To make format changes, you simply change the tab settings. For example, by editing the tabs in the Format Line in figure 6.9, you've turned unreadable data into readable data. Had you created the tables by pressing the space bar, your time spent editing would have been significantly longer.

Indents

If you spend time creating documents that include outlines, tables, contracts, or quotes, you will use indents often. To indent text,

1. Move the cursor to the desired position within a line.

2. Press **F4**.

This symbol will be displayed on your screen: →

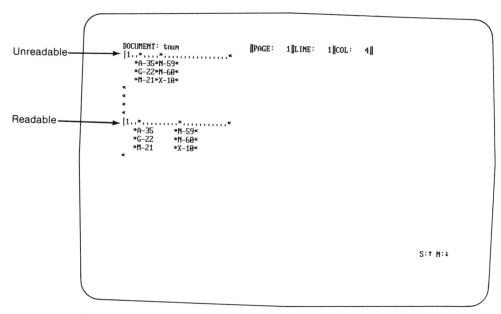

Fig. 6.9. Unreadable material made readable by editing the tabs.

This symbol does not appear in your printed document but serves as a re-minder (displayed on your screen) that the text ⤴ indented.

The Format Line controls indenting in the same way it controls tab settings. When you press F4 to indent, the indent symbol appears under the tab settings in the Format Line. Specifically, Format Line tab settings control both tabs and indents.

Inserting the indent symbol aligns *several* lines of text in response to the tab setting instructions in the Format Line. Alignment continues for as many lines as required.

   3. Type the text to be indented.

   4. Press **Return**.

A tab symbol aligns only *one* line of text. Use indents if you are creating a document with numbered paragraphs (a contract or an outline, for example). Use tabs if you are starting a paragraph or lining up text line by line. Figure 6.10 illustrates the difference between indents and tabs.

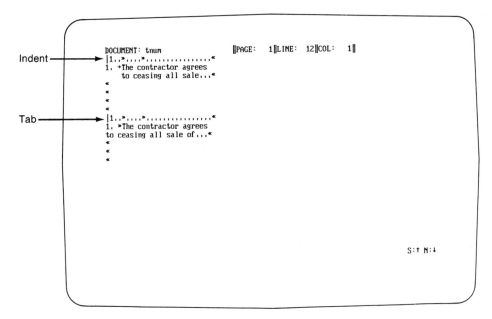

Fig. 6.10. The differences between indents and tabs.

Margins

The left and right margins govern how much white space appears on either side of the printed document. You set the left margin at the time you print the document. (See Chapter 10 to learn how to set the left margin from a print menu.) The Format Line controls the right margin.

Using a Positioning Ruler To Set Margins

A positioning ruler will help you set the margins and the length of the Format Line. You'll use the ruler with the following:

- The column information in the Status Line

- The paper on which you'll print the document

- The pitch you select to print the document

The *pitch* of your document refers to the number of characters that print in an inch. The MultiMate Advantage II pitch default is 10 characters per inch.

Some business documents are printed in a pitch of 12 characters per inch. (You set the pitch when you print a document. The procedure is discussed in Chapter 9.)

After you determine how many characters will print per inch and where the left margin will be, place the positioning ruler on the page horizontally and use the marked pitch values to determine how long the Format Line should be.

For example, suppose that your paper is 11 inches wide, and you want to print in 10 pitch, with a right margin of 10 spaces. By placing the "10 pitch" column of the positioning ruler horizontally across the page, you will see that a Format Line of 90 characters fits on the page and leaves enough space for the right margin.

To establish header and footer placement and to calculate the top margin and number of lines per page, place the positioning ruler vertically on the page and use the marked line values. (Chapter 8 describes headers and footers in detail.)

Setting the Right Margin

MultiMate Advantage II's right margin default is column 75. To lengthen the right margin, place the cursor in the Format Line:

1. Press **F9**.

2. Place the cursor at the desired column.

3. Press **F9**.

Or

1. Insert a Format Line.

2. Use the right-arrow key to move to the desired column.

3. Press **Return**.

Suppose that you want a right column of 90. (The maximum Format Line length is 156 characters.) As the cursor moves, watch the Status Line to determine when you have reached column 90. Then, with the cursor on column 90, press *Return* to mark the right margin.

Most monitors display 80 columns. Whenever you set the margin over 75, the Format Line moves left, but the text on your screen does not.

To shorten a margin,

1. Position the cursor in the Format Line at the desired column.

2. Press **Return** to mark the Format Line length.

3. Press **F9** to return the cursor to the line below the Format Line.

Or

1. Use **Del** to move the existing Return symbol to the desired location.

2. Press **Return**.

3. Press **F9** to return the cursor to the line below the Format Line.

MultiMate Advantage II reformats the text in the document up to the next Format Line according to the new margin setting.

Centering

MultiMate Advantage II makes centering text an easy task:

1. Press **F3**.

2. Type the text to be centered.

3. Press **Return**.

A double-ended arrow ↔ appears when you press F3.

Press *F3* on a blank line to place the centering symbol in the center of the screen. As you type your text, notice that the text moves left one space as you enter every other letter. After you finish typing the text, press *Return*.

To center existing text,

1. Position the cursor under the first letter that you want to center.

2. Press **Ins**.

MultiMate Advantage II prompts INSERT in the upper right corner of the screen.

3. Press **F3** to insert the centering symbol.

Now your text is centered. Any remaining text reappears on the screen.

The centering symbol affects only one line of text. If you try to center text that is too long for one line, MultiMate Advantage II automatically strikes over a character with a Return symbol at the maximum centering length and moves the rest of the text to the next line. Generally, text that you want to center must be three characters shorter than the Format Line. To center a block of text, you must center each line individually.

You can use the centering symbol more than once in a line (see fig. 6.11). For example, you can center a title and type the author's name to the right of the title. To use center more than once in a line,

1. Press **F3**.

2. Type the text.

3. Press **F3**.

4. Move the cursor to the location on the screen where you want the text to appear.

5. Type the text.

6. Press **Return**.

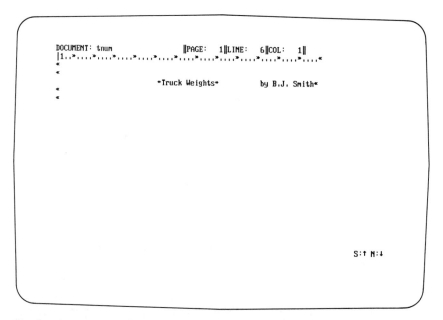

Fig. 6.11. Using the centering symbol twice in one line.

You may preview the appearance of your text before printing. The MultiMate Advantage II page appears without screen symbols and Format Lines. The headers, footers, and footnotes appear as they will print. You may preview text a page at a time or multiple pages at a time.

To preview a single page,

1. Place your cursor on the page.

2. Press **Alt-I**.

3. If the page is later in the document, a message like this one appears:

   `PLEASE WAIT -- Searching For Page 009 -- Page 003`

4. Press **any key** to halt the display or to bring up the next 25 lines.

5. Press **Esc** when you are done.

To preview multiple pages,

1. Place your cursor anywhere in the document.

2. Press **Alt-3**.

3. The Document Print Options screen appears.

4. Type in the starting page you want to preview after this prompt:

   `Start Print At Page Number`

5. Type in the ending page you want to preview after this prompt:

   `Stop Print After Page Number`

6. Type **C** for console after this prompt:

   `Use:`
   `(P)arallel/(S)erial/(F)ile/(L)ist/(A)uxiliary/(C)onsole`

7. Press **F10**.

8. If the page is later in the document, a message like this one appears:

   `PLEASE WAIT -- Searching For Page 009 -- Page 003`

9. Press **any key** to halt the display or to bring up the next 25 lines.

10. Press **Esc** when you are done.

7

Inserting, Deleting, Moving, and Copying Text

MultiMate Advantage II's unique features allow you to edit your documents quickly and easily. You can *insert* (add) text or *delete* (remove) text, as well as *move* or *copy* text to another page in your document. MultiMate Advantage II permits you to *copy* text from one document to another. Because MultiMate Advantage II has full copying capabilities, you can, with just a few keystrokes, identify a complex diagram or an important paragraph and place it wherever you want (and as many times as you want) within your document.

An important feature of MultiMate Advantage II is the ease with which you use the program to perform the Insert, Delete, Move, and Copy functions. To insert text, you simply press the *Ins* key; to delete text, you simply press the *Del* key. You also use a single key to copy or move text. As you use MultiMate Advantage II, these keys will become very familiar. And because the keystrokes are uncomplicated, you will have more time to devote to composing your text.

Inserting Text

You can add new material to your document in two ways: you can either strike over (replace existing characters with new characters) or insert new characters among the existing characters.

Strikeover is useful for correcting small errors. If you type a sentence and notice a typographical error, simply move the cursor to the incorrect character and strike over it with the correct character.

For example, to change the *a* in summ*a*r to an *e* using Strikeover,

    1. Place the cursor on the *a*.

    2. Type the lowercase **e**

To insert text,

1. Move the cursor to the position on the screen where you want to insert the first character.

2. Press **Ins**.

The prompt INSERT WHAT? appears on the screen.

Depending on your selection on the Modify System Defaults screen, the text after the cursor either drops to the bottom of the screen to make room for the text to be inserted or moves to the right as you insert text.

3. Type the text you want to be inserted.

4. Press **Ins**.

Pressing Ins takes you out of Insert Mode and back to Typewriter Mode. If necessary, text is reformatted.

To insert a space,

1. Move the cursor to the position on the screen where you want the blank space.

2. Press + on the numeric keypad.

The cursor does not move, but spaces are inserted. Once one or more spaces are inserted, you may strike over the space(s) with characters.

Deleting Text

To delete text,

1. Place the cursor under the first character of the text you want to delete.

2. Press **Del**.

The prompt DELETE WHAT? appears.

3. Move the cursor to highlight the text you want to delete.

The highlighting shows exactly what you will be deleting. To highlight more text for deletion, simply move the cursor—a character at a time, a line at a time, or more (as you will see in the next sections). When all of the characters are highlighted,

4. Press **Del** or **F10**.

The highlighted text will disappear.

If you begin to delete text and then decide against it, you can press *Esc* prior to actually completing the deletion. The highlighting disappears, and the cursor returns to where it was before you began deleting the text.

If you have set up the destructive backspace feature, you may press the backspace key to delete the character to the left of your cursor. Position the cursor to the right of the character to delete and press the *backspace* key.

Deleting Characters

To delete a single character,

   1. Place the cursor under the character you want to delete.

   2. Press **Del**.

   3. Press **Del** or **F10**.

The first keystroke highlights the character, and the second keystroke deletes the character. Here is another way to delete a character:

   1. Place your cursor under the character you want to remove.

   2. Press - on the numeric keypad.

You can delete several consecutive characters at a time:

   1. Position the cursor under the first character you want to delete.

   2. Press **Del**.

   3. Type the last character or space you want to delete.

MultiMate Advantage II moves to the first occurrence of the letter you have typed, so type an unusual letter (a *q* or a *z*, for example) near the spot where you want to stop deleting.

   4. Press **Del** or **F10** to finish deleting.

Deleting Words

To delete a word and the space following the word,

   1. Place the cursor under the first letter of the word.

   2. Press **Del**.

   3. Press the **space bar**.

MultiMate Advantage II highlights the word and the space following it.

   4. Press **Del** or **F10**.

The word and the space disappear. If you continue pressing the space bar, the program highlights words for deletion, one at a time.

You can delete words another quick way:

1. Position the cursor anywhere in the word you want to delete.

2. Press **Del**.

3. Press **Alt-F5**.

4. Press **Del** or **F10**.

Pressing Alt-F5 has the same effect as pressing the space bar, except that you can position the cursor anywhere in the word, not just on the first letter of the word. You can also use a cursor-movement key to delete text one word at a time:

1. Press **Del**.

2. Press **Ctrl** and the **right-arrow key** to highlight to just before the first letter in the word following the word you want to delete.

3. Press **Del** or **F10**.

Deleting Lines of Text

To delete lines,

1. Move the cursor to the position on the screen where you want to begin deleting lines of text.

2. Press **Del**.

3. Move the cursor down the lines you want to delete.

4. Press **Del** or **F10**.

If you want to delete a single line,

1. Press **Del**.

2. Move the cursor anywhere in the line you want to delete.

3. Press **Alt-F6**.

4. Press **Del** or **F10**.

Deleting a Sentence

You can delete sentences in two ways. Your first option follows:

1. Position the cursor anywhere in the sentence.

2. Press **Del**.

3. Press **Alt-F7**.

MultiMate Advantage II highlights the entire sentence, as well as the space after the sentence.

4. Press **Del** or **F10** to delete the highlighted sentence.

This is the second way to delete a sentence:

1. Place the cursor on the first character in the sentence.

2. Press **Del**.

3. Quickly move the cursor to the end of the sentence by pressing the key-equivalent of the punctuation mark that falls at the end of the sentence.

The cursor moves to that punctuation symbol, which may be a period, a question mark, or an exclamation point. (You may or may not have to adjust the cursor slightly to delete trailing spaces.)

4. Press **Del** or **F10**.

The sentence and spaces disappear, and MultiMate Advantage II reformats the text.

Deleting a Paragraph

To delete a whole paragraph, you could move the cursor slowly, line by line, character by character, until the entire paragraph is highlighted; however, MultiMate Advantage II provides two quicker ways to delete a paragraph.

If your cursor is at the beginning of the paragraph,

1. Press **Del**.

2. Press **Return**.

If your paragraph ends with a Return symbol, the cursor immediately moves to that Return.

3. Press **Del** or **F10**.

The paragraph is removed.

If your cursor does not rest at the beginning of the paragraph, MultiMate Advantage II highlights all the material between your cursor and the Return symbol.

To delete a paragraph another way,

1. Place your cursor anywhere in the paragraph.

2. Press **Del**.

3. Press **Alt-F8**.

MultiMate Advantage II highlights the entire paragraph.

4. Press **Del** or **F10**.

Deleting a Screenful of Text

To delete a screenful of text,

1. Press **Home**.

2. Press **Del**.

3. Press **End**.

4. Press **Del** or **F10**.

All the text on the screen disappears.

If you want to delete only a portion of the screenful of text,

1. Move the cursor to the first character of the text you want to delete. (Or, press **Home** to start with the first character on the screen.)

2. Press **Del**.

3. Move the cursor to the end of the text you want to delete. (Or, press **End** to go to the last character on the screen.)

4. Press **Del** or **F10**.

Deleting Pages

To delete single pages,

1. Place the cursor on the first character of the page you want to delete.

2. Press **Del**.

3. Press **Ctrl-End**.

4. Press **Del** or **F10**.

MultiMate Advantage II highlights the entire page through the last character on the page. To highlight through the first character on the next page,

1. Place the cursor on the first character of the page you want to delete.

2. Press **Del**.

3. Press **Ctrl-PgDn**.

4. Press **Del** or **F10**.

Deleting a Format Line

You cannot delete the Format Line at the top of the page (Line 0). You may delete Format Lines inserted in text:

1. Position your cursor under the Format Line.

2. Press **Del**.

3. Press **F9**.

4. Press **Del** or **F10**.

Undoing Deletions

If you delete using the Del key, the - key, or destructive backspace, you may undo your deletions starting with the most recent deletion. To restore,

1. Place your cursor where you want restorations to appear.

2. Press the * key on the numeric keypad.

3. The most recent character or character string appears.

4. Continue to press the * key until the text you want appears.

When you undo the deletion, the characters are replayed as they were deleted. For example, if you use destructive backspace to delete a line one character at a time, the Undo Delete function restores one character at a time. If you delete a paragraph by pressing Del, Return, and then Del or F10, the Undo Delete function restores the paragraph with one press of the * key.

How much deleted text is available to undo? The amount of text available is constrained only by the size of memory. When the last character available is

undone, the message NO DELETED TEXT TO UNDO appears. The Undo Delete
memory is cleared when you repaginate or exit the document.

Highlighting

Whether you are deleting, moving, or copying text, you can use the quick
cursor movements shown in table 7.1 to highlight characters, words, lines,
sentences, paragraphs, full screens of text, columns, and pages.

- Characters to be *deleted* are highlighted by first pressing **Del**.

- Characters to be *moved* are highlighted by first pressing **F7**.

- Characters to be *copied* are highlighted by first pressing **F8**.

You may want to take a moment to adjust the contrast of your screen so that
a good balance exists between the regular characters and the highlighted
characters. A very bright screen makes the highlighted characters fuzzy and
hard to read.

Table 7.1
Quick Cursor Movements for Highlighting Text

To highlight	Do this
Several characters	Highlight any character and type the last character to highlight. The cursor then moves to the first occurrence of that character.
A word	Highlight the first character in the word, press the space bar, and continue pressing the space bar to highlight as many words as desired. Or, with the cursor anywhere in the word, highlight it and press Alt-F5.
A line	Highlight a character and move the down-arrow key across lines. Or highlight a character and, with the cursor anywhere in the line, press Alt-F6.
A sentence	Highlight the first character of the sentence and press the key related to the punctuation mark at the end of the sentence. Or highlight a character and, with the cursor anywhere in the sentence, press Alt-F7.

A paragraph	Highlight the first character of the paragraph and press Return. Or highlight a character and, with the cursor anywhere in the paragraph, press Alt-F8.
A screenful	Press Home, highlight the first character, and then press End to mark the last character.
A column	See Chapter 12.
A page	Highlight the first character and then press Ctrl-End to mark through the end of the page. Or highlight the first character and then press Ctrl-PgDn to highlight up to the first character on the next page.
Several pages	Highlight a character, press F1, enter the page number, and press Return (see Chapter 9).

Moving Text

When you move text, MultiMate Advantage II transfers the highlighted text from one part of the document to another and deletes the text from its original location.

To move text,

1. Press **F7**.

The prompt MOVE WHAT? appears in the upper right corner of your screen.

To highlight the text you want to move,

2. Use any one of the cursor movements described in the preceding section of this chapter.

3. Press **F7** or **F10**.

The prompt TO WHERE? appears.

4. Move the cursor to the location within your document where you want the text to appear.

5. Press **F7** or **F10**.

MultiMate Advantage II moves the text.

If you are transferring large blocks of text or moving text close to the first or last line of the screen, the text on the screen may "jump" during the move. Don't worry, the Move function won't be affected.

If you try to move more text than MultiMate Advantage II can handle, a message appears in the lower left corner of the screen. When you move text, pay close attention to the spaces in your text. Moving text takes longer when you have to go back and add or delete spaces.

Moving Format Lines

If the text you are moving contains an inserted Format Line, MultiMate Advantage II moves the Format Line along with the other text.

Suppose that you want to move the current Format Line, but it does not lie within the text. Perhaps the inserted Format Line lies above the text you want to move, or perhaps it rests on Line 0. To move a copy of such a Format Line with your text,

   1. Press **F7**.

The prompt MOVE WHAT? appears.

   2. Press **F9**.

And continue with the rest of the Move function. MultiMate Advantage II moves both the current Format Line and the text. If you move text and forget to press F9 to move the appropriate Format Line, move the text back to the original position and start the move operation over.

Escaping a Move

If you want to stop a move and you have not pressed F7 or F10 for the final time, press *Esc*.

Copying Text

The Copy function, which is controlled by the F8 key, *duplicates* text in a different location in the document.

The move key (F7) and the copy key (F8) are side by side, so pressing one key when you meant to press the other is easy to do. The prompts in the upper right corner of the screen help you realize when you have made a mistake. For example, if you think you pressed F8 but the prompt says MOVE WHAT?, you know you pressed the wrong key.

To copy text,

1. Place the cursor at the beginning of the text to be copied.

2. Press **F8**.

The prompt COPY WHAT? appears on your screen. (Make sure this prompt says COPY, not MOVE.)

3. Highlight the text you want to copy.

4. Press **F8** or **F10**.

The prompt TO WHERE? appears.

5. Move the cursor to the location within your document where you want the text copied.

6. Press **F8** or **F10**.

MultiMate Advantage II copies the text to the second location and reformats it. At any point before step 6, you can stop the copying process by pressing *Esc*.

If you finish copying and do not like the results, simply delete the material you copied.

Copying the Format Line

If the Format Line lies within the text you are copying, MultiMate Advantage II copies the Format Line as well as the text. If the Format Line lies above the text you want to copy, copy both the Format Line and the text by pressing *F9* after you press *F8* to begin the copy.

If you forget to copy the Format Line and MultiMate Advantage II moves the text to a spot with a different Format Line, the result may be unsatisfactory—especially if you have used tabs or indents extensively. In this case, deleting the copied material and copying the material again is often the easiest solution to the problem. Or, you may copy the Format Line above the text you copied.

Using External Copy To Copy a Document

One of MultiMate Advantage II's unique features permits you to copy text from one document to another: the feature is called External Copy. The documents involved must be MultiMate Advantage II documents, but those documents do not have to reside on the same disk. (Chapter 19 discusses converting other documents into MultiMate Advantage II documents.)

To copy text from one document to another,

> 1. Position the cursor in the document where you want to place the copied text.
>
> 2. Press **Shift-F8**.

You press F8 for a regular copy, so Shift-F8 should be easy to remember. When you press Shift-F8, the prompt lines shown in figure 7.1 appear.

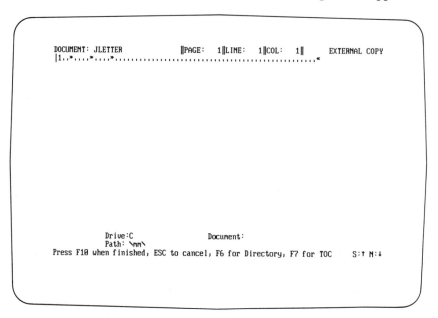

```
DOCUMENT: JLETTER              ‖PAGE:  1‖LINE:  1‖COL:  1‖     EXTERNAL COPY
|1..*.....*....*..........................................*




                 Drive:C              Document:
                 Path: \nn\
         Press F10 when finished, ESC to cancel, F6 for Directory, F7 for TOC    S:↑ N:↓
```

Fig. 7.1. Prompt that appears after you press Shift-F8.

> 3. Enter the drive and path, if necessary. If you are using a floppy disk system, place the floppy diskette on which the document resides in the appropriate drive.
>
> 4. Type only the first eight letters of the document name; you do not type the file extension *.DOC*.

If you do not remember the name of the document, press *F6* to see a directory of the documents on the drive and path.

If you want to copy from a table of contents, press *F7* and enter the name of the table of contents (in place of a document name).

If the document is not on the drive you have designated, or if you misspelled the name, MultiMate Advantage II displays Unable to find Document in the lower right corner of the screen.

    5. Press **F10**.

MultiMate Advantage II places the cursor at the beginning of the document and prompts this:

    START COPY WHERE?

    6. Move the cursor to the beginning of the text to be copied.

    7. Press **Shift-F8** or **F10**.

MultiMate Advantage II prompts this:

    COPY WHAT?

    8. Press **F9** if you want to copy the Format Line.

    9. Move the cursor to highlight the text you want to copy.

    10. Press **Shift-F8** or **F10**.

MultiMate Advantage II returns the cursor to the original document and moves the highlighted material.

If you want to stop the External Copy before you've completed the procedure, you must press Esc *before* you press Shift-F8 or F10 for the last time. If you accidentally copy material you do not want, simply delete it.

If you have a floppy disk system and removed the System disk to copy from a disk other than the one you are working on, replace the System disk now.

Using External Copy To Copy a Table of Contents

You may copy a table of contents from one document to another.

    1. Position the cursor in the document where you want to place the copied table of contents.

    2. Press **Shift-F8**. (The message F7 Switches to TOC at the bottom of the screen reminds you to press **F7** in order to copy a table of contents.)

3. Press **F7**.

4. Change the letter drive designation, if necessary.

5. You may press **Shift-F1** for a list of the table of contents on the drive.

6. Type the name of the table of contents.

7. Press **F10**.

8. Move the cursor to the beginning of the text to be copied.

9. Press **Shift-F8**.

10. Press **F9** if you want to copy the Format Line.

11. Move the cursor to highlight the text to be copied.

12. Press **Shift-F8** or **F10**.

Importing ASCII Files

Similar to the way you use External Copy, you may import ASCII files directly into MultiMate Advantage II documents.

1. Place the cursor in the document where you want to place the copied text. You may not copy into footnotes or libraries.

2. Press **Ctrl-6**.

3. Type in the drive, path, and ASCII file name (with extension).

If you do not know the file name, press *F6* to see a list of the file names. Or, enter a file name with a wildcard character (? for single characters or * for multiple characters) and then press *F6* for a directory of the files that match the entry. Type in the actual file name before proceeding.

4. Press **F10**.

To stop the import, press *Esc*. If text already has been imported, it remains in the MultiMate Advantage II document.

The entire ASCII file is entered at the cursor location. A new Format Line of 156 characters is created with tabs set every five characters through column 30. You may want to edit or delete the Format Line.

You may also use the ASCII File Conversion Utility to convert ASCII files to MultiMate Advantage II files. This method takes more time but may convert characters more accurately (such as underlines and Returns).

8
Enhancing Document Appearance

The kinds of word processing tasks you do with MultiMate Advantage II may require that you use special symbols either to improve the appearance of your documents or to accommodate scientific or mathematical text.

For example, if you work with technical documentation, you may already know that you can use the MultiMate Advantage II subscript symbols to move the number 2 below the regular print line in the scientific notation for water, H_2O. And, if you work in the marketing department, you may already know that special features of MultiMate Advantage II permit you to create sales reports that include bar charts and line drawings.

This chapter explores how you can use the features of MultiMate Advantage II to create a more polished document. By examining such topics as how to *underscore* (underline) text for greater impact, how to add subscripts and superscripts to your documents, how to add drama to your text using a variety of print sizes, how to use soft hyphens to provide a more pleasing format, and how to add headers and footers, you will discover how to use MultiMate Advantage II to produce more professional-looking documents.

Using Text Underline

MultiMate Advantage II provides you with two ways to underscore your text: *traditional underlining* and *auto-underlining*. To underline a few words, you use traditional underlining. If you want to underline many characters, use auto-underlining.

Traditional Underlining

To underline your text in the traditional manner, press *Shift* and the *Underline/Hyphen* key. If your computer does not have a color board, the underline appears as a regular underscore on your screen; if you have a color board, the characters you underline appear in reverse video.

To delete an underline, strike over the underlined characters or underline the characters again. When you underline characters twice, the characters stay in place, but the underline disappears. Underlining the characters a third time replaces the underline.

Auto-Underlining

Auto-underlining eliminates typing text and retracing your steps to underline it. When you specify auto-underlining, MultiMate Advantage II automatically underscores the characters *as you type them*. You can underline only letters and numbers, or you can auto-underline all symbols, including punctuation, spaces, mathematical symbols, international characters, and so forth.

To underline *only* alphabetical characters (A-Z and a-z) and numbers (0-9) automatically, press *Alt* and the +/= key. The Caps Lock/Num Lock key symbols in the lower right corner of your screen will appear to be underscored if your computer doesn't have a graphics board and monitor. They appear in reverse video if your computer is equipped with a graphics board and monitor.

Checking the Caps Lock/Num Lock symbol is an easy way to tell whether auto-underlining is on or off.

To end auto-underlining, press *Alt* and the +/= key again. The underline or reverse video of the Caps Lock/Num Lock symbols disappears.

To remove the underline in all or part of the text, retype the underlined characters. Another alternative is to press *Shift* and the *Underline/Hyphen* key to strike over the underlined characters.

To underline *all* letters, numbers, punctuation, spaces, and symbols with auto-underlining, press *Alt* and the *Underline/Hyphen* key. The Caps Lock/Num Lock key symbols appear underlined, and, from that point on, all the characters and spaces you type are underlined.

To end auto-underlining, press *Alt* and the *Underline/Hyphen* key

To remove the underline from parts of the text, use the same methods described earlier: either strike over the underline or use *Shift* and the *Underline/Hyphen* key.

Using Symbols in MultiMate Advantage II

Two kinds of symbols exist in MultiMate Advantage II:

- Regular symbols that you can use in the text to be printed

- Symbols that MultiMate Advantage II reserves for use with special functions

The symbols you can use in your text to be printed are those on the typewriter-like keys and include the percent symbol (%), the greater-than symbol (>), and so on.

Additional symbols become available if you edit the PAT (Printer Action Table). Essentially, you give up a symbol on your screen to be able to substitute another symbol. Chapter 10 explores this option. Other symbols are available only through alternate keyboards.

Alternate Keyboards

Six alternate keyboards are available for MultiMate Advantage II. They are the NORMAL, ROMANCE, GERMANIC, MATH, GRAPHIC1, and GRAPHIC2 keyboards.

Figure 8.1 illustrates the alternate keyboards and the symbols that you can display on your screen. Remember, your printer may not print each symbol.

To access an alternate keyboard,

1. Hold down **Alt-K** until the alternate keyboard of your choice is revealed in the upper right corner of your screen.

Although the keyboard prompt will disappear, you can select a symbol at any time.

2. Press **Ctrl** and the letter key identified in the table.

You do not need to turn off this function; the symbols will appear in text *only* when you press *Ctrl* with a letter key.

MultiMate Advantage II reserves some symbols for use with special functions. For instance, a double wavy line tells MultiMate Advantage II to use a particular type of hyphen. If you try to use any symbol MultiMate Advantage II reserves for special purposes, the message INVALIDKEY appears at the bottom of your screen.

Not all printers can print all the underlines and symbols that MultiMate Advantage II can display on the screen. Printing an underline without characters (just a line) is a particularly pesky problem for printers. Some printers print lines that appear as solid lines, and others print lines that appear as a series of dashes.

To find out what your printer can print, read your manual and experiment by printing symbols and underlines.

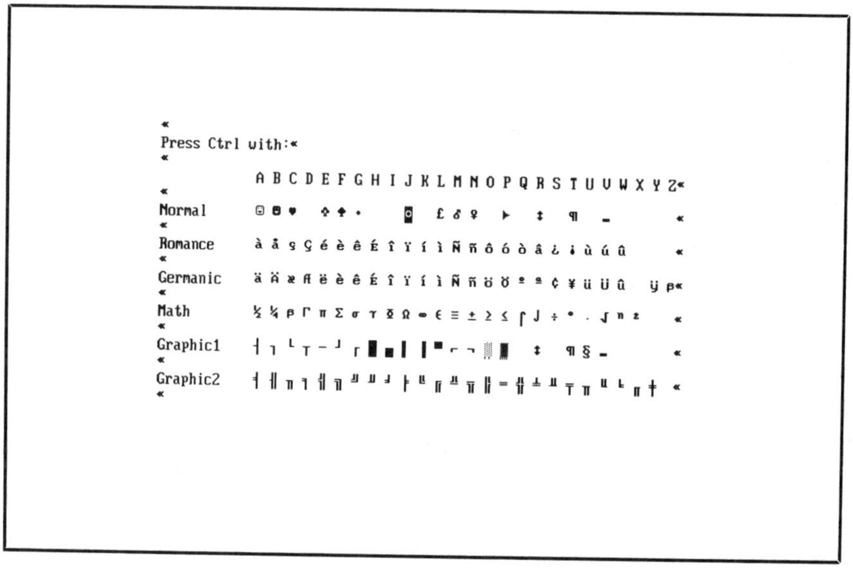

Fig. 8.1. Alternate keyboards and symbols.

Double Underscore

You can use screen symbols to double underscore text if your printer supports multiple printing (check your printer manual).

1. Place the cursor where the double underscore should begin.

2. Press **Ctrl** and the **Hyphen/Underline** key.

A double arrow appears.

3. Type the text to be double underscored.

4. Press **Ctrl** and the **Hyphen/Underline** key.

Using Hyphens: Hard and Soft

MultiMate Advantage II uses two kinds of hyphens: hard hyphens and soft hyphens. You use hard hyphens in words that *always* are hyphenated; words such as *ill-advised* and *fleur-de-lis*.

Words that include soft hyphens may move during reformatting, and the soft hyphen will be permanently removed (unless the word falls at the end of a line). If you reformat the text after additional editing changes, and you want soft hyphens in specific places, you must reinsert them. Soft hyphens allow parts of multisyllable words to be wrapped to the following line, which produces a less "jagged" right margin.

To create a hard hyphen (which assures you that the hyphenated word will remain hyphenated regardless of how the document is reformatted), you use the *Underline/Hyphen* key. If you are at the end of a line and want to hyphenate the syllables of a word, consider using soft hyphens instead.

To insert a soft hyphen,

1. Place the cursor on the character that follows the hyphen.

2. Press **Shift-F7**.

MultiMate Advantage II inserts a soft hyphen, which appears as a double curved line ($\approx$) on the screen but as a regular hyphen in your printed document.

Using Hard Spaces

The symbol for a hard space (ϕ) controls how text is handled at the end of a line.

There will be times when you won't want words to wrap around; for example, a proper name such as Mr. Smith should always appear in full in the line rather than separated on two lines. Dates (January 1, 1990) should not be divided. To prevent word wrapping for a specific space, insert a hard space.

1. Move the cursor to the location where you want the hard space to appear.

2. Press **Alt-S**.

During printing, the hard space symbol does not appear, but the space it occupies does appear. The hard space symbol represents a blank space, so you do not need to add another space to separate characters.

Using Strikeout Characters

You can automatically strike out characters by placing the characters you want struck between the strikeout symbols.

Pressing Alt-O creates a strikeout symbol (⊥). The strikeout symbol doesn't print, but any text between two strikeout symbols will print with slashes over the text like this: U̸s̸e̸/A̸l̸t̸/w̸i̸t̸h̸/O̸/t̸o̸/s̸t̸r̸i̸k̸e̸o̸u̸t̸.

Chapter 18 explains how to change the symbol for strikeouts.

Using Right-Justification

If you *right-justify* your text, you'll create a document in which all of the lines of text end precisely at the right margin. You control this feature from the Print Parameters for Document screen (see Chapter 10) rather than from the document itself. Your text appears right-justified only when you print it, not when it is displayed on the screen.

Using Print Modes

Your printer may support one or more of four print modes. These modes (which range from very dark print to very light print) are called *Shadow*, *Bold*, *Enhanced*, and *Draft*. Test your printer to see what modes it supports.

Shadow Print

Shadow is the darkest print mode. Each character is struck twice. The second time the character is printed, it is positioned slightly to the right, producing type similar to boldface type. To shadow-print text, insert the Shadow print symbol on both sides of the text (not just one side). The Shadow print symbol will not appear in your printed document.

To create Shadow print text,

1. Position your cursor at the point where you want to begin the Shadow print.

2. Press **Alt-X**.

A Shadow print symbol (⊩) appears.

3. Type in the text you want to appear as Shadow print in your document.

4. Press **Alt-X**.

Use *Ins* to insert the Shadow print symbol into existing text.

Bold Print

Bold print is slightly lighter than Shadow print but darker than Enhanced print. Your printer will print each letter twice, one on top of the other, to create text that will appear bold in your printed document:

1. Move the cursor to the location where you want to begin Bold print.

2. Press **Alt-Z**.

The Bold print symbol (▌) appears.

3. Type the text to be printed in Bold print.

4. Press **Alt-Z**.

As with all other print mode symbols, this symbol does not appear in your printed document. *Ins* can be used to insert the Bold print symbol into existing text. To remove Bold print, simply delete the beginning and ending Bold print symbols using the Delete character key.

Enhanced Print

Enhanced print emphasizes the text in your printed documents by creating text that appears darker than text generally appears. Enhanced print is a MultiMate Advantage II feature that causes characters to be printed in Double Strike print mode.

The menu you use to print your documents permits you to choose whether to print your document in Single Strike or Double Strike print mode (see Chapter 10). If you are printing in Single Strike Mode, you may want to use Enhanced print to make portions of the text stand out. If you are printing in Double Strike Mode, you would not use Enhanced print.

To create Enhanced print text,

1. Position the cursor where you want the Enhanced print to start.

2. Press **Alt-N**.

The Enhanced print symbol (∩) appears.

3. Type the text you want to print as Enhanced print.

4. Press **Alt-D**.

Alt-D tells MultiMate Advantage II where to end the Enhanced print and begin the regular Draft print. The Draft print symbol (δ) appears.

Ins can be used to insert the Enhanced print symbol, and *Del* can be used to delete the beginning Enhanced print symbol and the ending Draft print symbol.

When printing, MultiMate Advantage II ignores the space taken up by the Enhanced print symbol, so you must add the spaces needed between the characters and words in your text.

Draft Print

Draft print causes text between Draft print symbols to print in Single Strike Mode. You may want to print portions of your text in Single Strike Mode if you are going to choose the Double Strike print option when you print the document (see Chapter 10). To set Draft print,

    1. Move the cursor to the location where you want the Draft print to begin.

    2. Press **Alt-D**.

The Draft print symbol (δ) appears. To mark the end of the text to be printed in Draft print, insert the Enhanced print symbol:

    3. Press **Alt-N**.

Use *Ins* to insert the Draft print symbol into existing text. Remember to add any necessary spaces. MultiMate Advantage II does not print the Draft print symbols or the spaces they occupy.

Using Print Pitch

You can vary the look of your text by changing the pitch of the print. *Pitch* simply means the size and spacing of printed text measured by the number of characters per inch. You may want to change the pitch of your document from 10 pitch to 17.6 to add notes in smaller print, or you may want to use 5 pitch to emphasize characters in headings. MultiMate Advantage II defaults to 10 pitch.

The program assigns a special number called a *Pitch Indicator* to each of the most common print pitches. Your printer may support all or just some of the available print pitches; check your printer manual and experiment with your printer to find the pitch that prints closest to the one you have selected. Table 8.1 lists the print pitches MultiMate Advantage II supports.

Table 8.1
Print Pitches Supported by MultiMate Advantage II

MultiMate Advantage II Pitch Indicator	Equivalent Characters per Inch (CPI)	
1	5	Large
2	6	
3	8.5	
4 (default)	10	
5	12	
6	13.2	
7	15	
8	16.5	
9	17.6	Small

Altering Print Pitch

Character Print Pitch is a special effect you can turn on or off from your document. This feature is useful with dot-matrix printers only. To change the print pitch on a daisywheel printer, see the section *Using Printer Control Codes* in this chapter. You use the Print Parameters for Document screen (described in Chapter 10) to set the pitch in which your document will begin printing.

To use a different pitch in your document,

1. Position the cursor where you want the Character Print Pitch to begin.

2. Press **Alt-C**.

The print pitch symbol (P_t) appears.

3. Type the MultiMate Advantage II Pitch Indicator number.

Use the information from table 8.1 to determine which number you must type. Do *not* leave a space between the print pitch symbol and the Pitch Indicator, or the number of the Pitch Indicator will print out (instead of serving as a pitch symbol to the system).

4. Type the text you want to appear in the new pitch.

5. Press **Alt-C**.

In step 6, you'll type in the indicator number you want to switch to. The Pitch Indicator can be either the original default or another Pitch Indicator. If you do not insert another print pitch symbol and Pitch Indicator, your document continues printing in the last pitch you selected.

> 6. Type the MultiMate Advantage II Pitch Indicator number.

Figure 8.2 shows an example of a pitch changed from *10 pitch* (Pitch Indicator 4) to *5 pitch* (Pitch Indicator 1). Both the on-screen and printed appearances are illustrated. This particular example was generated using MultiMate Advantage II and a dot-matrix NEC Pinwriter P2™ printer.

You must pay close attention to spacing when you alter the print pitch. Remember, the smaller the pitch setting, the larger the print. For example, 5-pitch printing takes up more space than the 10-pitch printing.

The placement of the print pitch symbol is also very important. In figure 8.2, the print pitch symbols are positioned to create the same size space before and after the 5-pitch printing. The MultiMate Advantage II Pitch Indicator 4 controls the spacing between each sentence (for 10-pitch spacing).

Screen appearance (10 pitch print default, Print Indicator 4):

```
DOCUMENT: tnum                    ‖PAGE:  1‖LINE:  2‖COL:  1‖
|1..»....»....»....»....»....»....»....»....»....«
«
This is 10 pitch. ℝ1This is 5 pitch.ℝ4  This is 10 pitch.«
```

Printed appearance (10 pitch print default, Print Indicator 4):

This is 10 pitch. This is 5 pitch.   This is 10 pitch.

Fig. 8.2. Example of 10 pitch changed to 5 pitch.

Using Printer Control Codes

You will want to read your printer manual to find out if your printer will print special characters. If your printer does print these special characters, you can type a printer control character to use them.

Press the Printer Control Code keys where you want the special printing function to occur and press *Alt-A*. The Printer Control Code symbol (μ) appears.

Immediately after the Printer Control Code symbol, type the three-digit, decimal-value number that represents the code for the special character.

(Your printer manual lists the characters that can be sent and lists the codes representing those characters.) That code must be a number between *000* and *255*.

Pausing the Printer

If you want to use a different font or print pitch in a document printed by a daisywheel printer, the printer must pause at a certain point so that you can switch print wheels. The printer also must pause if you want to print part of a document in another color. To pause your printer,

1. Move the cursor to the location in the document where you want the printer to pause.

2. Press **Alt-P**.

When your printer encounters the pause symbol, the printer pauses (the symbol does not print), and you can make changes to the printer.

3. Press **Esc** to continue printing.

Using Superscripts and Subscripts

In MultiMate Advantage II, there are designated symbols that represent superscripts and subscripts. Superscripts are numbers or letters that appear half a line above the regular line; for example, the formula $E=MC^2$ includes the superscript 2. Footnotes frequently are marked with superscript numbers.

Subscripts are numbers or letters that appear half a line below the regular line, as in the formula for water, H_2O. The number 2 is a subscript. You use the same symbols for superscripts and subscripts, but you insert them in a different order.

To create a superscript,

1. Place your cursor where you want to insert the superscript.

2. Press **Alt-Q**.

An up-arrow symbol appears on the screen. The up-arrow tells MultiMate Advantage II to position the next character(s) above the line.

3. Type the character(s) for the superscript.

4. Press **Alt-W**.

Alt-W creates a down-arrow symbol on the screen, which instructs the system to return to regular print.

You create a subscript the same way you create a superscript but with the keys reversed. To create a subscript,

1. Move the cursor to the location where you want the subscript to appear.

2. Press **Alt-W**.

The down-arrow symbol appears.

3. Type the subscript text.

4. Press **Alt-Q**.

The screen displays an up-arrow symbol, which signals the system to return to regular print. MultiMate Advantage II does not print the up- or down-arrow symbols and ignores the spaces they occupy (see fig. 8.3).

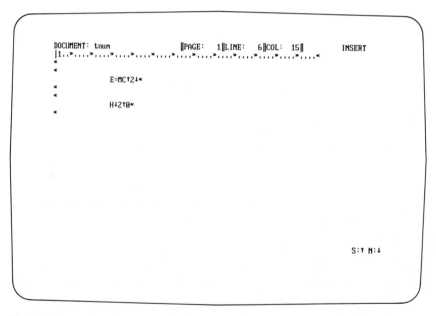

Fig. 8.3. Superscripts and subscripts.

Using Headers and Footers

When you create a document that is several pages long, you may want the same information to appear at the top or bottom of more than one page of your document.

Information appearing at the top of the page is called a *header*; information that appears at the bottom of the page is called a *footer*. Figure 8.4 illustrates a header and a footer as they would appear on your screen. Figure 8.5 illustrates a header and a footer as they would appear in your printed document.

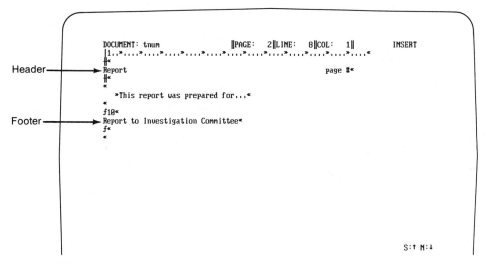

Fig. 8.4. On-screen header and footer.

Report   page 1

   This report was prepared for ...

Report to Investigation Committee

Fig. 8.5. Printed header and footer.

For a simple header or footer, you need to insert the header or footer only once in the document. MultiMate Advantage II automatically places the header or footer text on each page of the document as it prints.

Headers

To create a header,

1. Position the cursor at the top of the first page on which you want the header to appear.

This page does not have to be the first page of your document; putting the first header on the page following the cover page is common. Remember to place the header on the top line of the page; the header will not print if Return symbols or characters lie above it.

   2. Press **Alt-H**.

The header symbol appears on the screen as a stylized H ($\#$).

   3. Press **Return**.

   4. Type the information you want to appear in the header.

You can type a maximum of five lines in the header, using any MultiMate Advantage II regular features (centering, underlining, and so forth), with one exception: the # symbol. You use the # symbol to instruct the system to insert page numbers automatically.

Type # at the location in the header where you want page numbers inserted. If your document is 10 pages or longer, make sure enough room separates the symbol and the right-margin marker in the Format Line so that two or more digits can print. Otherwise, the page number digits will wrap around and appear on the next line.

You do not set the first page value in the header until you print the document using the Print Parameters for Document screen (described in Chapter 10).

   5. Press **Alt-H**.

   6. Press **Return**.

Your system will print the header on each page that follows in the document and will print the header that it most recently encountered.

If you want the header to print on only a few pages, you can create what is called an *empty header* on the first page that will not contain a header. Type the header symbol twice, without any text in between the symbols. In other words, go to the top of the page and press *Alt-H* and *Return*; then press *Alt-H* and *Return* again. You may enter a new header after the empty header.

If you want to print a different header on opposite pages, all you must do is set up the first header on one page and the second header on the following page. One page will be numbered with even numbers, and the other page will be numbered with odd numbers. The system will continue this pattern throughout the document, unless you create empty headers.

Footers

Setting up and using footers is similar to setting up and using headers. To create a footer,

1. Select the first page on which you want a footer to appear.

2. Using the **Return** key, space down to the beginning of the line on which you want the footer to appear.

3. Press **Alt-F**.

4. Type the line number on which you want the footer to start.

MultiMate Advantage II prints each footer on the line number you enter on this first page, so make sure to space down far enough to avoid printing over text on other pages of your document (but not so far as to print off the page).

5. Press **Return**.

The footer symbol appears as a stylized f (f) followed by the line number.

6. Type the footer text.

You can use all the regular MultiMate Advantage II features and symbols as you create the footer, except the # symbol. Wherever the # symbol appears in the footer, MultiMate Advantage II prints a page number. Page numbering begins on the page you indicate and continues on each page thereafter.

The program sets the value of the first page number when you print the document. (See the Print Parameters for Document screen described in Chapter 10.) If you use page numbers, make sure to leave enough room so that double, or even triple, digits print without wrapping around to the next line.

7. Press **Return**.

8. Press **Alt-F**.

9. Press **Return**.

The footer text must be the last text you type on the page.

You can create an empty footer to cancel a footer from continuing to print:

1. Locate the first page on which you do not want the footer to appear.

2. Press **Alt-F**.

3. Press **Return**.

4. Press **Alt-F**.

5. Press **Return**.

You may enter a new footer after the canceled footer. To print footers on alternating pages, put the first footer on either an even- or odd-numbered page, and put the second footer on the following page.

Drawing Lines and Boxes

One of the special features of MultiMate Advantage II is that the program permits you to draw lines and boxes in your documents.

Some printers, however, do not support the characters generated. Therefore, you must be sure that you test the characters on your own printer before you use the feature. Check the Printer Action Table and Character Translation Width Table used on your Parameters for Document screen.

To draw a line or a box,

1. Move the cursor to the location on your screen where you want to begin the drawing.

2. Press **Alt-E**.

You will see the screen display shown in figure 8.6.

3. Press the number of the style you desire.

4. Use the **arrow keys** to move the cursor to draw your line or box.

As illustrated in figure 8.6, you press 7 to erase a line, and you press 8 to move the cursor without drawing a line.

5. Press **Alt-E** to leave the Line Draw Mode.

Using System Print Commands

System print commands automatically place system print information into your document. By inserting the symbols shown in table 8.2, you can instruct your printer to print the information indicated.

You can use the system print commands anywhere in your document, including your headers and footers.

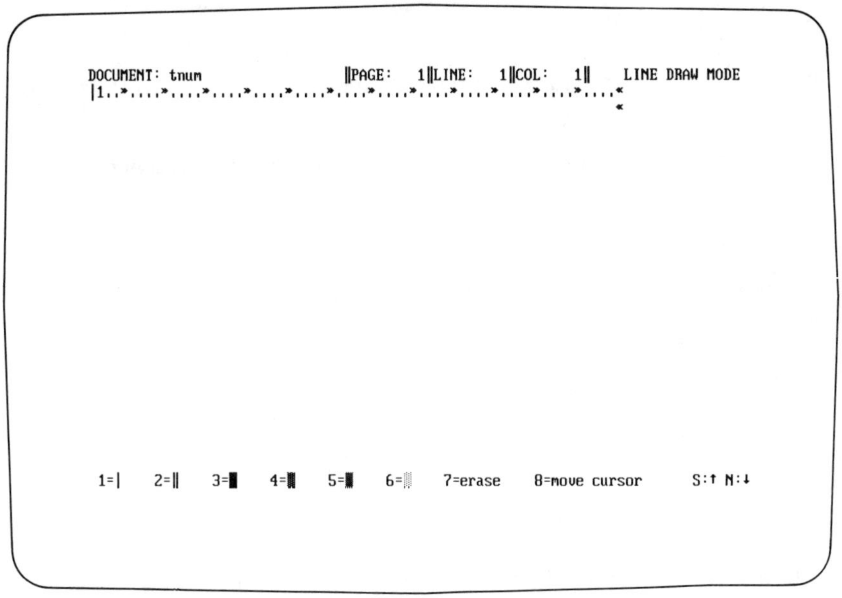

```
DOCUMENT: tnum              ‖PAGE:  1‖LINE:  1‖COL:  1‖   LINE DRAW MODE
|1..».....».....».....».....».....».....».....».....».....».....«
                                                          «


 1=|    2=‖   3=█   4=█   5=█   6=▒   7=erase   8=move cursor    S:↑ N:↓
```

Fig. 8.6. Line and box options.

Table 8.2
System Print Commands

Command	Information Printed
&DATE&	Prints the date entered when you started up the computer.
&TIME&	Prints the time entered when you started up the computer.
&PAGE&	Prints the page number that appears on the MultiMate Advantage II document screen.
&LPAGE&	Prints the page number on the last MultiMate Advantage II page in the document (the total page count).
&DOC&	Prints the document name.

Comments

You may enter comments in text. Comments must be on their own lines and cannot cross columns or pages.

1. Place the cursor in column 1 of the line where the comment will begin.

2. Press **Ctrl-[**

3. A double exclamation point appears (!!).

4. Press **Return**.

5. Enter any characters you want.

6. Press **Return**.

7. Press **Ctrl-[**

8. Press **Return**.

When you print the document, you may specify whether to print or skip the comments. (See the Print Comments option described in Chapter 10.) When you enter a comment, the lines are not counted in the page total. Repagination does not affect comments.

9
Paging

With MultiMate Advantage II, pages are arranged like those in a book. The top of each page starts on the first line of the screen. When you move from one page to the next, the previous page disappears from the screen, and the next page appears.

This chapter describes how to create individual pages, how to combine pages, and how to move between pages.

Document or Page Mode

Your pages may appear independently in Page Mode (the first line of each page is on the top of the screen) or in Document Mode (one page after another—paper-towel style). To control this, identify *D* for Document Mode or *P* for Page Mode on the Edit System Defaults screen. This screen is described in full in Chapter 18. You may change the mode at any time. Existing documents are affected.

Lines Per Page

MultiMate Advantage II's page-creating and page-deleting functions use either the system default of 55 lines per page or the number of lines you select as the maximum lines per page. If, while working on your document, you decide to change the number of lines per page of your entire document,

    1. Press **Alt-F2**.

This prompt appears in the bottom left corner of your screen. It displays the current maximum number of lines.

    `PAGE LINE LENGTH? [50]`

In the previous example, the prompt displayed the number of lines for a page currently set at 50 lines per page.

To change the page line maximum,

> 2. Strike over the number displayed with the number of lines per page you prefer.

> 3. Press **Return** or press **F10**.

Page Breaks

MultiMate Advantage II can insert an automatic page break for you, or you can insert a manual page break whenever you want to start a new page.

Automatic Page Breaks

The process of setting automatic page breaks (one of the steps you completed as you filled in the Create a Document screen) was discussed in Chapter 3.

To review briefly, the prompt Automatic Page Breaks? appears on the Modify Document Defaults screen. If you type *Y*, the system automatically ends each page either at the line number you type in the Number of Lines Per Page field, or the system ends each page at the system default value of 55 lines per page.

Manual Page Breaks

You have specified the number of lines per page when you create a document. If you do not select automatic page breaks, you must insert page breaks manually.

When you exceed the maximum number of lines per page that you elected as you created the document, the page number in the Status Line is displayed in reverse video and blinks; this signal indicates that you *should* insert a page break: press *F2*.

If you do not insert a page break, MultiMate Advantage II will let you continue to enter text—until you reach the 199 lines per page limit. Then, the system will insert the page break for you.

Remember that you can change the number of lines per page at any time. To do so,

> 1. Press **Alt-F2**.

> 2. Type the number of lines per page.

When you press F2 to create a page manually in Page Mode, you do not see a special page-break symbol.

Your cursor moves to the top of the new page. The Format Line at the top of that page is identical to the last Format Line on the previous page.

When you press F2 in Document Mode, the message PLEASE WAIT appears; then, a totally blank line and a new Format Line are inserted to mark the page break.

In addition to creating page breaks while you are creating a document, you can add page breaks to existing text:

1. Position your cursor under the first character of the text that you want to appear on the new page.

2. Press **F2**.

MultiMate Advantage II moves that character, and the text that follows, to the newly created page.

Additionally,

*   If you insert a page break in the middle of indented text, you do not need to insert indents on the new page to re-create the original indent; an indent is inserted for you.

*   If your cursor is on line 1 and column 1 of a page, and you press F2, the program creates a blank page prior to the page on which the cursor rests.

*   If you press F2 while your cursor is on the last line and column of a page, MultiMate Advantage II creates a blank page and moves your cursor to that page.

*   You can delete page breaks by combining pages. The *Combining Pages* section in this chapter will explain how it is done.

When you set your page breaks manually, try not to exceed the maximum lines per page suggested. You may remember from Chapter 3 that MultiMate Advantage II places limits on the number of lines in a page (199) and the number of pages in a document (250). The maximum data file size is 128K. If you exceed these limits, you run the risk of losing some of your text.

Last Page in a Document

If you allow for a page break on the last page of a document, your printer "prints" a blank page. If your document includes a header or footer, only the header or footer appears on the page. If you use continuous-form, perforated paper, you may find this arrangement useful. You can easily remove the printed pages without advancing the sheet feeder on the printer. If you use single-sheet paper, however, the extra page is a nuisance: you have to let the blank page print before you can print anything else.

It is important to press Return after you type the last line of your document; pressing Return assures you that the last line prints out completely. Generally, this procedure is an automatic response because documents usually end with a paragraph or punctuation; in this case, you press the Return key anyway.

Combining Pages

On occasion, you may want to combine pages in your document. You may have deleted enough text to make two short pages into one, or you may have inserted text that requires several subsequent pages be combined. Or, you may simply want to get rid of a blank page at the end of a document. You can combine pages manually, or you can combine pages automatically.

Combining Pages Manually

To combine two pages manually,

1. Place the cursor at the end of the first page you want to combine with another.

2. Press **Shift-F2**.

If you have not placed your cursor at the end of the first page, MultiMate Advantage II displays a warning:

```
 - ERROR: MUST BE AT END OF PAGE -
```

Format Lines carry over when you combine pages. If the Format Line on the second page differs from the Format Line on the first page, the Format Line on the second page also will be shown on the newly created page screen.

MultiMate Advantage II automatically renumbers the pages in your document to reflect the fact that you have combined pages.

Combining Pages Automatically

The second way to combine pages is to repaginate automatically several or all pages in the document. The *Automatic Repagination* function inserts and deletes page breaks to create pages that contain exactly the number of lines you have specified.

During automatic repagination, MultiMate Advantage II handles any required formatting. For example, if you specify that pages must be 45 lines long, and the 46th line of a page is the sixth of 10 lines of indented text, MultiMate Advantage II inserts the necessary indent symbols on the newly created page. Widows and orphans do not occur during automatic repagination.

To repaginate automatically,

1. Place your cursor at the beginning of the first page you want to repaginate.

2. Press **Ctrl-F2**.

The repagination window shown in figure 9.1 appears at the bottom of the screen.

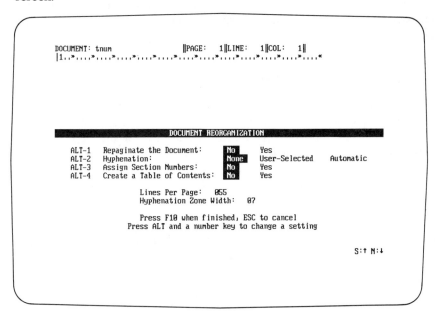

Fig. 9.1. The repagination window.

3. To change Repaginate the Document: press **Alt-1** between the words *No* and *Yes*.

4. Type the number of lines you want to appear on each page of your document after Lines per Page:

If you do not want to hyphenate, generate a table of contents, or reassign section numbers, select *No* or *None* in the other fields. These options are discussed later in this chapter.

5. Press **F10** to repaginate.

This message appears:

```
Repaginating - PLEASE WAIT
```

You may press *Esc* to cancel the Repaginate function and return to your document if you do it prior to step 5.

If you are carrying out *only* the Repaginate function, just those pages from the page where your cursor currently rests to the last page in the file will be repaginated. If you are creating a table of contents or renumbering sections, every page in the document will be repaginated if there is a *Y* in the Repaginate Document field.

Automatic Hyphenation

From the Document Reorganization screen (shown earlier), you may make one of the following choices for hyphenation: none, user-selected, or automatic. If you select none, no hyphens will be inserted when the document is repaginated. If you select user-selected, you will be able to select where the hyphen is entered. If you pick automatic, MultiMate Advantage II will insert a soft hyphen at appropriate points. Press *Alt-2* to switch among none, user-selected, and automatic.

If you will be adding hyphens, you may want to change the hyphenation zone width. This shows the longest blank space that will occur at the right margin. To change the hyphenation zone width,

1. Press the **up-** and **down-arrow** keys to move to the field.

2. Type in a new number; the minimum width is 3.

If you selected user-selected hyphenation, a screen like that shown in figure 9.2 appears whenever MultiMate Advantage II suggests a hyphen.

The cursor marks the suggested point of hyphenation. You may press *F10* to select the suggested point or *Esc* to cancel the operation. If you want to hyphenate at a different point than suggested, use one of the key presses shown in table 9.1 to move the cursor to the first character after the hyphen.

```
DOCUMENT: tnum              ||PAGE:  1||LINE:  4||COL: 61||
|1..».....».....».....».....».....».....».....».....»....«
This document is written to confirm the policies and procedures
used by the Ware Company relative to the continued questions
surrounding our methods of handling customer service.  It is
anticipated that the document will clear up ongoing misunderstandings
               and that the customer service record will
improve as a result.«




════════════════ DISCRETIONARY HYPHENATION ═══════════════

            Select The Desired Hyphenation Point

   <--        Previous Syllable    -->      Next Syllable
   Home       First Syllable       End      Last Possible Syllable
   Ctrl <--   Previous Character   Ctrl --> Next Character
                                   Ctrl End Last Possible Character

        Press F10 to select the current point, ESC to cancel


                                               S:↑ N:↓
```

Fig. 9.2. The User-Selected Hyphenation screen.

Table 9.1
Selecting the Hyphenation Point

Left-arrow	Previous syllable
Right-arrow	Next syllable
Home	First syllable
End	Last syllable
Ctrl with left-arrow	Previous character
Ctrl with right-arrow	Next character
Ctrl with End	Last possible character

Section Numbering and Table of Contents

Outlines, text with numbered paragraphs, and tables of contents are easy to produce with MultiMate Advantage II's Section Numbering feature. When you create a new document, you select the section number style (Roman or Numeric) on the Edit System Defaults screen.

To switch from one style to another after you have completed the Edit System Defaults screen,

1. Type **7**

2. Select **Edit System Defaults**.

3. Edit the default (**R** or **N**).

Instead of typing each section number (and editing all the section numbers if you add or delete a section), you enter symbols for section numbers. You can use MultiMate Advantage II to assign section numbers automatically.

To enter a section number symbol,

1. Move the cursor to the location on the screen where you want the section number to be positioned.

If you place your cursor after a tab or indent symbol, the section numbers for the document will be aligned by the tab or indent.

If you place your cursor after a decimal tab, the section numbers will be aligned by decimal tab (aligned on their decimal points). After positioning your cursor,

2. Press **Alt-U** as many times as required for the section of your outline.

The number of times you press Alt-U depends on the level of the section number you want to appear. For example, figure 9.3 illustrates the symbols that appear on the screen for either Roman or Numeric section numbers.

With Roman section numbers, one symbol creates a single Roman numeral (I., II., III., etc.), and two symbols create a single capital letter (A., B., C., etc.).

With Numeric section numbers, one symbol creates a single number (1., 2., 3., etc.), and two symbols create a double number (1.1, 2.1, 3.1, etc.).

Table 9.2 illustrates the types of section numbers MultiMate Advantage II will insert based on both the number of symbols you enter and the style you have selected. You can place from one to six symbols anywhere in your document.

Once the section symbols have been entered,

3. Press **Ctrl-F2**.

4. Press **Alt-3** to mark *Yes* in the Reassign Section Numbers field.

```
DOCUMENT: tnum                ‖PAGE:   1‖LINE:   1‖COL:   1‖
|1..ˮ....ˮ....ˮ....ˮ....ˮ....ˮ....ˮ....ˮ....ˮ....ˮ.............«
* →Types of Inventory«
«
    →There are three types of inventory in stock.  These are raw materials,
finished goods and preparation items.  Each is handled differently.«
«
   →** →Raw Materials«
«
    →    →Raw materials are the goods we buy from other suppliers.  When
     the goods are received at the loading dock, you must follow the dock
     procedures described later in this manual.«
«
   →** →Finished Goods«
«
    →    →Finished goods are the goods we produce.  These goods will reach
     the dock prepackaged and ready for shipment.«
«
   →** →Preparation Items«
«
    →    →Preparation items are raw materials that are in the process of
     being prepared to finished goods.  These materials are in the plant.«
«
* →Dock Procedures«
                                                        S:↑ M:↓
```

Fig. 9.3. Symbols for section numbers.

Table 9.2
Section Numbers Based on the Number of Symbols and Style

No. of Symbols	Roman	Numeric
1	I., II., III., . . .	1., 2., 3., . . .
2	A., B., C., . . .	1.1., 2.1., . . .
3	1., 2., 3., . . .	1.1.1., 2.1.1., . . .
4	a., b., c., . . .	1.1.1.1., 2.1.1.1., . . .
5	(1), (2), (3), . . .	1.1.1.1.1., 2.1.1.1.1., . . .
6	(a),(b),(c), . . .	1.1.1.1.1.1., 2.1.1.1.1.1., . . .

If you want to generate a table of contents that corresponds to the section numbers,

5. Press **Alt-4** to mark *Yes* in the Generate a Table of Contents field.

6. Press **F10** to continue the function.

This message appears on your screen:

```
Repaginating - PLEASE WAIT
```

(If you did not place a *Y* in the Repaginate Document field, the document is not repaginated. Only the section numbers are manipulated.)

Once the process is complete, the repagination window disappears. Section numbers and their symbols appear as shown in figure 9.4.

```
DOCUMENT: tnum                    ‖PAGE:   1‖LINE:   1‖COL:   1‖
|1..▸....▸....▸....▸....▸....▸....▸....▸....▸....▸....▸.............◂
◂
*I.▸Types of Inventory◂
◂
    ▸There are three types of inventory in stock.  These are raw materials,
finished goods and preparation items.  Each is handled differently.◂
◂
   ▸**A.▸Raw Materials◂
◂
    ▸    ▸Raw materials are the goods we buy from other suppliers.  When
    the goods are received at the loading dock, you must follow the dock
    procedures described later in this manual.◂
◂
   ▸**B.▸Finished Goods◂
◂
    ▸    ▸Finished goods are the goods we produce.  These goods will reach
    the dock prepackaged and ready for shipment.◂
◂
   ▸**C.▸Preparation Items◂
◂
    ▸    ▸Preparation items are raw materials that are in the process of
    being prepared to finished goods.  These materials are in the plant.◂
◂
*II.   ▸Dock Procedures◂
                                                        S:↑ N:↓
```

Fig. 9.4. Section numbers and their symbols.

You may want to edit the Format Line to align the section numbers before printing. If you want to edit the table of contents,

1. Press **Alt-1** to edit the document.

2. Press **F7** to switch to the Table of Contents Edit screen.

3. Use document editing procedures to edit the table of contents.

The system Format Line is used as the table of contents Format Line.

After you have completed editing on the section numbers and table of contents,

4. Print the table of contents and the document.

The section numbers print without the symbols. Figure 9.5 illustrates the appearance of the table of contents and section numbers when printed.

```
I.    Types of Inventory...................................................1
      A.   Raw Materials..................................................1
      B.   Finished Goods.................................................1
      C.   Preparation Items..............................................1
II.   Dock Procedures.....................................................1
      A.   Get the Purchase Order.........................................1
      B.   Inspect the Goods for Damage...................................1
      C.   Return Damaged Goods...........................................1
      D.   Inspect the Quality of the Goods...............................1
      E.   Forward Goods to Destination...................................1


I.     Types of Inventory

         There are three types of inventory in stock.  These are raw materials,
finished goods and preparation items.  Each is handled differently.

      A.    Raw Materials

            Raw materials are the goods we buy from other suppliers.  When the
goods are received at the loading dock, you must follow the dock
procedures described later in this manual.

      B.    Finished Goods

            Finished goods are the goods we produce.  These goods will reach
the dock prepackaged and ready for shipment.

      C.    Preparation Items

            Preparation itmes are raw materials that are in the process of
being prepared to finished goods.  These materials are in the plant.

II.    Dock Procedures
```

Fig. 9.5. Printout illustrating table of contents and section numbers.

Whenever you add or delete section numbers, use the repagination window to reassign section numbers. When you generate a new table of contents as the result of changing section numbers, you lose any edits that you performed on the old table of contents. The table of contents documents include the file extension *.TOC* instead of *.DOC*. You must use DOS commands to erase or copy the table of contents documents.

Footnotes

You can add footnote references that automatically appear at the bottom of the page of your printed document. A musical note symbolizes footnote text. When the document is printed, the symbol is replaced with a sequentially bracketed number (like [1]) if your printer doesn't support superscript, or the symbol prints as a superscript if your printer has that capability.

To add a footnote,

1. Move the cursor to the location on the screen where you want the footnote reference in the text to appear.

  2. Press **Alt-V**.

The footnote window shown in figure 9.6 appears.

  3. Type in your footnote text, up to a page in length.

  4. Press **F10**.

The musical note symbol appears in your text.

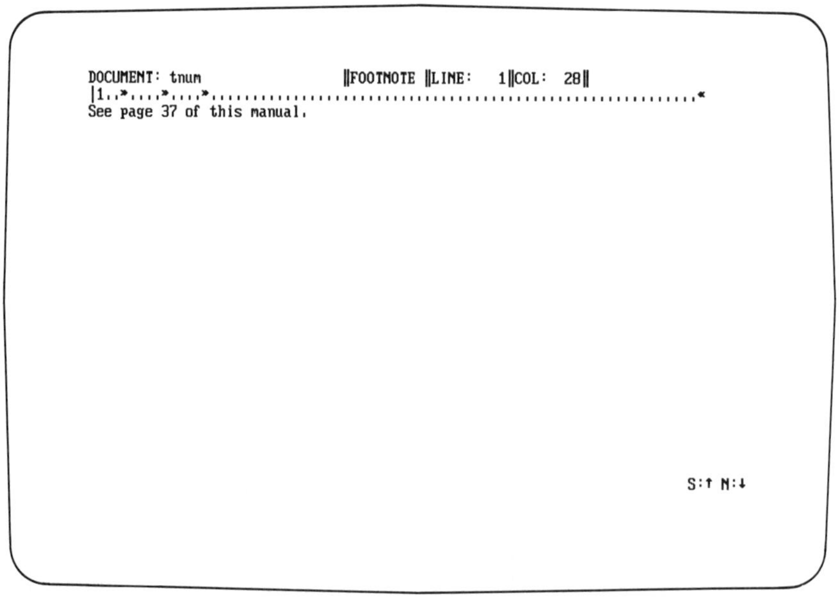

```
DOCUMENT: tnum                   ‖FOOTNOTE ‖LINE:    1‖COL:  28‖
|1..›....›....›....................................................‹
See page 37 of this manual.




                                                           S:↑ N:↓
```

Fig. 9.6. The footnote page.

Once you have entered the footnote, you must automatically repaginate the document. Footnotes are moved with the musical note reference during repagination.

The repagination process is not visible; the first screenful of text remains on the monitor while the system repaginates the remaining pages. You **cannot** press Esc to move out of the repagination process after you type the lines per page and press Return. If you make a mistake during repagination, simply repaginate again.

If you are unsure of the effects repagination will have on your document, make a copy of the document under another name. Or, create a backup document (see Chapter 13) and repaginate the copy or the backup. Your original document will remain unchanged.

There will be times when you won't want to repaginate the entire document. For example, you may not want to split a table (like table 9.2) between two pages. In such cases, you can insert a required page-break, which remains in place during automatic repagination. Regardless of the number of lines per page you specify, the required page-break symbol always instructs the system to insert a page break in the designated location. To insert a required page break,

1. Type the text.

2. Press **Return**.

3. Press **Alt-B**.

The required page-break symbol ($\perp$) appears on the screen. To remove a required page break,

1. Place the cursor under the page-break symbol.

2. Press **Del** twice.

To protect a page (such as table 9.2), you must insert a required page break twice: once at the end of the page preceding the page to be protected and once at the end of the page to be protected.

To delete a footnote, simply delete the musical-note symbol.

You may move or copy text from a footnote to the text in the document or from the text to a footnote. To move or copy from a footnote to the text, follow these steps:

1. Put the cursor on the footnote musical-note symbol.

2. Press **Alt-V**.

3. Place the cursor under the first footnote character to move or copy.

4. Press **F7** to move or **F8** to copy.

5. Highlight the footnote text to move or copy.

6. Press **F10**.

7. Press **Alt-V**.

8. Place the cursor where you want the text moved or copied in the body above the footnote.

9. Press **F10** (or **Esc** to cancel the operation).

To move or copy from the text to a footnote, follow these steps:

1. Place the cursor under the first character of the text you want to move or copy.

2. Press **F7** to move or **F8** to copy.

3. Highlight the text to move or copy.

4. Press **F10**.

5. Place the cursor on the musical-note symbol of the footnote you want to copy or move to.

6. Press **Alt-V**.

7. Move the cursor to the position to place the text.

8. Press **F10** (or **Esc** to cancel the operation).

When you print a page with a footnote, you may find a separator line on the page as shown in figure 9.7. The text/footnote separator line (between the text and footnote) is a dashed line. The footnote/footnote separator line (after one footnote to separate it from the next footnote) is a blank line. The default Format Line is used unless you edit it. You may edit the separator lines or the Format Line.

```
I.  Types of Inventory

    There are three types of inventory in stock.  These are raw materials,
finished goods and preparation items.  Each is handled differently.

    A.   Raw Materials

         Raw materials are the goods we buy from other suppliers.  When
    the goods are received at the loading dock, you must follow the dock
    procedures described later in this manual.¹

    B.   Finished Goods

         Finished goods are the goods we produce.  These goods will reach
    the dock prepackaged and ready for shipment.

    C.   Preparation Items

         Preparation items are raw materials that are in the process of
    being prepared to finished goods.  These materials are in the plant.

II.      Dock Procedures

---------------
¹See page 37 of this manual.
```

Fig. 9.7. Printout illustrating footnote separator line.

To change the Format Line or the text/footnote separator line (between the text and first footnote),

1. Press **Alt-V**.

2. Press **Alt-H**.

3. Press **F9** to enter the Format Line. Edit it and press **F10** to save the Format Line as edited.

4. Edit the text/footnote separator as desired (up to 80 characters).

5. Press **F10**.

6. This message appears:

   `Do you want this separator to be the system default?`

7. Type **Y** to make the separator the system default or press **N** to make the separator relevant to that footnote only.

8. The cursor is returned to the footnote text page.

To change the footnote/footnote (between footnotes) separator line,

1. With the cursor over the musical note symbol, press **Alt-V**.

2. Press **Alt-F**.

3. Edit the footnote/footnote separator as desired (up to 80 characters).

4. Press **F10**.

5. This message appears:

   `Do you want this separator to be the system default?`

6. Type **Y** to make the separator the system default or press **N** to make the separator relevant to that footnote only.

7. The cursor is returned to the footnote text page.

The MultiMate Advantage II default is to print footnotes on the page where they are referenced. You may print the footnotes as endnotes (at the end of the document) instead. To control this option, change the Footnotes/Endnotes field on the Modify Document Defaults screen. See Chapter 18 for more information.

Endnotes

Endnotes are footnotes printed either at the end of the document or at the end of sections within a document (rather than at the bottom of each foot-noted page). To print the footnotes as endnotes,

1. Create the footnotes.

2. On column 1 of the line after which you want endnotes to print, press **Ctrl-]**

All the notes from the beginning of the document or from the last endnote symbol print at that point.

3. Add endnote symbols for other sections within the document if appropriate.

4. Print the document.

Another way to specify endnotes is to enter an *E* in the Endnotes field on the Modify Document Defaults screen when the document is created.

Text and Page Associated Headers and Footers

When you create a document, you indicate whether headers and footers should be repaginated by Text Association or Page Association. On the Edit System Defaults screen, you can type *T* for text or *P* for page.

If you type *P*, the header and footer lines are included in the total page-length count, and the headers and footers remain on the page where they were originally entered.

If you type *T*, the header and footer lines are not included in the total page-length count. The headers act as page breaks and remain with the original text. Figure 9.8 illustrates the effect of repagination on text associated headers and footers and page associated headers and footers.

Repagination Results Based on Text or Page Association

Test document:	Document Repagination Result with Text Association:	Repagination Result with Page Association:
Line 1	Line 1	Line 1
Line 2	Line 2	Line 2
Line 3	Line 3	Line 3
Line 4	Line 4	Line 4
Line 5	Line 5	Line 5
Line 6	*Page 1.*	*Page 1.*
Page 1.	Line 6	ǂ
ǂ	ƒ	This is the header
This is the header	This is a footer	ǂ
ǂ		Line 6
Line 7	*Page 2.*	Line 7
Line 8		Line 8
Line 9	ǂ	ƒ
Line 10	This is a header	This is the footer
Line 11	ǂ	ƒ
Line 12	Line 7	*Page 2.*
Line 13	Line 8	
ƒ	Line 9	Line 9
This is the footer	Line 10	Line 10
ƒ	Line 11	Line 11
Page 2.	*Page 3.*	*Page 3.*
	Line 12	Line 12
	Line 13	Line 13
	Page 4.	*Page 4.*

"P"
Headers/Footers remain on the page where originally entered

"T"
Headers act as page breaks and remain with the original text

Fig. 9.8. Repagination results based on text or page association.

10

Saving and Printing Documents

At one time or another, almost everyone who uses a computer has "lost" an important document or a portion of a document. The fear of losing text is especially common among users new to computers. Generally, the fear of losing work is groundless. If you take good care of your disks, and you are careful when you save documents, you can reduce the chances of lost time, lost effort, and lost text significantly.

Lost work is most often the result of an obvious error, such as formatting over an important disk or copying an old file over a new one—users lose work simply because they do not save files properly.

To save your documents, you must move them from your computer's random-access memory (RAM) to more permanent storage: document disks (if your computer has floppy disk drives) or the hard disk (if your computer has a hard disk drive). While you create and edit MultiMate Advantage II documents in your computer's random-access memory, you must remember that this memory is temporary; RAM is erased when you turn off your computer or reboot the system.

Saving

Suppose that you have been working on a 10-page document for the past three hours. Suddenly, without warning, the lights flicker and the power fails. During the power failure, your system's random-access memory is lost.

With some word processors, your document and your three hours of labor would have been lost. With MultiMate Advantage II, you may set a default on the Edit System Defaults screen to save automatically each page as you move to a new page. Moving from page to page will take longer, but you may need the added safety. (See Chapter 18 for more information.)

You may edit a document only to decide you like the original version of the document better. If the document is only one page, you can press *Esc* to "lose" the edited changes you made. When you press *Esc*, the following prompt appears at the bottom of the screen:

```
Do you wish to escape without saving this page? (Y/N)
```

If you type *Y* (yes), MultiMate Advantage II *does not* save your edited changes. However, it will save the page that was previously created. You would type *N* (no) if you had accidentally pressed Esc while working on the document or if you decided that the edited version wasn't so bad after all.

Save and Exit

If you want to stop work on your document and turn off your computer, or if you want to use another Main Menu option (such as printing), you can save your work and *exit* (return) to the Main Menu by pressing *F10*. If you press F10 by mistake, you will have to reenter the document to continue working on it.

Save and Continue

When you instruct the system to save and continue, MultiMate Advantage II saves your work; your document remains on the screen so that you can continue to work on it. Saving and continuing takes only seconds and protects your work. If, for example, you spend several hours developing a complicated multi-page document or single-page table, and somebody trips over the power cord and unplugs your computer, you'll lose that diagram unless you save and continue as you work.

To save and continue, press *Shift-F10*. This message flashes on your screen:

```
<<<PLEASE WAIT>>>
```

MultiMate Advantage II is saving your work—either to the disk in the disk drive or to the hard disk. When the message leaves the screen, the light on the disk drive will be off. (**Never** open the disk drive door while the light is on.) The screen and cursor position have not changed, and you can continue working.

Printing

MultiMate Advantage II offers you many printing options. After you determine how you want to print a document, you'll complete the information on two screens:

- The first screen will name the document you want to print.

- The second screen will identify the print option values.

This list of steps describes the printing process:

1. Make sure MultiMate Advantage II can identify the brand and the model of the printer you are using. MultiMate Advantage II must be able to access the PAT (Printer Action Table) file.

2. Get the printer ready for printing.

3. Select Option 3, Print a Document, on the MultiMate Advantage II Main Menu and specify the document to print on the Print a Document screen.

4. Change options as necessary on the Document Print Options screen.

5. Send the document to the printer.

Identifying the Printer

The first step in printing a document is to make sure MultiMate Advantage II can identify both the make and the model of the printer you are using.

As discussed in Chapter 2, you must install (on your MultiMate Advantage II *System Working Disk*) the Printer Action Table file that corresponds to your printer. You need to type the PAT only once at the Document Print Options screen (which is accessed for printing). The PAT files are located on the Printer Tables diskette.

If the files are not on your hard disk, copy the PAT file(s) you need to the hard disk containing the MultiMate Advantage II system programs. If you have trouble finding a particular PAT file, use the *DOS DIR* command to look at the directory listing of the disk.

Readying the Printer

After you install the appropriate PAT file, you can print a document. Make sure of the following:

- The printer is **ON**.

- A ribbon has been installed.

- You have printer paper.

Using the Print a Document Screen

1. Type **3** to access Option 3 (Print a Document) on the Main Menu.

The system will display the Print a Document screen. (See fig. 10.1.)

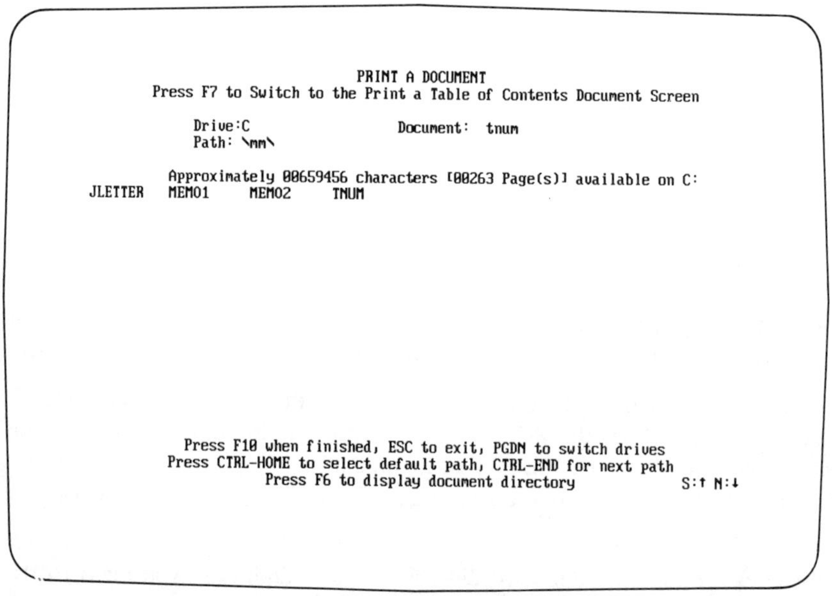

```
                              PRINT A DOCUMENT
              Press F7 to Switch to the Print a Table of Contents Document Screen

                  Drive:C                    Document: tnum
                  Path: \mm\

                  Approximately 00659456 characters [00263 Page(s)] available on C:
        JLETTER    MEMO1      MEMO2     TNUM










                  Press F10 when finished, ESC to exit, PGDN to switch drives
                Press CTRL-HOME to select default path, CTRL-END for next path
                      Press F6 to display document directory      S:↑ N:↓
```

Fig. 10.1. The Print a Document screen.

2. Type the name of the document you want to print.

3. Type the letter of the drive on which the document resides and type the path, if necessary.

If you need to change the drive designation,

    4. Press **PgDn**.

The letter of the drive changes, and the drive directory lists the documents available on that drive.

To change to a subdirectory,

    5. Press **Ctrl-End**.

To select the default directory,

    6. Press **Ctrl-Home**.

If you want to print a table of contents,

    7. Press **F7**.

In figure 10.1, the directory for drive C contains two documents, *JLETTER* and *MEMO1*.

The line above the drive directory shows how much space, in terms of characters and pages, is available on the drive. This information is important when you create and edit documents but not essential when you print documents. The key status symbols (*S* and *N*) in the lower right corner of your screen show the status of the Caps Lock key (*S*) and the Num Lock key (*N*).

    8. Press **F10**.

The second and final screen used in printing a document is displayed.

Using the Document Print Options Screen

The Document Print Options screen displays the options available to you at the time of printing (see fig. 10.2). While it may seem that you must remember a number of options, most of the time you will use the system defaults. Only a few options change each time you print a document. You can alter almost all of the values on the Document Print Options screen either by changing the values before you print the document or by changing the system defaults.

To alter the options before you print the document,

    1. Move the cursor to the desired option using the cursor arrow key.

Do not use the space bar to move from option to option. You will delete the options you move through.

    2. Type the value.

```
Document:  TNUM           DOCUMENT PRINT OPTIONS

Start Print At Page Number       001  Left Margin                     000
Stop Print After Page Number     013  Top Margin                      000
Enhanced [N] / Draft [Y]           N  Double Space The Document [N or Y]  N
Number Of Original Copies        001  Default Pitch [4 = 10 CPI]        4

Printer Action Table (PAT)   LJETFS1  Sheet Feeder Action Table(SAT)
Use:(P)arallel/(S)erial/(F)ile/(L)ist  Sheet Feeder Bin Numbers [0 - 3]
    (A)uxiliary/(C)onsole          P     First Page 0  Middle 0  Last Page 0
Device Number                    001  Char. Width/Translate (CWT)
Pause Between Pages [N or Y]        N  Background / Foreground [B or F]   B

Print Comments [N or Y]            N  Justification [N or Y or (M)icro]   N
Print Doc. Summary Screen [N or Y] N  Proportional Spacing [N or Y]       N
Print This Screen [N or Y]         N  Lines Per Inch [6 or 8]             6
Header / Footer First Page Number 001  Paper Length (lines per page)     066
Starting Footnote Number[1 - 749] 001  Default Font                      A
                                      Remove Queue Entry When Done [Y or N] Y

Current Time Is     15:39:09       Delay Print Until Time Is   15:39:09
Current Date Is     08/28/1987     Delay Print Until Date Is   08/28/1987

            Press F10 when finished, ESC to exit
          Press F1 for PATs, F2 for SATs, F3 for CWTs        S:↑ N:↓
```

Fig. 10.2. The Document Print Options screen.

If you change the values of some options and then leave the screen by pressing Esc, MultiMate Advantage II does not save those values. The program does, however, save most of those values when you send the document to be printed.

Document and Drive

The first line holds the screen title, identifies the drive on which the document resides, and displays the name of the document. This information is identical to the information you provided on the Print a Document screen.

Pages To Print

The first two options that you fill in specify the page number on which the program begins printing your document (Start Print At Page Number) and the page number on which the program stops printing your document (Stop Print After Page Number).

The Start Print Page default is *1*, and the Stop Print Page option defaults to the last page in your document. These page numbers correspond to the page numbers shown in the Status Line while you type your document, not page numbers you may have assigned to the document. To complete the Start Print Page option, type the number—between *1* and *999*—that corresponds to the document page number up to which you want to print.

When you type values and send the document to the printer, MultiMate Advantage II saves the Start Print Page Number.

The Stop Print Page Number, however, reverts to the default (the last page of the document). If you print a document that stops printing before the last page, and you then want to reprint the pages, you must reenter the page number on which you want the printer to stop printing the document.

Draft/Enhanced Print

Draft print occurs when a document is printed in Single Strike Mode; in other words, the printer prints each character only once. Enhanced print occurs when a document is printed in Double Strike Mode.

To select Draft print, type *Y*. To signal the printer to print your document in Enhanced print (Double Strike Mode), type *N*.

When you select Enhanced print, each character is struck twice, creating a darker, bolder print.

Enhanced Mode is useful with dot-matrix printers; many of them tend to have light characters that can be difficult to read and to photocopy. (Some daisy-wheel printers do not support Double Strike Mode, so your printer generates a Single Strike document whether you type *Y* or *N*.)

If you insert Draft print or Enhanced print symbols into your document, those symbols will override the printer menu option, and the text marked with the symbols won't look the same as the print in the rest of the document. For example, inserting Enhanced print symbols and then printing in Double Strike Mode defeats the purpose of the symbols. In such a case, you should select Draft print mode to make the Enhanced print characters stand out.

Number of Original Copies

In the Number of Original Copies field, type the number of copies you want to print.

You can print up to 999 original copies of a document. Using your computer and a printer to print original copies can be as inexpensive as making a copy on a photocopy machine, especially if you must send your document out to be copied.

Printer Action Table

In the Printer Action Table field, type the PAT file name that corresponds to your printer. Type the name exactly as it appears in your MultiMate directory. If your PAT file is installed correctly, the system displays the PAT file name at the bottom of the Document Print Options screen.

MultiMate Advantage II can list 16 PAT files. Press *F1* to see the list of PAT files installed for your use.

Parallel and Serial Print

Most printers used with personal computers are parallel printers; some, however, are serial. Check the manual that came with your printer to determine whether to type *P* for a parallel printer or *S* for a serial printer.

In unusual circumstances, you may want to send your print request through DOS. To print through DOS, type *L* if you have a parallel printer. If you have a serial printer, type *A*.

To send the print request to a file, type *F*.

To create an ASCII file with the extension *.prn*,

1. Type **F**

2. Enter the Printer Action Table (PAT) as **TTYCRLF**

3. Set the left and top margins to **0**.

4. Set Draft print to **Y**.

To see the text on your screen without the nonprintable characters (such as the Return symbol), type *C*.

Device Number

If more than one printer is available, type the number of the printer port connection. Type *1* if you are using only one printer.

Pause Between Pages

If you are printing on single sheets of paper, you must tell the printer to pause after printing each page so that you can insert the next sheet. Type *Y* in the Pause Between Pages field.

While the document prints, MultiMate Advantage II displays the Main Menu, and the following message appears:

`PRINTER PAUSE BETWEEN PAGES. PRESS <ESCAPE> TO CONTINUE`

This blinking, boxed message signals that you can press *Esc* when the paper is in place. The printer prints the first page, the message reappears, and you can put the next sheet of paper in the printer.

If you are using continuous-form paper, you *do not* want the printer to pause between each page but, rather, to advance immediately to the next page. Type *N* in the Pause Between Pages field.

Print Comments

Enter *N* if you do not want to print comments that are embedded in the text. Enter *Y* to print the comments. If *Y* is chosen, the comments are printed between rows of exclamation points (!!). If the comments were not added into the total line count when the text was divided into pages, and you decide to print them, the comments may make the pages run over to partial pages.

Print Document Summary Screen

The Document Summary screen appears just before you see your document. The screen includes the following:

- Document Name, Author, Addressee, and Operator
- Identification Key Words
- Comments
- Creation Date and Modification Date
- Total Editing Time and Editing Time Last Session
- Keystrokes Last Session and Total Keystrokes
- Total Pages

If you want to print both your document and the Document Summary screen, type *Y*.

Print this Screen (Document Print Options)

If you want to print the Document Print Options screen before you print your document, type *Y*.

Header/Footer First Page Number Option

Chapter 8 explains how to type the # symbol in a header or a footer so that your system numbers pages automatically.

If either a header or a footer contains the # symbol, you can use the header/footer First Page Number option to specify which page number you want to print on the first header or footer.

MultiMate Advantage II prints the first page number, and then it increments by one and prints the next page number. The page number you type does not have to correspond to the page number in the Status Line of your document.

If your document has no header or footer, or if the header or footer has no # symbol, the value in this print option is of no consequence because no page number is printed.

Starting Footnote Number

Enter the number that should be used with the first footnote in the document. Remaining footnotes will be numbered automatically and placed on the appropriate pages.

Left Margin and Top Margin

Use the next two options to set the left margin and the top margin. To set the left margin, place a positioning ruler horizontally on the sheet of paper you will print on and note the space number based on the pitch you will use for printing. Business letters have left margins between 10 and 15 spaces; standard envelopes have left margins of approximately 45 spaces.

To measure the top margin of your document, place the positioning ruler vertically on the paper. Note the number of lines from the top that you want to remain blank. *Type this number as the value for the top margin.*

If you are printing on single sheets of paper that you insert by hand, you may want to specify a top margin of zero and position the paper to begin printing on the line you have chosen. An alternative is to use the blank lines for the top margin in the header of the document and set the top margin at zero.

Double-Space the Document

If you enter *N*, the spacing indicated in the Format Line is used during the print. If you enter *Y*, the Format Line spacing is ignored, and the entire document is printed in double-space.

Default Pitch

MultiMate Advantage II supports nine print pitches, which vary from five characters per inch to 17.6 characters per inch. Check your printer manual to see which print pitches your printer supports. If your printer uses a daisy wheel or a print ball, make sure the printing element matches the print pitch you are using; otherwise, you run the risk of damaging your printer.

Rather than typing the pitch number on the Document Print Options screen, you type the number identified as the MultiMate Advantage II Pitch Indicator, which is assigned to each print pitch (see table 10.1). Your system defaults to a print pitch of four (10 characters per inch).

Table 10.1
Pitch Indicators

MultiMate Advantage II Pitch Indicator	Equivalent Characters Per Inch (CPI)	
1	5	Large
2	6	
3	8.8	
4 (default)	10	
5	12	
6	13.2	
7	15	
8	16.5	
9	17.6	Small

Sheet Feeder Bin Numbers and Sheet Feeder Action Table

Some printers have electronic sheet feeders with bins that feed single sheets of paper to the printer.

Three options on the Document Print Options screen affect sheet feeders:

- Sheet Feeder Action Table
- Sheet Feeder Bin Numbers
- First Page/Middle/Last Page

If you are **not** using a bin with your printer, use the MultiMate Advantage II default of *0* for each option.

If you have a sheet feeder, you can print on paper from as many as three bins. You can print the first page of the document on the paper from one bin, the middle pages on paper from another bin, and the last page of the document on paper from a third bin.

In the Sheet Feeder Action Table field, type the name of the Sheet Feeder Action Table (SAT) you want to use. (The MultiMate Advantage II Utilities diskette contains a listing of Sheet Feeder Action Tables. If the Sheet Feeder Action Table you need does not appear on the diskette, contact Multimate International Technical Support personnel.) Press *F2* to see a list of the SATs installed for your use.

Each bin has been assigned a number. To access a bin, type the appropriate number in the Sheet Feeder Bin Numbers field.

In the First Page field, enter the number of the bin with the paper for the first page. In the Middle field, enter the number of the bin with the paper for the middle pages. In the Last Page field, type the number of the bin with the paper for the last page of the document.

Character Width/Translation Table

To access special characters with your PAT file, you must write special commands.

Enter the value of the Character Width/Translation Table (CWT). Chapter 19 describes this option in greater detail. Some Character Width/Translation Tables come on your MultiMate Advantage II System diskette. If you are using a laser printer or want to try using a CWT file for line and box drawing, check your MultiMate *Printer Guide*. Press *F3* to see the CWTs installed for your use.

Experiment with your printer. For example, the printed result shown in figure 10.3 was generated using a Hewlett-Packard LaserJet Printer and cartridge F. On the Document Print Options screen, the PAT file was entered with *Y* for proportional spacing, as well as the CWT file.

Figure 10.4 shows how print pitch characters (press *Alt-C* and enter the identifier) were embedded in the text to create a variety of font styles on one page.

This is font I

This is font J

This is font K

This is font L

This is font M

HP LaserJet Series II
Ljetps1
Proportional Space
Default pitch 4
No CWT
Draft print

Fig. 10.3. Print using Hewlett-Packard LaserJet Printer.

```
DOCUMENT: MEMO1              ‖PAGE:  2‖LINE:  12‖COL:   3‖         INSERT
|1..»....»....»...........................................................«
RI«
This is font I«
RJ«
This is font J«
RK«
This is font K«
RL«
This is font L«
RM«
This is font M«
«
RKHP LaserJet Series II«
Ljetps1«
Proportional Space«
Default pitch 4«
No CWT«
Draft print«
«



                                                        S:↑ N:↓
```

Fig. 10.4. Screen entries used for the print shown in figure 10.3.

Background and Foreground Modes

When you print documents in *Background* Mode, you can work on other documents while a document is printing. When you work in *Foreground* Mode, you cannot do any other work on the system until your document has printed.

Justification

When you choose *justification*, MultiMate Advantage II prints the lines in your document with right margins that are even, as well as left margins that are even. Although your pages do not appear right-justified on the screen, they will be when they are printed. Two types of right-justification are available.

If you want the text to be right-justified with extra spaces between words, type *Y*.

If you want spaces between both words and characters, type *M*. Typing *M* instructs your system to microjustify the text. Test your printer to make sure it handles microjustification.

If you want a ragged-right margin, type *N*.

Figure 10.5 illustrates the differences among text printed with ragged-right margins, text that is right-justified, and text that is microjustified.

Proportional Spacing

Proportional spacing gives each character an amount of space on the printed page equal to the width of the character. For instance, the letter *w* will occupy more space on the printed page than the letter *i*. Proportional spacing can make your documents look as though they have been typeset by a professional printer.

Test your printer to make sure that it supports proportional spacing. If your printer does permit proportional spacing, type *Y*.

If you want each character to occupy the same amount of space (fixed spacing) when your document is printed, type *N*.

Figure 10.5 shows how proportional spacing can improve the appearance of your documents.

```
The quick brown fox jumped over
the lazy dog.  After resting, the
same quick brown fox jumped a
river called the muddy
Mississippi.
```

(The text above is not justified;
the right margin is ragged.)

```
The quick brown fox jumped over
the lazy dog.  After resting, the
same quick brown fox jumped a
river called the muddy
Mississippi.
```

(The text above is not justified,
but is proportional spaced.)

```
The  quick  brown  fox  jumped over
the  lazy  dog.  After resting, the
same   quick  brown  fox  jumped  a
river     called      the     muddy
Mississippi.
```

(The text above is right justified;
space is placed between words.)

```
The  quick  brown  fox  jumped over
the  lazy  dog.   After resting, the
same  quick  brown  fox  jumped  a
river     called      the     muddy
Mississippi.
```

(The text above is right justified
and proportional spaced.)

```
The quick brown fox jumped over
the lazy dog.  After resting, the
same quick brown fox jumped a
r i v e r   c a l l e d   t h e   m u d d y
Mississippi.
```

(The text above is microjustified;
space is placed between words and
letters.)

```
The  quick  brown  fox  jumped over
the  lazy  dog.  After resting, the
same  quick  brown  fox  jumped  a
r i v e r   c a l l e d   t h e   m u d d y
Mississippi.
```

(The text above is microjustified
and proportional spaced.)

Fig. 10.5. Justification and proportional spacing options.

Lines Per Inch

By either increasing or decreasing the space between lines, you can fit additional lines (or fewer lines) on a page. The Lines Per Inch default on the Document Print Options screen is 6.

MultiMate Advantage II calculates six lines to an inch. If you want to print lines closer together, you can change this value to 8; your system then calculates eight lines to an inch.

Paper Length (Lines Per Page)

The Document Page Length option tells your system how far to advance continuous-form paper after one page is printed. The value you enter for this option should reflect the number of lines on the paper you use for printing. The standard 8 1/2-by-11-inch page has 66 lines, so the MultiMate Advantage II system default is 66 lines.

Here is a hint to help you avoid unnecessarily changing the Document Page Length option:

If you are using single-sheet paper (*not* continuous-form paper) and must pause between pages, you can specify a longer line length. Longer line lengths cause the printer to eject the document. If you pause between pages to print individual envelopes, for example, use a line length of 66.

Default Font

Some printers (like laser printers) are capable of multiple type styles. Select the type style you want as a default for the document. The MultiMate Advantage II default is A. You may change the font style from within the document (see Chapter 8).

Remove Queue Entry When Done

To delete your document from the printer queue after printing is complete, type *Y*. To place your document back in the printer queue with an "on hold" status after the first printing is complete, type *N*.

Delay Print

The final field on the Document Print Options screen is Delay Print, which you use to tell the system when to print the document.

For example, you can instruct the system to print your document at noon, and, while you are out for lunch, the document will print.

The cursor cannot change the current time and current date values. If you want to use the Delay Print option, you must enter the correct day and time when DOS comes up (unless you have an automatic time device installed).

Type the time (hour/minute/second) and the date (month/day/year); then type the time and date when you want MultiMate Advantage II to print the document. Leave your system on so that the printer can print your document at the desired time.

Sending the Document to the Printer

After you fill out the options on the Document Print Options screen, press *F10* to send the document to the printer queue.

If your printer is on and ready to print, and no other documents are in the queue, your document is printed right away. If other documents are queued, your document goes to the end of the queue and "waits its turn" before printing.

Stopping a Printing Document

You can stop a document that is being printed. If the document is printing in Foreground Mode, press *Esc*. If the document is printing in Background Mode, press *Ctrl-Break*.

Pressing these two keys takes you to the Printer Queue Control screen (see fig. 10.6). Type *1* to remove the first document in the queue (that is, the document that is printing).

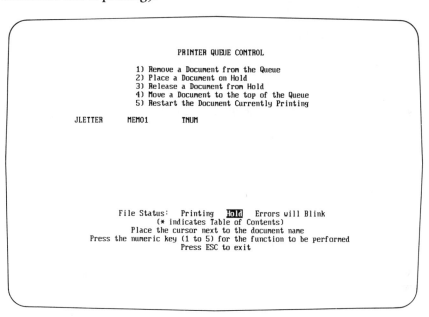

```
                    PRINTER QUEUE CONTROL

             1) Remove a Document from the Queue
             2) Place a Document on Hold
             3) Release a Document from Hold
             4) Move a Document to the top of the Queue
             5) Restart the Document Currently Printing

   JLETTER      MEMO1        TNUM




             File Status:   Printing   Hold   Errors will Blink
                     (* indicates Table of Contents)
                  Place the cursor next to the document name
       Press the numeric key (1 to 5) for the function to be performed
                        Press ESC to exit
```

Fig. 10.6. The Printer Queue Control screen.

Changing the Print Defaults

As mentioned earlier, you can change the default values on the Document Print Options screen. To edit the defaults,

1. Type **4** on the Main Menu.

2. Type **2** on the submenu.

MultiMate Advantage II displays the Edit Printer Defaults screen.

3. Move the cursor to the default you want to change.

4. Strike over the option with your choice.

After you finish editing the screen,

    5. Press **F10** to complete the process.

If you begin editing and then decide not to save the changes you made, press *Esc*.

Defaults for documents already printed do not change.

Controlling the Documents in the Queue

To control the documents in the printer queue,

    1. Type **4** on the Main Menu.

    2. Type **1** on the screen that appears after the Main Menu screen.

MultiMate Advantage II displays the Printer Queue Control screen, which shows the names of the documents in the queue.

    3. Place your cursor on the name of the document you want to control and select one of the five numbered options (descriptions follow).

Removing a Document from the Queue

If you type *1* on this screen, the document marked by the cursor is removed from the queue.

If the printer is running, the first document is the one that is printing, and that document's name is highlighted. If you want to remove another document from the queue, move the cursor to that document's name and type *1*.

Sometimes, however, typing *1* will not remove the document from the printer queue. Should this occur, you may delete the entire queue file (all the documents in the printer queue) using this procedure:

    1. Return to DOS.

After the DOS prompt appears,

    2. Type **DEL WPQUE.SYS**

    3. Press **Return**.

Placing a Document on Hold

To place a document on hold, type *2*. The document's name (marked by the cursor) appears on the screen in reverse video, and other documents in the queue move ahead of that document. Then type *3* to release the document from hold.

If you are working on a Local Area Network system, *1* is the only available option.

Moving a Document

You can move a document to the front of the queue by typing *4*. The selected document and the next document to print switch places in line.

Restarting a Document Currently Printing

A document currently printing can be restarted from the beginning. Suppose, for example, that you are printing the final copy of a 15-page document. While the document is printing, you decide that you want to make two more copies. Select *5*.

Error Checking

If some of the document names are blinking on the Printer Queue Control screen, an error has occurred. Your system components may have a bad connection, your printer may not be functioning correctly, or you may have typed incorrect values on the Document Print Options screen.

Check the connections on your hardware and make sure that the printer is operational. If the connections and the printer appear to be functional, send another document to the printer; if that document prints without error, carefully check each item on the Document Print Options screen. If you still cannot locate the error, contact Multimate International Technical Support personnel. Press *Esc* to exit the Printer Queue Control screen.

Using the HP LaserJet Printer

MultiMate Advantage II uses many of the HP LaserJet Printer features. General guidelines and a test for the fonts you may print are presented here. Consult the MultiMate Advantage II *Printer Guide* for specific information about the font letters (identifiers) and Document Print Options fields to use with your LaserJet cartridges or downloadable fonts.

You may use up to 26 fonts per document (including cartridge and downloadable fonts). Press *Alt-C* and enter the letter of the font change you desire. That font will print until you press *Alt-C* and enter another font letter.

The Document Print Options screen presents several selections for your consideration. These are described in table 10.2.

Table 10.2
Document Print Options with the LaserJet

Enhanced [N] /Draft [Y]	Enter *Y.*
Printer Action Table (PAT)	Enter *Ljetfs1*, *Ljetfs2*, or *Ljetfs3* for fixed space.
	Enter *Ljetps1* or *Ljetps2* for proportional space.
	See the *Printer Guide* for your cartridge or downloadable font PAT.
Use:(P)arallel/(S)erial...	Enter *S* for serial.
	Enter *P* for parallel if you have a Series II printer that is set up as a parallel printer.
Default Pitch	Enter the pitch with fixed space PATs.
	Enter *4* (default) with proportional space PATs.
Char. Width/Translate (CWT)	Do not enter a CWT.
	With fixed space, the pitch is used.
	With proportional space, the PAT calls the appropriate CWT.
Proportional Space (Y or N)	Enter *Y* with proportional space PAT.
	Enter *N* with fixed space PAT.
Default Font	Enter the font letter you want as the default; this font style will print until a font change (Alt-C and a letter) is encountered in the document.

Line/Box Drawing can be used with several cartridges and downloadable fonts. Consult the *Printer Guide* for information on the cartridges and downloadable fonts currently supported.

Here's a quick way to test which fonts and boxes are available:

1. Create a document called *LJETTEST*.

2. Press **Alt-C**.

3. Type **A**

4. Type **A font**

5. Press **Return**.

6. Repeat steps 2 through 5 for the font letters you want to test. (You can enter a line for each letter A through Z.)

7. Using Line/Box Drawing (Alt-E), enter a box using each box style you want to test; make sure to embed a font letter (Alt-C followed by a letter) before the box.

Use the font letters suggested in the *Printer Guide* for the cartridge or downloadable font you will use. You may want to type words inside the boxes to test that feature.

8. Save the document.

9. Print the document using the selected settings on the Document Print Options screen.

You may want to print the document more than once using different settings (such as different PAT files) to see the effect of the settings. Because a new sheet of paper is used every time you change from Landscape to Portrait Mode, testing can consume a good deal of paper. You may want to use scrap.

Using the Typewriter Mode

With MultiMate Advantage II, you may use your printer like a typewriter and print the text as it is typed. Addressing an envelope and creating a label are good examples of the kinds of tasks MultiMate Advantage II handles easily in Typewriter Mode.

Not all MultiMate Advantage II functions may be used in Typewriter Mode, although you may use most functions, including an alternate keyboard (to type symbols) and key procedures (to replay keystrokes). It is also true that not all printers work in Typewriter Mode. Experiment with your printer.

To use Typewriter Mode,

1. Type **4**, Additional Print Functions, from the Main Menu.

2. Type **3**, Typewriter Mode (Single Character), to print a character at a time.

Or

2. Type **4**, Typewriter Mode (Line), to print a line at a time.

Note that some printers do not support Single Character Mode but will support Line Mode.

Whether you select Single Character or Line Mode, the bottom left corner of the screen shows the printer the line and column position on which the next text will print. If the printer is being used, this message will appear on your screen:

```
Cannot use Typewriter Mode while printing
```

Single Character Typewriter Mode

From the Additional Print Functions Menu, you may select item 3 to access the Typewriter Mode (Single Character) screen shown in figure 10.7.

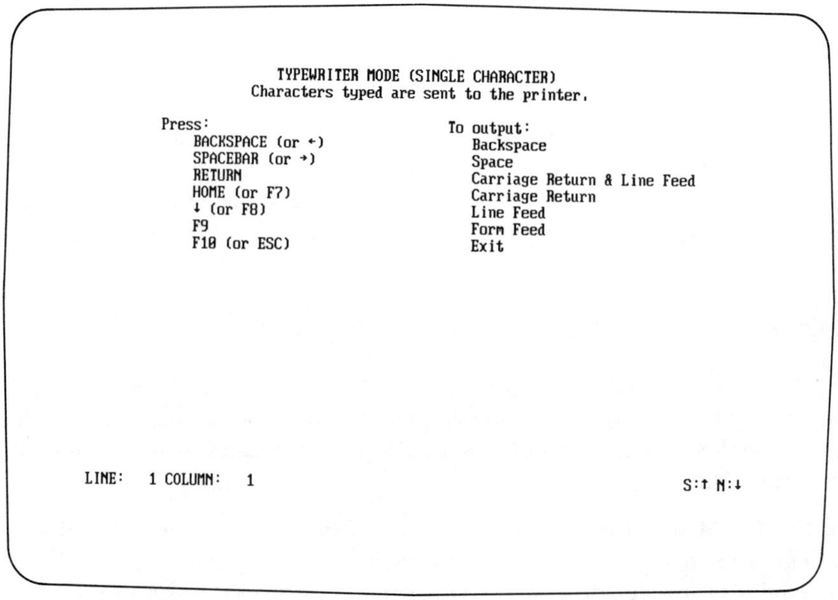

```
                    TYPEWRITER MODE (SINGLE CHARACTER)
                    Characters typed are sent to the printer.

          Press:                        To output:
            BACKSPACE (or +)              Backspace
            SPACEBAR (or +)               Space
            RETURN                        Carriage Return & Line Feed
            HOME (or F7)                  Carriage Return
            + (or F8)                     Line Feed
            F9                            Form Feed
            F10 (or ESC)                  Exit




          LINE:  1 COLUMN:  1                              S:↑ N:↓
```

Fig. 10.7. Typewriter Mode (Single Character) screen.

The Typewriter Mode (Single Character) screen identifies the keys you may use. Those keys are presented for easy reference in table 10.3.

Table 10.3
Typewriter Mode (Single Character) Keys

Key	Action
Backspace or **Left-Arrow**	Backspace and delete.
Space Bar or **Right-Arrow**	Enter a space.
Return	Enter a carriage return and line feed (to advance the paper one line).
Home or **F7**	Enter a carriage return with no line feed.
Down-Arrow or **F8**	Enter a line feed (the printer head stays in the same column position).
F9	Enter a form feed that will advance the paper in your printer the equivalent lines of a regular piece of paper or the number of lines set in your printer as a form feed.
F10 or Esc	Exit Typewriter Mode.

Line Typewriter Mode

When you select item 4 from the Additional Print Functions Menu, the screen shown in figure 10.8 appears on your screen.

The keys presented in table 10.4 are the keys you will use to edit your work in Line Typewriter Mode.

As text is entered, it is held in a buffer and appears after the label Current Line. The previous five lines you entered appear after F1 through F5 on the screen. You may select any of the print options shown in table 10.5.

```
                    TYPEWRITER MODE (LINE)
              Up to 80 characters may be entered per line

Press:          To:
     RETURN         Print Current Line ending with Carriage Return & Line Feed
     F6             Print Current Line
     F7             Print Current Line ending with Carriage Return
     F8 (or ↓)      Print Current Line ending with Line Feed
     F9             Print Current Line ending with Form Feed
     F10 (or ESC)   Exit


F1 sends the following line to the printer:
Jim Smith
F2 sends the following line to the printer:
The Launders Company
F3 sends the following line to the printer:
3200 Ash Street
F4 sends the following line to the printer:
Lincoln, Nebraska 56444
F5 sends the following line to the printer:
Sue Linder
Current Line:

LINE:   6 COLUMN:   1                                    S:↑ N:↓
```

Fig. 10.8. Typewriter Mode (Line) screen.

Table 10.4
Typewriter Mode (Line) Editing Keys

Keys	Action
Backspace	Destructive: delete text as the cursor moves to the left.
Left-Arrow	Move cursor one character to the left.
Right-Arrow	Move cursor one character to the right.
Home	Move cursor to the beginning of the line.
End	Move cursor to the end of the line.
Ins or **Keypad +**	Insert a space in the text.
Del or **Keypad -**	Delete a space in the text.

Table 10.5
Print Options in Typewriter Mode (Line)

Key	Option
Return	Print the line and return the print head to the next line on the paper in the beginning column position.
F6	Print the line and leave the print head at the end of the line without moving the paper up.
F7	Print the line and move the print head to the beginning of the line.
F8 or **Down-Arrow**	Print the line, move the paper up, and leave the print head at the end of the line.
F9	Move the paper to the top of the next page.
F10 or **Esc**	Exit Typewriter Mode.
F1 to **F5**	Reprint any line shown on the screen.

Hot Print

Using the Hot Print option permits you to print a single page without leaving your document. The print parameters set on the Document Print Options screen are used.

To use the Hot Print option,

1. Display the page you want to print on your screen.

2. Press **Ctrl-PrtSc**.

This prompt appears on your screen:

    HOTPRINTING

3. Press **Esc** to stop the Hot Print process.

11
Search and Replace

MultiMate Advantage II's Search and Replace features permit you to do the following:

- Search for text (called character strings).

- Search for character strings and replace those strings with different character strings.

Suppose you have just finished a seven-page document in which you mistakenly referred to the *Hartford Company, Inc.*, as *Hartford Company*. You know that the name *Hartford Company* appears several times in the document, but you do not know precisely how many times or where it appears.

You could read through the document, looking for and editing every occurrence of the name *Hartford Company*. In a seven-page document, correcting your mistake would be very time-consuming, and you could easily overlook one of the errors. With MultiMate Advantage II's Search function, you can search for *Hartford Company* and edit the name to read *Hartford Company, Inc.* With MultiMate Advantage II's Replace function, you can either automatically replace all occurrences of *Hartford Company* with *Hartford Company, Inc.*, or change the name in specific instances only.

MultiMate Advantage II's Search Technique

MultiMate Advantage II interprets a word as a character string; a *character string* is any series of characters, including letters, numbers, spaces, punctuation marks, tabs, returns, and so forth. Your system can search for as many as 49 characters at a time.

For example, suppose that you are looking for the word *is* in your document. After you type the letters *i* and *s*, the program locates every occurrence of these two characters, not only in the word *is* (with spaces on either side), but also in words such as can*is*ter, *Is*tanbul, and re*is*sue.

If you do not want the system to find embedded letters, you must place blank spaces both before and after the character string. The procedure for instructing MultiMate Advantage II to look for *is* follows:

1. Press the **space bar**.

2. Type **is**

3. Press the **space bar**.

MultiMate Advantage II will locate *is* only when it is preceded and followed by a space. If *is* happens to be followed by a comma, the system won't identify it because that character string is read as *is,*

Your system also can find an entire phrase, a useful capability if the words you are searching for are common. For example, if you are looking for the phrase *where is the*, the individual words *where* and *is* and *the* will probably appear frequently throughout the document; however, the character string *where is the* occurs less frequently.

Remember: To search for a specific word or phrase, type that word or phrase—including spaces and punctuation—exactly as it appears.

MultiMate Advantage II permits you to search for footnote symbols, numbered sections, and double underscore as well.

Case Significance

MultiMate Advantage II does not distinguish between uppercase letters and lowercase letters while executing a simple search or a search and replace.

For example, if you want to replace the title *manager* with the new string *Director*, your system will find *manager, Manager, MANAGER*, or any combination of uppercase and lowercase letters.

As the system replaces the incorrect string with your replacement string, the replacement string will appear exactly as you have typed it. In this case, the capitalized title *Director* will replace the lowercase title *manager*.

The Case Significance feature forces your system to search for an exact match of the replacement string you have specified.

The Search Function

Now that you understand what a character string is, try using the Search function to locate a string:

1. Move the cursor to the location within your document where you want the search to begin.

2. Press **F6**.

This prompt appears in the upper right corner of the screen:

SEARCH MODE

If the prompt does not appear, press *Esc* and start again.

This prompt and the cursor appear in the lower left corner of the screen:

SEARCH FOR:

Figure 11.1 illustrates the search options that appear.

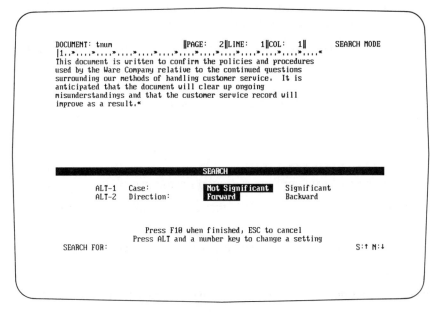

Fig. 11.1. The Search Mode screen of options.

3. If you want to search according to case (requiring an exact match of upper- and lowercase letters), press **Alt-1** to highlight the word *Significant*; otherwise, highlight *Not Significant*.

4. Press **Alt-2** to highlight whether you want to search forward or backward from your cursor position.

5. Type the word or character string you want MultiMate Advantage II to locate.

You can use the editing keys—arrow keys, Del, backspace, and so forth—to correct any typing mistakes in the search word or phrase.

To prevent the program from locating a word or character string embedded in other words, be sure to include spaces both before and after the word or character string; also place spaces between words in a character string and include any identifying symbols or punctuation.

6. Press **F10**.

If your system has to search through several pages before finding the first occurrence of the character string, you will see the pages go by on the screen; while this is happening, the program is in Search Mode.

When MultiMate Advantage II locates the first occurrence of the character string, the cursor stops on the first character in the string. You then have two options:

7. Press **F6** to skip the character string and move to the next occurrence.

Or

7. Press **Esc** to stop the search to edit the occurrence (or otherwise move your cursor around on the page).

As soon as you move the cursor off the first character in the string, the search stops.

If you edit the string and then want to resume the search,

8. Press **F6**.

The character string reappears at the bottom of the page for your visual check.

9. Press **F10**.

The Search function begins again.

If MultiMate Advantage II cannot find further occurrences of the character string, the cursor stops on the last line of the document, but the character string is held in memory until you specify a different character string or turn off your computer.

To search for a different character string,

   1. Press **F6**.

The prompts and the character string most recently used reappear on the screen.

   2. Strike over the old character string.

If the new string is shorter than the old string, use *Del* to delete trailing characters.

To cancel Search Mode, press *Esc*.

Use Search to make a quick visual check of several pages. Search for a nonsense character string (such as *lksdjf*). Watch the screen as MultiMate Advantage II moves quickly from page to page; when you see what you are looking for, press *Esc* to stop.

Searching from Page to Page

You can use the Search function to move from one page to another. If you know what text you are looking for but do not know which page contains the text, you can use the Search function to find the text.

Such a search resembles the Go to Page feature, but MultiMate Advantage II searches by *unique character identifier* rather than page number.

For example, if you are on the first page of a 25-page document, and you must find the section of the document that discusses *purchasing personal computers*, you can search for the words *purchasing personal computers*. After you type the Search command, MultiMate Advantage II moves the cursor to the first occurrence of the words *purchasing personal computers*. You can check to see if it is the page you want; then you can either search for the next occurrence of the words or stop.

The Search function permits you to move your cursor to specific locations on a single page. By searching for Returns or tab markers, you can move from paragraph to paragraph on a page and the pages that follow it. By inserting a specific number of spaces in a chart and then searching for that number of spaces, you can move the cursor from one part of a chart to another.

Searching for a Format Line

You use the Search Format Line function to search for Format Lines. This feature is helpful if you want to locate a specific Format Line and copy it to another location, if you want to edit the next Format Line, or if you have developed a chart with a new Format Line and want to find the chart quickly. You cannot search for a specific Format Line—the system stops at each one.

To search for a Format Line,

1. Move the cursor to the location within your document where you want to begin the search.

2. Press **F6**.

This prompt appears in the upper right corner of your screen:

    SEARCH MODE

The search options appear. Also, this prompt appears in the lower left corner of the screen:

    SEARCH FOR:

Do not worry about any characters that may appear in the SEARCH FOR: prompt area.

3. Press **F9**.

When you press F9, MultiMate Advantage II concentrates on finding only Format Lines. The system places the cursor on the first character or symbol under the Format Line.

4. Press **F6** to look for the next Format Line.

Or

4. Press **F9** to edit the Format Line.

And

5. Press **F9** again to set the Format Line.

If you want to stop the search after the system finds a Format Line, move the cursor off the identified spot or press *Esc.*

The search process stops when you edit the Format Line.

To resume the Search Format Line function,

    1. Press **F6**.

    2. Press **F9**.

To exit the Search Format Line function, press *Esc*.

The Replace Function

In the example illustrating the use of the Search function, the name *Hartford Company* was used incorrectly throughout a seven-page document. The Search function was implemented to change *Hartford Company* to *Hartford Company, Inc.* Using the Replace function is an even quicker way to correct the name: with the MultiMate Advantage II Replace function, you can locate an incorrect character string and automatically replace it with the appropriate character string.

To carry out the Replace function,

    1. Move the cursor to the location within your document where you want the replacement to begin.

In most of these operations, you start replacing on the first page of the document. Like the Search function, the Replace function moves forward in your document, not backward.

    2. Press **Shift-F6**.

This prompt appears in the upper right corner of your screen:

    REPLACE MODE

Figure 11.2 shows the options that appear.

    3. If you want to search according to case (requiring an exact match of upper- and lowercase letters), press **Alt-1** to highlight the word *Significant*; otherwise, highlight *Not Significant*.

    4. Press **Alt-2** to highlight whether you want to search forward or backward from your cursor position.

    5. Press **Alt-3** to select a discretionary or global replace.

If you want a global replace,

    6. Type **1**

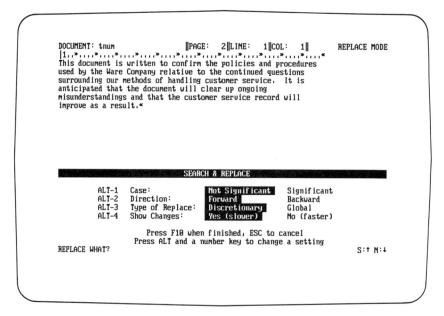

```
DOCUMENT: tnum                    ||PAGE:  2||LINE:  1||COL:  1||     REPLACE MODE
|1..»....»....»....»....»....»....»....»....»....»....«
This document is written to confirm the policies and procedures
used by the Ware Company relative to the continued questions
surrounding our methods of handling customer service. It is
anticipated that the document will clear up ongoing
misunderstandings and that the customer service record will
improve as a result.«




                            SEARCH & REPLACE
          ALT-1   Case:            Not Significant   Significant
          ALT-2   Direction:       Forward           Backward
          ALT-3   Type of Replace: Discretionary     Global
          ALT-4   Show Changes:    Yes (slower)      No (faster)

                   Press F10 when finished, ESC to cancel
                   Press ALT and a number key to change a setting
REPLACE WHAT?                                              S:↑ N:↓
```

Fig. 11.2. The Replace Mode screen of options.

During a global replace, the system automatically moves through your entire document, replacing every incorrect character string with the appropriate character string.

You see the cursor moving through the text and the pages changing as MultiMate Advantage II works. Use this option only if you are sure you want to replace **every** occurrence of a character string.

For example, changing *Hartford Company* to *Hartford Company, Inc.*, is generally a safe global replace because the name *Hartford Company* was used by mistake.

Globally replacing common words with less frequently used words (changing book to manuscript, for example) can be dangerous. In such cases, use the Discretionary Replace option so you can check the context of the passage before MultiMate Advantage II performs the replacement.

During a discretionary replace, MultiMate Advantage II searches through the document, stopping at each occurrence of the character string you want to replace. Each time, this prompt appears:

REPLACE? Y/N/ANY OTHER KEY TO CANCEL

- If you press *Y*, the system replaces the incorrect character string and moves on to search for the next occurrence of the string.

- If you press *N*, the program ignores that character string and searches for the next occurrence of the string.

- If you press any key other than *Y* or *N*, the system aborts Replace Mode.

7. If you selected global replace, press **Alt-4** to select whether you want to see each change as it is made (Yes) or whether you do not want to see each change (No).

Typing Characters for Replacement

At the bottom of the screen, MultiMate Advantage II prompts REPLACE WHAT? and the cursor appears after the prompt.

8. Type the character string you want the program to search for and replace.

You can use the editing keys to correct any mistakes you make. Remember to put spaces before and after a character string if you do not want the system to locate occurrences of the character string within words.

9. Press **Shift-F6**.

This prompt and the cursor appear on the bottom of the screen:

> REPLACE WITH?

10. Type the replacement string.

11. Press **F10**.

Using MultiMate Advantage II's Replace feature, you can easily alter letters and documents. For example, if you have a sales letter prepared for *Ajax Company* and decide you can send the same sales letter to *Jones Distributors*, simply replace the name *Ajax Company* with *Jones Distributors*. Another trick is deleting a word or phrase by replacing it with nothing. Suppose you find out that one of your customers, *Jackson P. Smith*, never uses his middle initial; by replacing *P.* with nothing, you can quickly delete all occurrences of the middle initial.

Replacing Format Lines

Using the Replace function to automatically replace Format Lines can be a real time-saver. Suppose, after typing a 25-page document, you decide the Format Line is too long—you want to reposition the first tab to fall in column

8 instead of column 5. Without the Replace function, you would have to change each Format Line. With the Replace function, you can automatically replace each Format Line.

To replace the Format Line,

1. Place the cursor anywhere in the page.

2. Press **Shift-F6**.

3. Set the options as you desire.

Respond to the prompt REPLACE WHAT? with one of the following keystroke combinations:

4. Press **Shift-F9** to show the most recent Format Line.

Or

4. Press **Ctrl-F9** to show the system (default) Format Line.

Or

4. Press **Alt-F9** to show the Format Line at the top of the page.

Regardless of the option you choose, you may edit the Format Line.

5. Edit the Format Line.

The system prompts you about line spacing (single, double, and so on) and displays the column number at the end of the Format Line.

6. Press **F10**.

If you chose a global replace, MultiMate Advantage II changes the Format Line that your cursor is resting upon, as well as the rest of the Format Lines in the document.

If you chose a discretionary replace, the program stops at each Format Line and asks whether you want to replace it.

To exit the Replace function, press *Esc*.

Place Marks

To insert a place mark in your document, use the Set Place Mark function. You might set a place mark in your document to indicate where additional text will be added later in the editing process.

For example, you may be writing a speech and want to use a famous quotation that is not available to you as you write. By inserting a place mark in your document, you can later access your document, find the place mark, and add the text of the quotation. You can set as many place marks as you like in a document.

Setting Place Marks

To set a place mark,

1. Position the cursor on the character you want to identify as the place mark.

2. Press **Alt-F1**.

The character flashes and the place mark is set. You can continue typing and editing text, or you can set another place mark.

Using the Go to Place Mark Function

You use the Go to Place Mark function to find the place marks you have placed in your document: press *Ctrl-F1*.

MultiMate Advantage II starts searching from your cursor position forward. When the cursor stops on a place mark, you have two options: strike over the letter to remove the place mark or press *Ctrl-F1* to continue the search.

The Go to Place Mark function stops automatically at each place mark; you cannot search for a specific letter place mark.

Deleting Place Marks

To delete a place mark, position the cursor on the place mark. Then, type over the character with the same character or press *Alt-F1*. The character stops flashing and is no longer considered a place mark.

To clear all of the place marks you've set in your document, press *Alt-Y*.

These messages appear on your screen:

```
CLEARING PLACE MARKS <<PLEASE WAIT>>
```

MultiMate Advantage II clears all place marks in your document, no matter where the cursor happens to be.

12
Columns

MultiMate Advantage II offers a number of sophisticated column manipulation functions that you can use to align columns of numbers either by decimal point or by comma. These features are useful for maintaining lists of figures, for creating tables, for generating financial reports, and for developing statistical reports. MultiMate Advantage II offers a Column Mode feature that permits you to manipulate as many as eight columns of text and numbers.

The tab marks you inserted in the Format Line when you created the document determine whether columns line up by decimal point or by comma. The Decimal Tab function can be used to right-justify columns of text and to right-justify the labels in charts of financial reports.

Another MultiMate Advantage II feature is the power to perform arithmetical calculations on rows of numbers or columns of numbers. In addition, you can move entire columns of numbers to a new location within a page, duplicate columns of numbers within a page, delete columns of numbers, and insert spaces for new columns of numbers.

With the assistance of MultiMate Advantage II's word wrapping feature, you can create as many as eight columns that will appear side by side in your document.

If you are responsible for creating newsletters, sales reports, brochures, flyers, or other forms of written communication, you'll find MultiMate Advantage II's Bound and Snake Column functions helpful.

The Snake Column feature allows you to create newspaper-like columns of text. You select the number of columns and the width of those columns, and your system "spreads" the text across those columns for professional-looking results. The Bound Column feature permits you to create a page containing columns of varying widths and lengths. The Bound Column option provides you with an opportunity to create a document that is both graphically interesting and logically arranged.

Aligning Columns by Decimal Point or Comma

Before you can align columns, you must insert tabs in the Format Line to specify where the decimal points will align. (Chapter 6 provides directions for setting up tabs in the Format Line.)

To use the Decimal Tab function,

1. Press **Shift-F4**.

The decimal tab symbol (▌) appears just before the next tab mark in the Format Line, and the cursor appears directly under the tab mark in the Format Line. The decimal tab symbol is not printed; on the screen, it simply serves to remind you of the method you've selected to align the columns.

2. Type the number.

Each time you type a number, the decimal tab symbol and the numbers shift left, until you type the decimal point (or a comma).

Figure 12.1 illustrates this process. The decimal point remains at the tab setting, and any numbers you type after the decimal point do not shift left; they stay to the right of the decimal place.

After you type a number,

3. Press **Shift-F4**.

4. Continue to type numbers and press **Shift-F4** to move to the next tab until you've completed the first row.

5. Press **Return**.

6. Move to the next line.

Type any subsequent rows using steps 1 through 5—until you reach the last line.

Left-Justifying and Right-Justifying Columns of Text

You can left-justify columns of text using the Indent function:

1. Press **F4**.

2. Type the text.

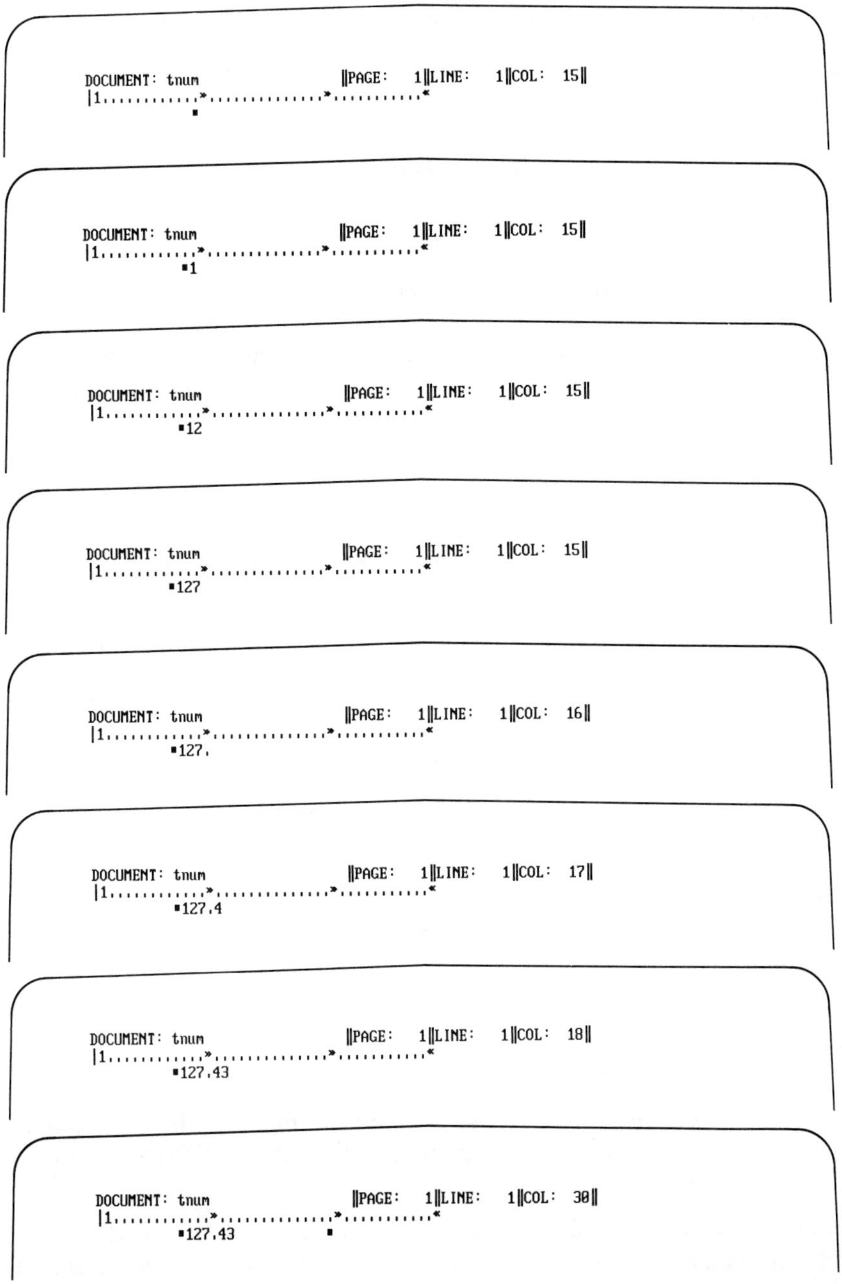

DOCUMENT: tnum   ‖PAGE: 1‖LINE: 1‖COL: 15‖
|1...........».............».............«
        ▪

DOCUMENT: tnum   ‖PAGE: 1‖LINE: 1‖COL: 15‖
|1...........».............».............«
      ▪1

DOCUMENT: tnum   ‖PAGE: 1‖LINE: 1‖COL: 15‖
|1...........».............».............«
      ▪12

DOCUMENT: tnum   ‖PAGE: 1‖LINE: 1‖COL: 15‖
|1...........».............».............«
      ▪127

DOCUMENT: tnum   ‖PAGE: 1‖LINE: 1‖COL: 16‖
|1...........».............».............«
      ▪127,

DOCUMENT: tnum   ‖PAGE: 1‖LINE: 1‖COL: 17‖
|1...........».............».............«
      ▪127,4

DOCUMENT: tnum   ‖PAGE: 1‖LINE: 1‖COL: 18‖
|1...........».............».............«
      ▪127,43

DOCUMENT: tnum   ‖PAGE: 1‖LINE: 1‖COL: 30‖
|1...........».............».............«
      ▪127,43   ▪

Fig. 12.1. Each time you type a number, the decimal tab symbol and the numbers shift left until you type the decimal mark.

Figure 12.2 illustrates left-justified text with column alignment.

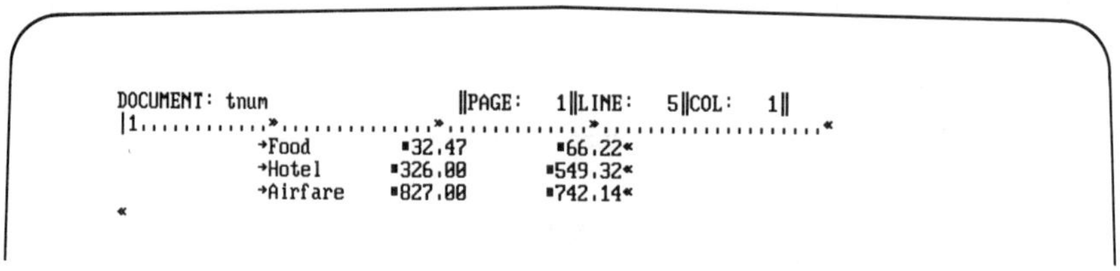

```
DOCUMENT: tnum              ‖PAGE:  1‖LINE:  5‖COL:  1‖
|1............*..............*..............*..............*
           →Food        ■32.47      ■66.22◄
           →Hotel       ■326.00     ■549.32◄
           →Airfare     ■827.00     ■742.14◄
      ◄
```

Fig. 12.2. Left-justified text with column alignment.

You also can use the Decimal Tab function to right-justify text, but, before you do this, make sure your Format Line has a tab mark just before the Return symbol. To right-justify the text,

1. Press **Shift-F4**.

2. Type the text.

3. Press **Shift-F4** to type additional characters on the line or press **Return** to end the line.

Figure 12.3 shows two right-justified lines of text with column alignment.

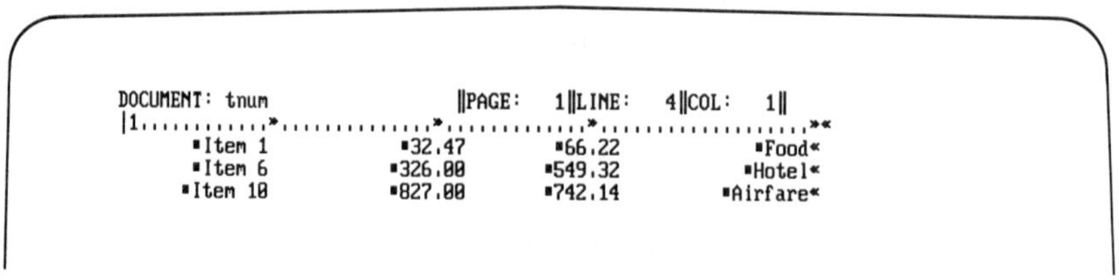

```
DOCUMENT: tnum              ‖PAGE:  1‖LINE:  4‖COL:  1‖
|1............*..............*..............*..............*◄
         ■Item 1      ■32.47      ■66.22        ■Food◄
         ■Item 6      ■326.00     ■549.32       ■Hotel◄
         ■Item 10     ■827.00     ■742.14       ■Airfare◄
```

Fig. 12.3. Right-justified text with column alignment.

Column Math

After you have created the rows and columns of numbers with the decimal tab key, you can use MultiMate's calculations. Six math functions are available and listed in table 12.1.

The functions can be used horizontally or vertically on a page and may be combined. You cannot perform calculations between MultiMate Advantage II pages. If you are using Bound or Snake columns, you may only perform the calculations in the column group or the column containing the cursor. Up to 16 digits may be in a number, and commas and dollar signs may be used.

Table 12.1
Types of MultiMate Advantage II Calculations

Addition
Subtraction
Multiplication
Division
Percentages
Exponents

Entering Numbers and Math Symbols

All numbers are entered after decimal tab symbols, which are created by pressing *Shift-F4*.

To enter a number for addition, just enter the number after the decimal tab.

You can show a number to be subtracted in three ways. The minus sign may be placed on the left or on the right, or you may enclose the number in parentheses. Table 12.2 shows the options.

Table 12.2
Ways To Show Numbers To Be Subtracted

-300
300-
(300)

Try not to mix the subtraction formats you use. If you do, MultiMate Advantage II will select the format in the priority shown in table 12.2.

Show a number to be multiplied by pressing *Shift-8* for the asterisk symbol (*) or *Shift-2* for the at symbol (@). Be sure to use the 8 and 2 on the letter keyboard, not the numeric keyboard. Place the symbol after the second number to be multiplied.

You may divide by using the slash key (/) or the division symbol (÷) in front of the second number in the calculation. You may get the division symbol (÷) by using the alternate keyboard. (Press *Alt-K* to select Math; then press *Ctrl-S*.)

To make a number a percent, place the percent symbol (%) after the number. The math notation in front of the number will determine how the percentage is used in calculation.

To show an exponent, type the whole, non-negative number inside superscript and subscript symbols. Press *Alt-Q*, enter the exponent, and press *Alt-W*. When printed, the number appears as a superscript. When calculated, the exponent is converted into a whole number.

Order of Calculation

When the calculation is performed, horizontal math is calculated from left to right, and vertical numbers are calculated from top to bottom. Table 12.3 shows the order that math symbols are applied, as well as a reminder of the keys used for the math symbols.

Table 12.3
The Order of Calculation

Order (first to last)	On-screen appearance	Keys used to get symbol
Exponent	3↑2↓	Alt-Q, Alt-W
Percent	5%	%
Multiplication and Division	* or @ / or ÷	Shift-8 or Shift-2 / or Alt-K (Math) then Ctrl-S
Addition and Subtraction	+ or no symbol ( ) or -	+ or no symbol entry ( ) or - before or after number

Decimals

The answer is rounded to two decimal places if no decimals are used and division is performed.

If decimal places are identified in the number for calculation, the answer is rounded to the maximum number of decimals used.

Horizontal Math

You may calculate numbers horizontally. Use decimal tabs to align the numbers (press *Shift-F4* for the decimal tab).

1. Place tabs in the Format Line to identify where you will place numbers and the answer.

2. Type in the numbers using decimal tabs to align the number under the tab positions; enter dollar symbols, commas, and decimal points as desired.

3. Since horizontal math is performed left to right, place a decimal tab to the right of the last number entered; place the cursor under that decimal tab by pressing the left-arrow key.

4. Press **Ctrl-F3** to perform the calculation; the answer appears.

Dollar symbols, commas, and decimal points are carried into the answer. You may recalculate horizontal math by changing numbers, placing the cursor back under the "answer" decimal tab, and pressing *Ctrl-F3* again.

Figure 12.4 shows examples of horizontal math.

```
DOCUMENT: tnum                ‖PAGE:  1‖LINE:  2‖COL:  1‖        INSERT
|1.........►.........►.........►.........►.........►.........◄
     ■1,000.00  ■*10    ■/2    ■-20.00 ■4,980.00◄
```

Fig. 12.4. Column calculations using horizontal addition and subtraction functions.

Vertical Math

You may calculate numbers vertically. Use decimal tabs to line up the numbers vertically. Press *Shift-F4* for the decimal tab.

1. Place tabs in the Format Line to identify where you will place numbers and the answer.

2. Type in the numbers using decimal tabs to align the numbers under the tab positions; enter dollar symbols, commas, and decimal points as desired.

3. Since vertical math is performed top to bottom, place a decimal tab under the last number entered; place the cursor under that decimal tab by pressing the left-arrow key.

4. Press **Ctrl-F4** to perform the calculation; the answer appears.

Dollar symbols, commas, and decimal points are carried into the answer. To recalculate vertical math, change numbers, place the cursor back under the "answer" decimal tab, and press *Ctrl-F4*.

Figure 12.5 shows examples of vertical math.

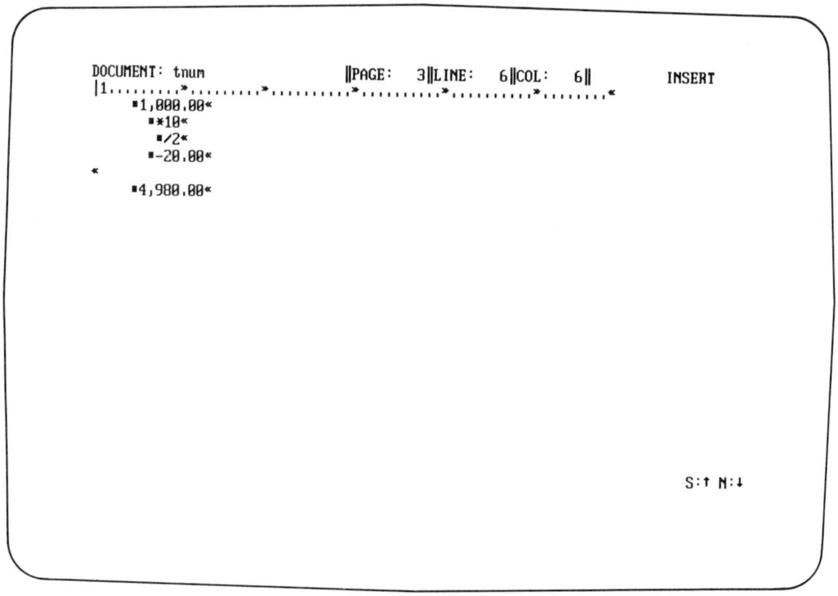

```
DOCUMENT: tnum                    ||PAGE:   3||LINE:   6||COL:   6||      INSERT
|1..........»..........».........».........».........».».......«
        ■1,000.00«
          ■*10«
           ■/2«
          ■-20.00«
      «
        ■4,980.00«
```

```
                                                          S:↑ N:↓
```

Fig. 12.5. Column calculations using vertical addition and subtraction functions.

Inserting, Deleting, Moving, and Copying Columns

You can use MultiMate Advantage II to insert, delete, move, or copy columns of characters. Those columns of characters and text include columns that you have created with the Decimal Tab function (or the Insert or Tab functions).

You may want to add data to the original data typed in the columns. Perhaps you have created columns seven characters wide and want to expand one column to 10 characters in width. Or you may have created a page of five columns and want to make room for a sixth column between the first and second columns. To perform these kinds of activities, you'll use the *Column Insert function.*

You also can delete numbers from columns, remove columns of text you no longer need, and move or copy whole columns or parts of columns. Remember that you can use these features only **within a single page**; you cannot move or copy a column from one page to another.

Character Marking

When inserting, deleting, copying, or moving columns, you use your cursor to mark the top left character and bottom right character to be affected.

By marking these two points, you specify where you want to use the Insert, Delete, Copy, or Move function. Figure 12.6 illustrates how you can mark certain areas of text and numbers.

The last example in the figure illustrates an important point: if you are going to use columns of numbers created with the decimal tab symbol, you should insert spaces to make all the numbers the same number of characters long. Otherwise, when you mark the upper left character, MultiMate Advantage II may split subsequent numbers that are longer.

Column Insert

To insert a new column between existing columns, you could lengthen the Format Line and add the necessary spaces manually (line by line), but this is a time-consuming process. Using MultiMate Advantage II's Column Manipulation-Insert feature, you can add all the spaces automatically.

```
DOCUMENT: tnum                    ‖PAGE:  1‖LINE:  4‖COL:  23‖      COLUMN COPY
|1..........⋗.....................⋗............⋗...................◄
Animals:◄
            →Cat and Dog    ▪   32      ▪32◄
            →Bird and Cat   ▪1,000      ▪1,000◄
            →Bird and Dog   ▪   89      ▪89




        <←> and <→> to Define Width THEN <↓> to Define Length.          S:↑ N:↓
```

Fig. 12.6 (cont. on next page). How to mark text.

```
DOCUMENT: tnum                    ‖PAGE:   1‖LINE:   4‖COL:  32‖      COLUMN COPY
|1.........▸....................▸...........▸..................◂
Animals:◂
              →Cat and Dog    ▪   32      ▪32◂
              →Bird and Cat   ▪1,000      ▪1,000◂
              →Bird and Dog   ▪   89      ▪89




              <←> and <→> to Define Width THEN <↓> to Define Length.          S:↑ N:↓
```

```
DOCUMENT: tnum                    ‖PAGE:   1‖LINE:   4‖COL:  43‖      COLUMN COPY
|1.........▸....................▸...........▸..................◂
Animals:◂
              →Cat and Dog    ▪   32      ▪32◂
              →Bird and Cat   ▪1,000      ▪1,000◂
              →Bird and Dog   ▪   89      ▪89




              <←> and <→> to Define Width THEN <↓> to Define Length.          S:↑ N:↓
```

Fig. 12.6 (cont.). How to mark text.

Before getting started, make sure your Format Line has enough tab marks and space between tab marks to accommodate the characters you want to insert; otherwise, the changes that result may place the existing text in a state of disarray. Then, follow these steps:

1. Move the cursor to the column in which you want to insert spaces.

2. Place the cursor on the character or symbol immediately following the characters you want to insert.

3. Press **Shift-F3**.

This prompt appears in the upper right corner of your screen:

COLUMN MODE

4. Press **Ins** to insert.

This prompt appears in the upper right corner of the screen:

COLUMN INSERT

At the bottom of the screen, you see the following prompt:

INSERT # of Columns 00 # of Lines Press F10 to Continue

In this prompt, the word *Columns* refers to the character columns defined in the system Status Line, not columns you have created with numbers or letters.

In the # of Columns 00 field,

5. Type the width of the column—any number from *01* to *99*. MultiMate Advantage II adds that number of spaces prior to your cursor position.

6. Press **Return**.

The cursor moves to the # of Lines 00 field.

7. Type the number of lines for the inserted area—any number from *01* to *99*.

You should type the exact number of lines; if you specify more lines than necessary, the lines appear as spaces at the end of the text or are inserted into any text that might follow.

After you define the number of character columns and lines,

8. Press **F10** to execute the Insert function.

The specified number of spaces are inserted and become part of the document. MultiMate Advantage II automatically adjusts existing text to accommodate the spaces. If your columns do not line up, adjust the Format Line.

Figure 12.7 illustrates a column insert. Fifteen columns of spaces (shown by dots) were inserted for two lines. This insert allows another column of numbers to be added. The format line was altered prior to the column insert to accommodate the additional spaces.

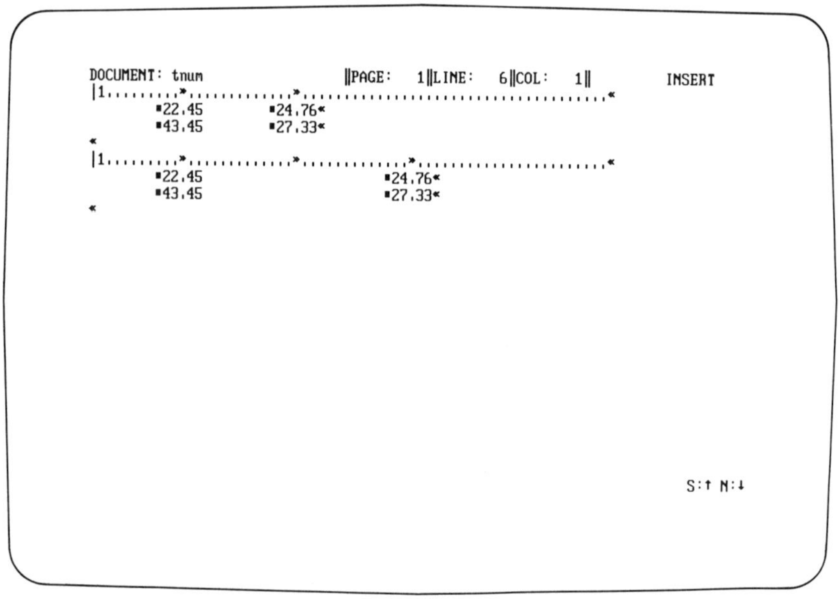

```
DOCUMENT: tnum              ‖PAGE:  1‖LINE:  6‖COL:  1‖        INSERT
|1.........►.............►..................................◄
      ■22.45    ■24.76◄
      ■43.45    ■27.33◄
  ◄
  |1.........►.............►...........►....................◄
      ■22.45              ■24.76◄
      ■43.45              ■27.33◄
  ◄



                                                    S:↑ N:↓
```

Fig. 12.7. A column insert.

If you want to exit the Insert function before execution, press *Esc*.

Column Delete

You use the Column Manipulation-Delete function to delete columns of text or numbers. When MultiMate Advantage II deletes columns, the material remaining on each line moves left. If you use word wrapping, the program reformats the remaining text within the margins. Like the Insert function, the Column Manipulation-Delete function cannot move across pages.

To begin,

1. Move the cursor under the top left character you want to delete.

2. Press **Shift-F3**.

This prompt is displayed in the upper right corner of the screen:

    COLUMN MODE

3. Press **Del**.

This prompt appears in the upper right corner of the screen:

    COLUMN DELETE

This prompt appears at the bottom of the screen:

`<←><→> to Define Width THEN <↓> to Define Length`

To highlight the width and length of the block of characters you want to delete,

4. Move the cursor, using the **right-arrow** key, to define the rightmost character column to be deleted.

To redefine the leftmost character column to be deleted,

5. Move the cursor, using the **left-arrow** key.

After you define a right and left character column for deletion, you **cannot** remove the highlight. If you highlight too many characters, press *Esc* and begin again.

6. Define the length of the column to be deleted, using the **down-arrow** key to highlight the lines.

Check to be certain (before pressing the key) that the column width is defined properly. After you press the down-arrow key, you **cannot** use the right- or left-arrow keys to change the highlighting on the right and left columns.

If you highlight too many lines, remove the highlight using the up-arrow key. To start again, press *Esc*.

7. Press **Del** to finish the delete.

MultiMate Advantage II deletes the highlighted text and adjusts the remaining text automatically.

Column Move

You use the Column Manipulation-Move function to move a column to another position on the same page. You cannot use this function to move a column from one page to another. Look at table 12.4. Suppose you want to reposition the *Check #* column to appear after the *Amount* column.

Table 12.4
A Check Listing

Date	Check #	Description	Amount
2/3	10932	JK Travel	432.67
2/3	10933	Postage	108.00
2/4	10934	Supplies	679.03

To use the Move function,

1. Check the Format Line to be sure enough tabs and spaces are available.

2. Place your cursor under the top left character you want to move.

3. Press **Shift-F3**.

This prompt appears in the upper right corner of the screen:

```
COLUMN MODE
```

4. Press **F7**.

This prompt replaces the prompt in the upper right corner of the screen:

```
COLUMN MOVE
```

And this prompt appears at the bottom of the screen:

```
<←> and <→> to Define Width THEN <↓> to Define Length
```

5. Highlight the left and right margins of the block to be moved, using the **right-** and **left-arrow** keys.

After you highlight a right and left character column, you can remove the highlight only by pressing *Esc*.

6. Using the **down-arrow** key, highlight the length (by line) of the column to be moved.

Remember, after you press the down-arrow key (Step 6), you cannot use the left- and right-arrow keys to highlight text. Use the up-arrow key to remove the highlighting from the lines. Press *Esc* if you want to start the process over.

7. Press **F7**.

This prompt appears in the upper right corner of the screen:

```
TO WHERE?
```

8. Move the cursor to the location on the screen where you want to insert the highlighted text.

9. Press **F10**.

Your system moves the text to the new location and adjusts the existing text on the screen. If the columns do not line up, change your Format Line.

Column Copy

If you want to copy text to a new location **and** keep that text in the old location, use the Column Manipulation-Copy function. Like the Insert, Delete, and Move functions, the Copy function can be used only within one page.

Before getting started, be certain that your Format Line has enough tabs and spaces to accommodate the text to be copied. To be absolutely sure, try copying a column to see whether the Format Line accommodates it. If the Format Line is not set correctly, you can delete the copied column, adjust the Format Line, recopy the column, and delete it in its old location.

To perform the Column Copy function,

1. Move the cursor to the upper left character column you want to copy.

2. Press **Shift-F3**.

This prompt appears in the upper right corner of the screen:

    COLUMN MODE

3. Press **F8**.

This prompt replaces the prompt in the upper right corner:

    COLUMN COPY

This prompt appears at the bottom of the screen:

    <←> and <→> to Define Width THEN <↓> to Define Length

4. Using the **right-** and **left-arrow** keys, highlight the width of the text you want to copy.

If you move too far left or right, press *Esc* and begin the procedure again.

5. Define the length of the column to be copied.

Before you press the down-arrow key, make sure the column width is defined properly. You **cannot** change the highlighted left and right character columns after you press the down-arrow key. If you highlight too many lines, use the up-arrow key to remove the highlighting.

6. Press **F8**.

This prompt appears in the upper right corner of the screen:

    TO WHERE?

7. Move the cursor to the location on the screen where you want to insert the highlighted text.

8. Press **F10**.

Your system inserts the copied text and adjusts the existing text around it. The original columns remain as they were. If your columns do not line up, adjust the Format Line.

Column Sort

You may sort columns of text in order:

1. Place the cursor on the upper left character letter of the column you want to sort.

2. Press **Shift-F3**. The prompt COLUMN MODE appears.

3. Press **F5**. The prompt COLUMN SORT appears.

4. Press the **left-** and **right-arrow** keys to identify the width of the column to sort.

5. Press the **down-arrow** key to highlight the number of lines to sort. (Make sure the left and right boundaries are identified before pressing the down-arrow key.)

6. Press **F5**.

The sort options shown in figure 12.8 appear.

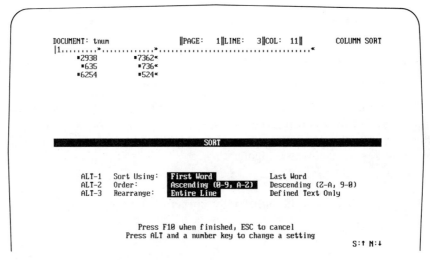

Fig. 12.8. The Sort by Column options.

Press the Alt key combination to highlight the choices desired. You may press *Alt-1* to select between sorting by the first word or the last word in the highlighted block you have marked. Press *Alt-2* to choose between sorting in ascending order (A-Z and 0-9) or descending order (Z-A or 9-0). If lines with the same value are encountered, the original "presorted" order is maintained. You may press *Alt-3* to select whether to move entire lines during the sort or whether to move only the defined (highlighted) text.

7. Highlight the sort options needed; press **Alt** with the number shown to change the sort options.

8. Press **F10** to complete the sort.

Bound and Snake Columns

There is a MultiMate Advantage II feature that permits you to create (using word wrapping) as many as eight columns of text on your screen. Depending on their purpose in your document, these columns of text are called either *Bound columns* or *Snake columns*.

Bound columns are used when each column may be a different size and the information at the end of one column does not lead into the next. Snake columns are similar in appearance and in function to newspaper columns. The columns are of the same width and are comprised of text that automatically "wraps up" to the beginning of the next column.

Using Snake Columns

To set up the Format Line for Snake columns,

1. Press **F9** or another Format Line combination.

2. Using the **arrow keys**, select the left column boundary.

The Format Line will begin at column 1 unless you place a left bracket symbol ([) at column 3 or further to the right. (You cannot begin the left boundary at column 2.) You may use tab symbols in the Format Line.

3. Press the **left bracket** symbol if you are beginning the left boundary at any position other than column 1.

4. Position the cursor at the right column boundary using the **arrow key**.

5. Press the **right bracket** symbol (]) to indicate the end of the column.

6. Type in the number of columns (from two to eight) that you want to appear on the page.

For example, you would type *3* to indicate that the page will contain three columns of text. The system automatically inserts two spaces between columns. If you want more than two spaces,

7. Press the **space bar** once for each additional space you want inserted between columns.

8. Press **Return**.

9. Press **F10** to leave the Format Line.

Figure 12.9 illustrates how different spacing between columns may be controlled with the Format Line spaces.

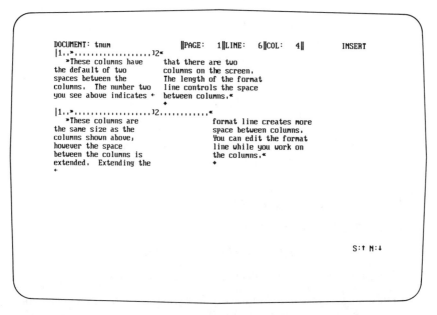

Fig. 12.9. The effect of the Format Line length on spacing between columns.

If your columns and the spaces between columns will not fit the maximum Format Line of 156 columns, this message appears on your screen:

TOTAL SIZE OF COLUMNS IS GREATER THAN 156

You must edit the Format Line.

10. Type in the text to create a single, long column.

When the text that you want divided into three columns has been entered,

11. Press **Ctrl-Return**.

The End Column Group symbol (◆) appears. To "spread" the text,

12. Press **Shift-F3** (to repaginate).

13. Press **Ctrl-F2** (column balancing).

Your system reformats the single, long column into three evenly spaced columns across the page.

What if, however, you don't want the text to be spread evenly across the columns? In formatting a newspaper or newsletter, you may know that one column must be five inches long and the second column only three inches long. You can determine the length of the column using this procedure:

1. Place the cursor at the location on your screen where you want the column to end.

2. Press **Shift-F3**.

3. Press **Return**.

The column will end at this point. A Hard Column Break symbol (◄) appears, and the cursor moves to the beginning of the next column.

The disadvantage inherent in this method is that you cannot use repagination without scrambling the text. You must plan the text carefully before typing it into column format.

If you type over an End Column Group symbol or over a Column Break symbol, your text will readjust.

Using Bound Columns

Bound columns (each column independent of the others) may be of different lengths. Eight columns may be created on one screen, each column with its own Format Line. To create Bound columns,

1. Press **F9** or another Format Line key combination.

2. Select the left column boundary using the **arrow key**.

The Format Line will begin at column 1 unless you place a left bracket ([) symbol at column 3 or further to the right. (You cannot create a column beginning at column 2.) You can use tab symbols in the Format Line.

3. Move the cursor to the location on your screen where you want the column to end.

4. Type a **right bracket** (]) symbol at the right column boundary.

5. Press the **space bar** to create space between the first and second columns.

6. Type a **left bracket** ([) to identify the beginning of the second column.

7. Type a **right bracket** (]) to identify the end of the second column.

8. Repeat Steps 4, 5, and 6 until you have all of the columns arranged.

9. Press **Return** rather than a right bracket to end the last column.

10. Press **F9** when the Format Lines are set.

11. Type in the first column text.

12. Press **Shift-F3** for a Hard Column Break.

13. Press **Return** to go to the next column.

To end Column Group and return to the first column position,

14. Press **Ctrl-Return**.

The End Column Group symbol appears.

If you type over an End Column Group symbol or a Column Break symbol, the text will readjust.

Moving Between Columns and Moving Within Columns

The keystrokes presented in table 12.5 can be used to move within a column, within a column group, and between column groups. (The regular editing keys also can be used.)

Table 12.5
Moving within and between Columns

Key	Action
Shift-F3-Home	Go to the first character in the column.
Shift-F3-End	Go to the last character in the column.
Shift-F3 Up-Arrow	Go to the previous column group, last line, same character position.
Shift-F3 Down-Arrow	Go to the next column group, same line, same character position.
Shift-F3 Right-Arrow	Go to the next column, same line, first character.
Shift-F3 Left-Arrow	Go to the previous column, same line, last character.
Shift-F3 Alt-F3	Go to the same line of the column group, first character.
Shift-F3 Alt-F4	Go to the same line of the column group, last character.
Ctrl-Home	Go to the first character on the page.
Ctrl-End	Go to the last character on the page.
Ctrl Right-Arrow	Go to the first letter of the next word.
Ctrl Left-Arrow	Go to the first letter of the previous word in the column.

To leave Column Mode and resume regular editing, press *Esc*.

13
Document-Handling Utilities

There are seven MultiMate Advantage II Utilities to help you perform disk and document-management activities:

- Copying documents
- Moving documents
- Deleting documents
- Renaming documents
- Printing Document Summary screens
- Searching through Document Summary screens
- Restoring backed-up documents

To access Utilities, select item 6 on the Main Menu, and MultiMate Advantage II displays the Document Management Menu, shown in figure 13.1.

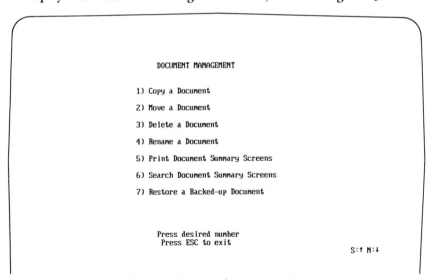

```
                    DOCUMENT MANAGEMENT

           1) Copy a Document

           2) Move a Document

           3) Delete a Document

           4) Rename a Document

           5) Print Document Summary Screens

           6) Search Document Summary Screens

           7) Restore a Backed-up Document




              Press desired number
              Press ESC to exit
                                              S:↑ N:↓
```

Fig. 13.1. The Document Management Menu.

Copy a Document

To duplicate an existing document, use the Copy a Document utility. Your document can be copied under its original name, or it can be copied under a new name. You do **not** have to use the DOS copy command for document duplication.

The Copy a Document utility can be used in many ways to help you be more efficient. As an example, you can copy a document to a separate disk to be used as a backup document. You can use a copy of a document to transfer data from one computer to another. You can copy documents to a disk and mail it to another office; the recipient can print as many copies of the document as needed, without retyping them.

To copy a document,

1. Type **1** on the Document Management Menu (see fig. 13.1).

The screen shown in figure 13.2 is displayed on your monitor.

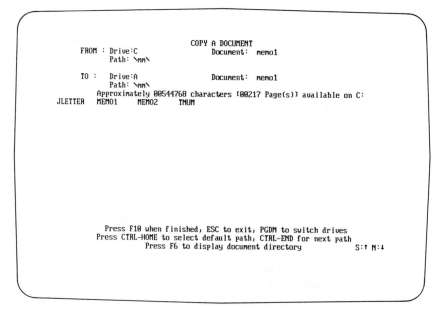

```
                              COPY A DOCUMENT
            FROM : Drive:C          Document:  memo1
                   Path: \mm\

            TO :   Drive:A          Document:  memo1
                   Path: \mm\
                   Approximately 00544768 characters [00217 Page(s)] available on C:
   JLETTER   MEMO1     MEMO2     TNUM




                    Press F10 when finished, ESC to exit, PGDN to switch drives
                Press CTRL-HOME to select default path, CTRL-END for next path
                       Press F6 to display document directory          S:↑ N:↓
```

Fig. 13.2. The Copy a Document screen.

Under the COPY FROM: prompt,

2. Type the letter of the disk drive on which the document resides and enter the path.

3. Type the name of the original document.

Use the arrow keys to move your cursor between fields.

Under the TO: prompt,

4. Type the letter of the drive to which you will copy the document and enter the path.

You may have noticed that the Copy a Document screen contains a document drive directory. The documents displayed in the directory reside on the drive identified in the directory line. If you want to see the directory of another drive, press *PgDn*. If you want to change paths, press *Ctrl-End* or *Ctrl-Home*.

5. Type the name of the new (copied) document.

The name that you assign to the copy can be the same as the name of the existing document, or you can give the document a new name. If you want to make two copies of one document on one disk, you must change the name of the copied document because you cannot copy a document to itself.

If you do want two (or more) copies of the same document on a single disk, assign the copies a name similar to the first copy. For example, if the copied document is named *TARK1*, call the second copy *TARK2*, the third copy *TARK3*, and so on.

After you type the drive designation and the names of the document to copy from and the document to copy to,

6. Press **F10**.

This prompt may appear on your screen:

    INSERT DISKETTE(S), STRIKE ANY KEY WHEN READY

7. Place the original disk and the copy-to disk in the specified drives.

If you have a floppy disk system, you can remove the MultiMate Advantage II *System Working Disk*, if necessary.

8. Press **any key** on the keyboard.

While MultiMate Advantage II is copying the document, a system prompt warns you not to type any characters from your keyboard:

    OPERATION IN PROGRESS
    - DO NOT INTERRUPT -

Another prompt lets you know when you can remove the disks:

```
- OPERATION COMPLETE -
<ESCAPE> to abort, any other key to continue
```

The copy is complete. If you removed the MultiMate Advantage II *System Working Disk* for the copy operation, you can replace it.

To return to the Document Management Menu,

> 9. Press **Esc**.

If you press any other key on the keyboard, the program clears the document names on the copy screen so that you can type the names for another copy.

Move a Document

You use the Move a Document function to move—not copy—a document from one disk to another disk. Select this option if you need to free space on your disk by moving selected documents to another disk. The Move a Document option can be used to create a permanent set of archive disks that contain just those documents that are no longer being used.

To begin the Move a Document procedure,

> 1. Type **2** on the Document Management Menu and press **Return**.

The screen that appears is shown in figure 13.3.

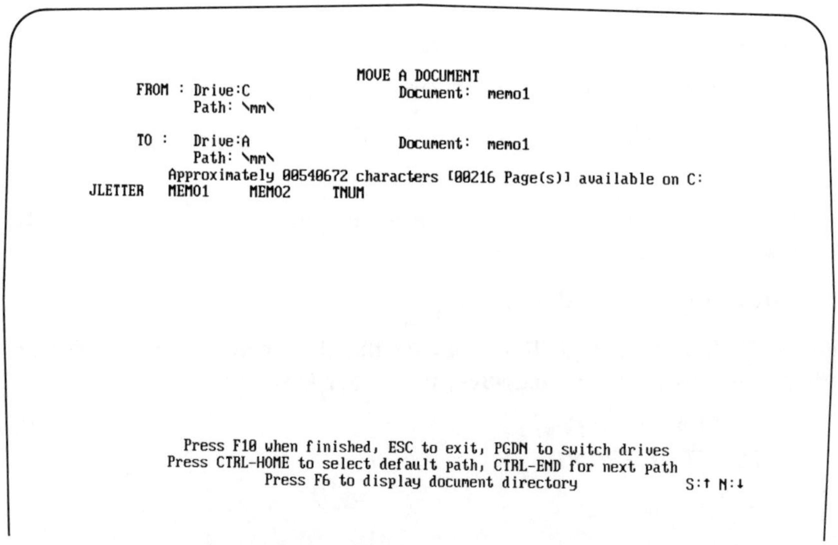

```
                              MOVE A DOCUMENT
        FROM : Drive:C              Document: memo1
               Path: \nm\

        TO :   Drive:A              Document: memo1
               Path: \nm\
               Approximately 00540672 characters [00216 Page(s)] available on C:
JLETTER    MEMO1     MEMO2     TNUM




                Press F10 when finished, ESC to exit, PGDN to switch drives
              Press CTRL-HOME to select default path, CTRL-END for next path
                      Press F6 to display document directory        S:↑ N:↓
```

Fig. 13.3. The Move a Document screen.

Under the MOVE FROM: prompt,

2. Type the letter of the disk drive on which that document resides. Enter the path.

3. Type the name of the document to be moved.

Under the TO: prompt,

4. Type the letter of the disk drive to which you want to move the document and enter the path.

5. Type the name of the document.

Use the arrow keys to move from field to field. If you want both to move a document and change its name, type the new name under the TO: prompt. Your system will assign a new name to the document to be moved.

If you want to access a different drive, press *PgDn*. Press *Ctrl-End* or *Ctrl-Home* to change paths. Again, review your MultiMate Advantage II documentation for a detailed explanation of moving between directories.

You can move documents from one disk to another, but the TO: prompt designations and the FROM: prompt designations must be different.

6. Press **F10**.

This prompt may appear:

    INSERT DISKETTE(S), STRIKE ANY KEY WHEN READY

7. Place the original disk and the destination disk in the specified drive.

If you are using a floppy disk system, you can remove the MultiMate *System Working Disk*, if necessary.

8. Press **any key**.

A prompt reminds you not to disturb the disks while MultiMate Advantage II moves the document:

    OPERATION IN PROGRESS
    - DO NOT INTERRUPT -

This prompt lets you know when you can remove the disks:

                - OPERATION COMPLETE -
    <ESCAPE> to abort, any other key to continue

If you removed the System disk for the Move function, you can replace it now. If you want to return to the Document Management Menu, press *Esc*.

To move another document,

    9. Press **any key**.

MultiMate Advantage II clears the document names on the Move a Document screen, and you can begin another move.

Delete a Document

Think twice about the documents you choose to delete. Once you have deleted a document, you cannot recover it. If you are unsure about deleting a document, store it on another disk.

It is wise to delete inaccurate and out-of-date documents from your active disk. Deleting these documents creates space on your disk for new documents and eliminates the possibility that you will confuse an old document with an updated version.

To erase a document permanently from a disk,

    1. Type **3** on the Document Management Menu and press **Return**.

The screen shown in figure 13.4 appears.

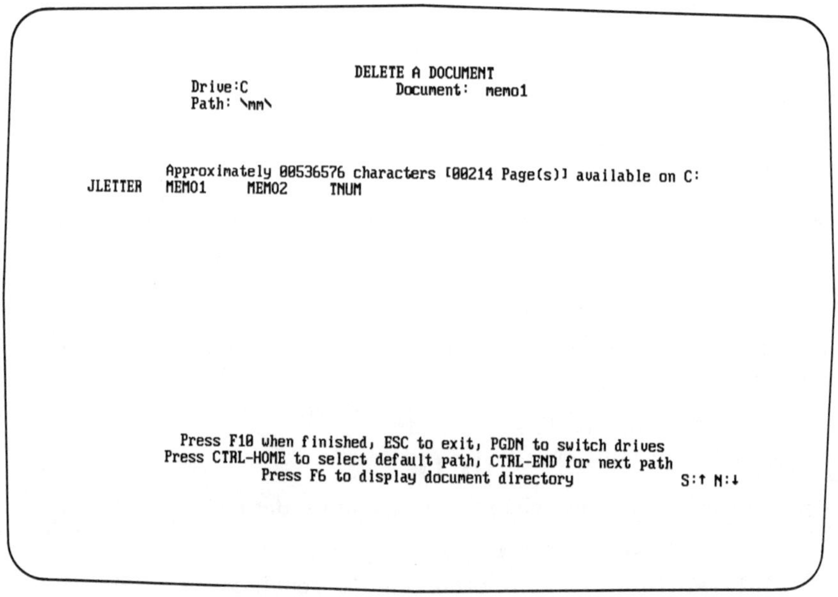

```
                              DELETE A DOCUMENT
            Drive:C              Document:  memo1
            Path: \mm\


            Approximately 00536576 characters [00214 Page(s)] available on C:
    JLETTER  MEMO1      MEMO2      TNUM








            Press F10 when finished, ESC to exit, PGDN to switch drives
         Press CTRL-HOME to select default path, CTRL-END for next path
                Press F6 to display document directory        S:↑ N:↓
```

Fig. 13.4. The Delete a Document screen.

Using the arrow keys to move from field to field,

>   2. Type the letter of the disk drive on which the document resides and enter the path.

>   3. Type the name of the document to be deleted.

MultiMate Advantage II displays the names of the documents residing on the drive indicated. To change drives, press *PgDn*. Press *Ctrl-Home* or *Ctrl-End* to change paths. After you type the disk drive designation and the document name,

>   4. Press **F10**.

This prompt may appear on your screen:

```
INSERT DISKETTE(S), STRIKE ANY KEY WHEN READY
```

>   5. Insert the disk in the drive you have specified.

>   6. Press **any key**.

Deleting the document takes only a few seconds; during this time, the following prompt appears:

```
OPERATION IN PROGRESS
- DO NOT INTERRUPT -
```

When it is safe to remove the disk, this prompt appears:

```
        - OPERATION COMPLETE -
<ESCAPE> to abort, any other key to continue
```

To return to the Document Management Menu,

>   7. Press **Esc**.

To delete another document,

>   8. Press **any key**.

>   9. Type the name of the document.

Rename a Document

You may want to change the name of one of your documents for a number of reasons. The name you originally assigned to the document may be less appropriate at the present time or difficult to remember; the name may be too similar to another document, or it may be difficult to type the document name without error. Changing the name of a document is a simple process:

1. Type 4 on the Document Management Menu and press **Return**.

The screen shown in figure 13.5 appears.

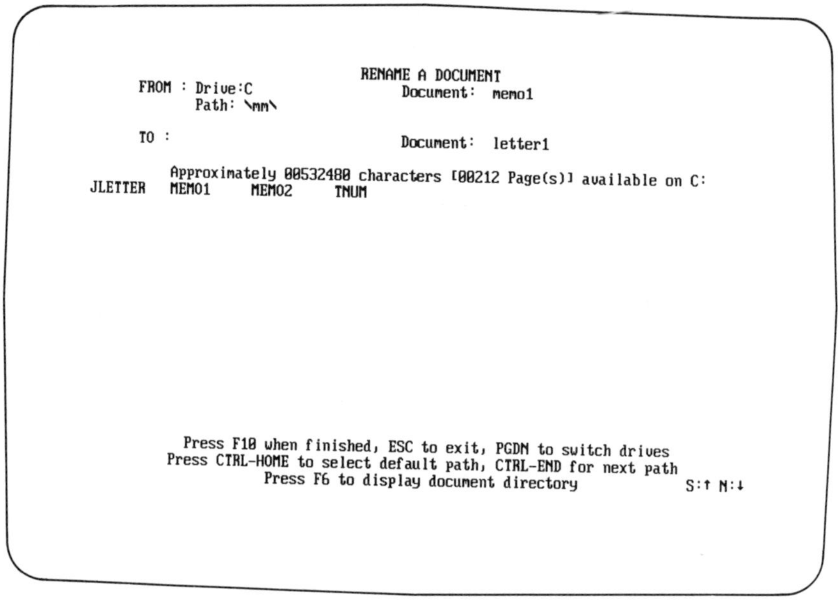

```
                              RENAME A DOCUMENT
           FROM : Drive:C            Document:  memo1
                  Path: \mm\

           TO  :                     Document:  letter1

                Approximately 00532400 characters [00212 Page(s)] available on C:
    JLETTER   MEMO1      MEMO2      TNUM









                Press F10 when finished, ESC to exit, PGDN to switch drives
              Press CTRL-HOME to select default path, CTRL-END for next path
                       Press F6 to display document directory        S:↑ N:↓
```

Fig. 13.5. The Rename a Document screen.

Under the RENAME FROM: prompt,

2. Type the letter of the disk drive on which the document resides and enter the path.

3. Type the name of the document you want to rename.

Under the TO: prompt,

4. Type the new document name.

Use the arrow keys to move from field to field. To change the drive specified in the document directory, press *PgDn*. Press *Ctrl-Home* or *Ctrl-End* to change paths. After you fill in the new name,

5. Press **F10**.

MultiMate Advantage II may prompt the following:

INSERT DISKETTE(S), STRIKE ANY KEY WHEN READY

Be certain that the document disk is in the drive you specified. Then,

>   6. Press **any key**.

This prompt may appear on your screen:

```
OPERATION IN PROGRESS

- DO NOT INTERRUPT -
```

After renaming the document, your system prompts the following:

```
- OPERATION COMPLETE -
<ESCAPE> to abort, any other key to continue
```

To return to the Document Management Menu,

>   7. Press **Esc**.

To rename another document,

>   8. Press **any key**.

Print Document Summary Screens

When you create a new document or edit an old document, MultiMate Advantage II displays the Document Summary screen—the screen that records the Document Name, Author, Addressee, and the Operator Name, as well as the Identification Key Words, Comments, Creation and Modification Dates, Total Editing Time, Editing Time Last Session, Total Keystrokes, and Keystrokes Last Session.

The Print Document Summary Screens utility gives you two options:

- You can *view* all of the Document Summary screens on a disk.

- You can *print* all of the Document Summary screens on a disk.

To review the contents of a disk, you may want to view all the Document Summary screens on a disk. To do so, follow these steps:

>   1. Type **5** on the Document Management Menu and press **Return**.

MultiMate Advantage II displays the screen shown in figure 13.6.

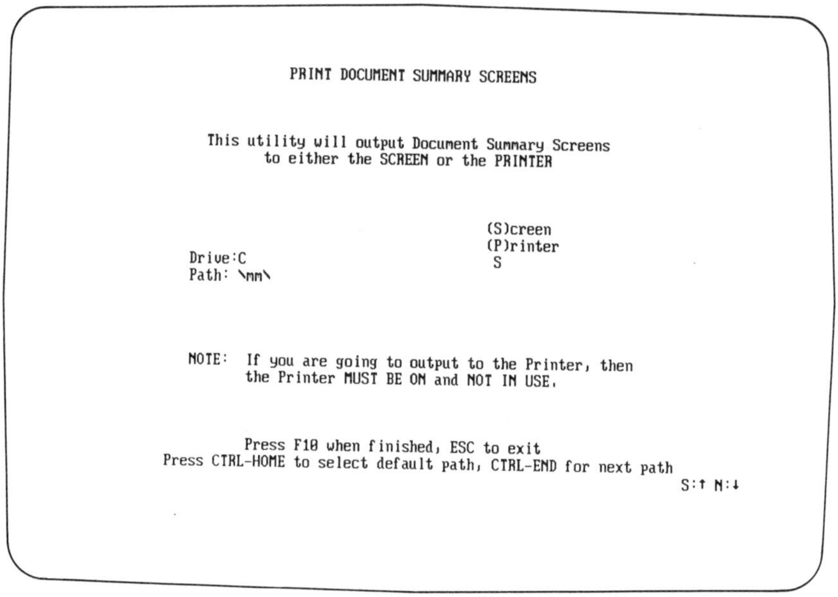

```
                    PRINT DOCUMENT SUMMARY SCREENS


             This utility will output Document Summary Screens
                   to either the SCREEN or the PRINTER


                                        (S)creen
                                        (P)rinter
          Drive:C                       S
          Path: \mm\




          NOTE:  If you are going to output to the Printer, then
                 the Printer MUST BE ON and NOT IN USE.



                  Press F10 when finished, ESC to exit
          Press CTRL-HOME to select default path, CTRL-END for next path
                                                    S:↑ N:↓
```

Fig. 13.6. The Print Document Summary Screens screen.

2. Type the letter of the drive containing the Document Summary screens you want to view.

3. Press **Return** to move to the next field.

If you are using subdirectories,

4. Press **Ctrl-End** for the next path or press **Ctrl-Home** to select the default path.

5. Type **S** to display the Document Summary screens or type **P** to print the Document Summary screens.

6. Press **F10**.

In response to your instructions, the system either prints or displays the Document Summary screens.

If you want to print the Document Summary screens, make sure your printer is on and ready. MultiMate Advantage II prints two Document Summary screens on each page. To stop the printing, press *Esc*.

If you want to view the Document Summary screens on your monitor,

1. Press **any key** to move from screen to screen.

If you find a document you want to work on,

>   2. Press **Esc** twice.

You then return to the Document Management Menu, and from there you can move to the Main Menu and then to the Edit a Document screen. The document name on this screen appears as the name of the document you want to edit.

Search Document Summary Screens

The Search Document Summary Screens option is used to search for specified information on all the Document Summary screens on a disk. You may want to identify those documents that reference a particular author, addressee, or operator. Or, you may want to find documents that have a specific key word. You can search for any information on the Document Summary screen except keystroke data.

The Search utility selects those documents that match the elements of document specification you supply. MultiMate Advantage II lists the names of the matching documents on the screen or prints them.

To search Document Summary screens, you fill in the fields on a blank Document Summary screen, and the system matches these fields with those on existing Document Summary screens. You can use one field for a match, or you can use several fields.

For example, you may want to search all the documents that have the author *K. Smith* and/or all the documents that have the author *K. Smith* and/or the comment *bus trip*. Notice that the word *or* is used. If you type *K. Smith* as the author and *bus trip* as a comment, MultiMate Advantage II lists all the documents that have the author *K. Smith*, all the documents that have the comment *bus trip*, and all the documents that have both the author *K. Smith* and the comment *bus trip*.

MultiMate Advantage II compares each field you select with the corresponding field in the Document Summary screens stored on the disk. For example, if you type *K. Smith* in the Comment field, your system does not match that name with *K. Smith* in the Author field. Whether you use uppercase or lowercase letters is not important; MultiMate Advantage II does not distinguish among *K. Smith*, *k. smith*, and *K. SMITH*.

The system may find a match if you type only part of a character string (see table 13.1). If you type a character string that is longer than the character string for which you are searching, MultiMate Advantage II will not find a match. Table 13.1 includes examples of the characters you may type for the search, as well as the field content in the actual Document Summary screens.

Table 13.1
Matching in Document Summary Screen Searches

Typed for Search	*Field in Document Summary Screen*	*Match? Why or Why Not*
Smith	K. Smith	Match - identical words
SMITH	K. Smith	Match - case insignificant
Smi	K. Smith	Match - partial word match
Smithy	K. Smith	No Match - excessive number of characters

To perform a search,

1. Type **6** on the Document Management Menu and press **Return**.

MultiMate Advantage II displays the screen shown in figure 13.7.

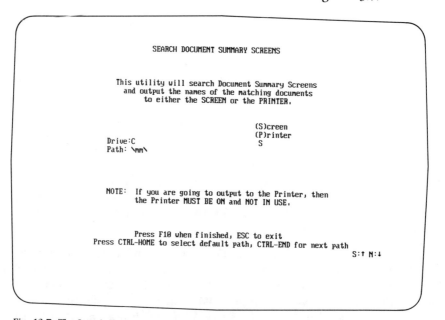

Fig. 13.7. The Search Document Summary Screens screen.

In the Drive field,

2. Type the letter of the drive containing the Document Summary screens to be searched and enter the path.

If you are using multiple directories, press *Ctrl-End* or *Ctrl-Home* to select the directory.

Use the next field to indicate whether you want MultiMate Advantage II to display the document names on the screen or to display them on the screen and print them.

3. Type **S** for screen display or type **P** for screen display and print.

4. Press **F10**.

Your system displays a blank Document Summary screen (see fig. 13.8).

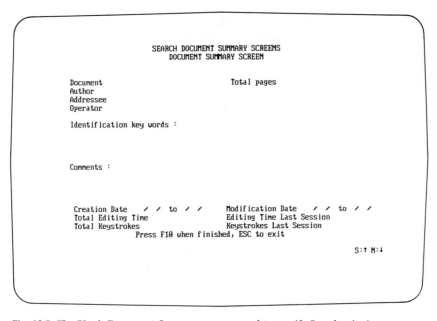

```
                    SEARCH DOCUMENT SUMMARY SCREENS
                       DOCUMENT SUMMARY SCREEN


      Document                        Total pages
      Author
      Addressee
      Operator

      Identification key words :




      Comments :




      Creation Date    / / to / /     Modification Date    / / to / /
      Total Editing Time               Editing Time Last Session
      Total Keystrokes                 Keystrokes Last Session
                    Press F10 when finished, ESC to exit

                                                         S:↑ N:↓
```

Fig. 13.8. The Blank Document Summary screen used to specify Search criteria.

Use this screen to specify the criteria to be used in the search. If you want to find all documents authored by *Jack Jones*, skip the Document field:

5. Type **Jack Jones** in the Author field.

6. Press **F10**.

(You do this because *Author* is the only criterion you want to search for.)

The system searches all of the Document Summary screens on the specified disk, finds all the documents authored by Jack Jones, and displays (and/or prints) the names of these documents.

If you fill in more than one field, MultiMate Advantage II lists the names of the documents with a match between one or more of the entries in the fields. If you type two comments (*fiscal* and *accountant*, for example), your system lists the names of documents that contain either the word *fiscal* or the word *accountant* or both.

Use the Creation and Modification Dates to specify a range of dates that matches any document created or modified within that range. Type the dates in MM/DD/YY (month/day/year) format and be sure to include the slashes.

You may enter more than one name in the Document field. Separate the names by a space.

After all the Document Summary screens have been searched, and the system has identified matching documents, this prompt appears:

```
PRESS ANY KEY TO EXIT
```

Restore a Backed-Up Document

When creating a new document, you press *Y* or *N* in the field called Backup Before Edit Document on the Modify Document Defaults screen. If you press *Y*, MultiMate Advantage II automatically creates a backup copy of your document. The backup document name contains the extension *.DBK*. Each time you edit the document, the "old" *.DBK* file is replaced with the new version of the document, and it is stored on the same disk as the new document.

Having the capability to restore a backed-up document is an important option if, for instance, you edit a document and then decide you want to use an earlier version. The procedure is also useful when a document somehow becomes damaged.

To restore a backed-up document,

    1. Type **7** on the Document Management Menu and press **Return**.

The screen that appears is illustrated in figure 13.9.

All backed-up files (files with the extension *.DBK*) are listed in the document directory.

    2. Type the letter of the drive on which the backed-up document is stored and enter the path.

```
                        RESTORE A BACKED-UP DOCUMENT
           Drive:C                    Document:
           Path: \mm\


           Approximately 00516096 characters [00206 Page(s)] available on C:
  TEST1








           Press F10 when finished, ESC to exit, PGDN to switch drives
          Press CTRL-HOME to select default path, CTRL-END for next path
                   Press F6 to display document directory        S:↑ N:↓
```

Fig. 13.9. The Restore a Backed-Up Document screen.

If you need to check the contents of other drives,

   3. Press **PgDn**.

A new document directory is displayed. To change hard disk paths, press *Ctrl-End* or *Ctrl-Home*, and the new document directory will be displayed. Only documents that have been backed up after editing appear in the directory.

   4. Move the cursor to the appropriate field on the screen.

   5. Type the document name.

   6. Press **F10**.

MultiMate Advantage II replaces the existing document with the backed-up document of the same name. The table of contents and footnote files are replaced as well. You cannot delete backup documents from your disk by using the Delete a Document option on the Document Management Menu. Instead, you must use the DOS Delete command to delete the documents. (For more information, see *Using PC DOS*, 2nd Edition, or *MS-DOS User's Guide*, 2nd Edition, both published by Que Corporation.)

14

Spell-Checking Documents and Using the Thesaurus

MultiMate Advantage II's Spell-Check feature furnishes you with a fingertip dictionary—literally! You can use this timesaving feature to check individual words or blocks of words either as you work on your document or after you have entered all of the text.

MultiMate Advantage II checks each word against the Merriam-Webster Dictionary located on your disk. Medical and legal terms are included. If the Spell-Check function identifies a misspelling, and you are not certain of the correct spelling, you can call up a list of words from which to choose the accepted spelling.

MultiMate Advantage II's dictionary doesn't contain all words, however. Proper names, professional jargon, and obscure technical phrases, for instance, cannot be found in the dictionary. MultiMate Advantage II permits you to create custom dictionaries to house the special words, names, and character combinations that you frequently use in your work.

The default custom dictionary is *CLAMFL*. To create another custom dictionary, use the Edit System Defaults screen to assign it a unique name (see Chapter 18). You may switch from one custom dictionary to another as well.

Two methods are used to add or delete words in a custom dictionary. You may add or delete as you perform a spell-check on a document, or you may add or delete words through the Custom Dictionary utilities on the Utilities and Conversions Menu (see Chapter 19). Disk space is all that limits the size of your custom dictionary.

MultiMate Advantage II offers you a 40,000-word thesaurus, a 110,000-word dictionary that includes legal and medical terms, and a custom dictionary editor.

Spell-Checking

Before the system can correct misspelled words, it must identify them. The program checks each word against *The Merriam-Webster Linguibase*™ *Dictionary* and your custom dictionary.

MultiMate Advantage II marks (with a place mark) those words or characters that do not appear in either dictionary, and it registers these words as misspelled. For example, when I used a previous version of MultiMate to write a book, many of the keyboard key names, document names, and letters did not appear in either the program dictionary or in a custom dictionary. When the system spell-checked the manuscript, the misspelled word count was high even though many of the words marked as misspelled were, in fact, correct.

You have two options for identifying misspelled or unidentifiable words:

- Work with blocks of text from within your document.

- Spell-check your entire document, either from within the document or through the Main Menu.

Spell-Checking Portions of Your Document

To spell-check from within your document after you have typed some of the text,

1. Position the cursor under the first word you want to check.

2. Press **Ctrl-F10** (spell-check).

This prompt appears in the upper right corner of your screen:

    CHECK WHAT?

You must highlight the words you want to check. You can highlight one word or many words—you could even highlight all the words in your document. Use any of the quick cursor movements used for highlighting (see Chapter 7). For example, if you press Return, your system will highlight the remaining words in a paragraph.

3. Highlight the text you want to spell-check.

4. Press **F10**.

If your computer has a hard disk drive, MultiMate Advantage II immediately begins processing the spell-check. If your computer has two floppy disk drives, the prompt INSERT DICTIONARY DISK IN DRIVE A - PRESS ANY KEY appears. At this point, you must replace the MultiMate Advantage II System disk with the Dictionary disk.

As the system checks the spelling, it displays both the number of misspelled words and the total number of words checked:

    [00000] misspelled words [00000] words total

When the spell-check is complete, this prompt appears:

    SPELL CHECK COMPLETE - PRESS ANY KEY TO CONTINUE
    [00009] misspelled words [00035] words total

  5. Press **any key**.

The prompt disappears and you return to the Main Menu.

MultiMate Advantage II marks any unidentified words with a blinking first letter called a *place mark*. At this point, you can use the Spell-Edit feature, which is described later in this chapter.

Another way to spell-check words from within a document is to spell-check a single word.

  1. Place the cursor under the first letter of the word you want to spell-check.

  2. Press **Alt-F1** to mark the word.

Use the Spell-Edit feature, which is described in *The Spell-Edit Feature* section of this chapter, to check the word.

Spell-Checking Your Entire Document

You can spell-check a specific number of pages in a document, or you can spell-check all of the pages in your document.

If the Main Menu is displayed on your screen,

  1. Type **8**

  2. Press **Return** to move to the Spell Check a Document screen (see fig. 14.1).

Or, if the document that you want to spell-check is displayed on your screen,

  1. Press **Alt-8** to move to the Spell Check a Document screen.

Now, on the Spell Check a Document screen,

1. Type the name of the document you want to spell-check.

2. Type the letter of the disk drive on which the document resides and type the path.

Use the arrow keys to move between fields. This screen has a document directory for reference. Press *PgDn* to change the document directory to reflect another drive. Press *Ctrl-Home* or *Ctrl-End* to change paths. The document you want to spell-check must appear on the document directory.

3. Press **F10**.

4. Type the numbers of the pages you want to spell-check.

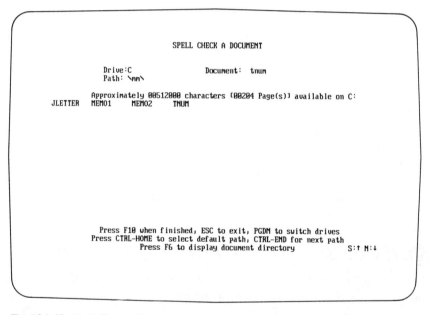

Fig. 14.1. The Spell Check a Document screen.

If you leave the Start Page number at *1* and the End Page number at *999*, the entire document will be spell-checked.

If you change the Start Page and End Page numbers, use the tab key or the arrow keys to change fields. These page numbers reflect the numbers in the MultiMate Advantage II Status Line, not the page numbers you may have assigned in the document itself.

5. Press **F10**.

If you have a hard disk, MultiMate Advantage II begins to spell-check the document. If you have a dual floppy disk drive system, the program prompts the following:

```
INSERT DICTIONARY DISK IN DRIVE A - PRESS ANY KEY
```

Remove the System disk, insert the Dictionary disk, and press any key.

As the system spell-checks the document, this prompt appears on your screen:

```
OPERATION IN PROGRESS
[00000] MISSPELLED WORDS [00000] WORDS TOTAL
```

If you press *Esc*, this prompt appears:

```
OPERATION DISCONTINUED AT PAGE 000
```

When MultiMate Advantage II finishes spell-checking, this prompt appears:

```
OPERATION COMPLETE - PRESS ANY KEY TO CONTINUE
[00009] MISSPELLED WORDS [00035] WORDS TOTAL
```

6. Press **any key** to move to the Main Menu.

7. Type **1** to view the document you just spell-checked.

MultiMate Advantage II first displays the Edit a Document screen and then the Document Summary screen. In the document, you will see that the first letter of each unidentified word is blinking.

Correcting Misspelled Words

You can correct misspelled words in two ways:

- Strike over the word and use Insert/Delete.

- Use the Spell-Edit feature.

Strikeover

If you know the corrections for some small errors, you can make changes quickly—simply strike over the blinking place mark and correct the word. If your document has a number of blinking place marks, or if you do not know the correct spelling of the word, use MultiMate Advantage II's Spell-Edit feature.

The Spell-Edit Feature

Use the Spell-Edit feature to correct words that are indicated by place marks. Your cursor moves quickly from one identified misspelling to the next, gives you several options for handling the misspelling, and provides at your request a list of possible spellings.

To use the Spell-Edit feature,

1. Move the cursor to the beginning of the text you want to spell-edit.

2. Press **Alt-F10**.

If you are working on a hard disk system, MultiMate Advantage II finds the first identified misspelling. If you have a dual floppy disk drive system, the prompt INSERT DICTIONARY DISK IN DRIVE A - PRESS ANY KEY appears.

You do not need the System disk to spell-edit. Make sure the Dictionary disk is in drive A and press any key.

After MultiMate Advantage II finds the first place mark, you have several choices (see fig. 14.2).

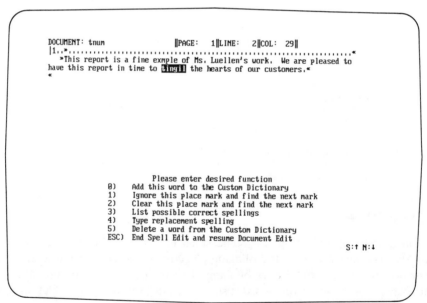

Fig. 14.2. The prompt displayed after MultiMate Advantage II finds the first place mark.

When the system cannot find any other unidentified words, the prompt UNABLE TO FIND NEXT MISSPELLING - PRESS ANY KEY appears.

Adding a Word to the Custom Dictionary

If you press *0* (zero), MultiMate Advantage II removes the place mark and adds the marked word to your custom dictionary; during this time, a prompt appears. For instance, suppose that you are adding the name *Luellen* to your custom dictionary. You would see this prompt:

```
Adding to Custom Dictionary: Luellen
```

Because *Luellen* is capitalized, this prompt appears:

```
Is capitalization required? (Y/N)
```

Proper names, some professional jargon, and some technical terms always are capitalized; other words are not. Type the appropriate response to the prompt.

If the word appears at the end of a sentence, this prompt appears:

```
Is the ending period required? enter Y for yes, N for no
```

Choose the appropriate response. The program then displays the following prompt:

```
Press any key to search for the next misspelling or press Esc
to end Spell Edit and resume Document Edit
```

If you want to continue the search, press any key. To end the spell-edit, press *Esc*.

Ignoring the Place Mark

Another option for dealing with a marked word is to ignore the place mark by typing *1*. MultiMate Advantage II leaves the place mark intact and continues the Spell-Edit function.

You may select this option if you know the word is misspelled but do not know the correct spelling. For example, you may know that the name of a company is misspelled, but you cannot make the correction because the letter that will verify the spelling is at home.

If you leave a place mark in the document, you can easily find it later by using the Go to Place Mark keys: *Ctrl-F1*.

Clearing the Place Mark

Choose number *2* to clear the place mark and find the next place mark. You use this option when the word is correctly spelled, but it is not one that you want to add to the custom dictionary. The place mark disappears, and the spell-edit continues.

You may clear all place marks by pressing *Alt-Y.*

Listing Possible Spellings

If you want MultiMate Advantage II to list all possible correct spellings for the misspelled word, choose option *3*. The program consults the dictionary, and a system prompt appears. (In this next example, MultiMate Advantage II cannot identify the word *tingil*.)

```
Looking for correct spelling for : tingil
```

After the system identifies possible correct spellings, the program presents you with several options (see fig. 14.3).

```
DOCUMENT: tnum                    ‖PAGE:   1‖LINE:   2‖COL:  29‖
|1..>...........................................................«
      *This report is a fine exmple of Ms. Luellen's work.  We are pleased to
have this report in time to tingil the hearts of our customers.«
«




              Enter the number of the word to replace the misspelled word
                    or press ESC to return to Spell Edit menu.
     1) tingle          4) tinnily          7) atingle
     2) tingly          5) tangly           8) tunnel
     3) tinily          6) tangelo          9) tangle
                                                          S:t N:↓
```

Fig. 14.3. The prompt displaying possible correct spellings.

Type the number that is to the left of the word you want to substitute for the misspelled word.

If the word in the text is underlined, MultiMate Advantage II replaces that word with an underlined, corrected word and retains any capitalization. If the replacement word is longer or shorter than the misspelled word, the program reformats the paragraph within the margins.

MultiMate Advantage II has an auto-correction feature that automatically corrects identical, multiple spelling errors after the first occurrence is corrected. Of course you may elect not to use this feature if it is inconvenient or might cause problems. After the system replaces the word, this prompt appears:

```
Press any key to search for the next misspelling or press ESC
to end Spell Edit and resume Document Edit
```

To continue, press any key except *Esc*. If you press *Esc*, the spell-edit ends.

If the word does not appear in the list that the program generates, press *Esc*. Use option *4* (described next) to alter the word.

If MultiMate Advantage II cannot find any correct spellings, the following prompt appears:

```
No correct spellings were found, press any key to continue
```

Typing Replacement Spelling

You may type a replacement spelling for a word while you are in the Spell-Edit Mode. Choose option *4* (see fig. 14.2); a line like that in figure 14.4 appears on the screen. In the example shown in figure 14.4, the word *excite* has been chosen to replace *tingil*. Type the word you desire and press *F10*. The word is inserted in the text and replaces the marked word.

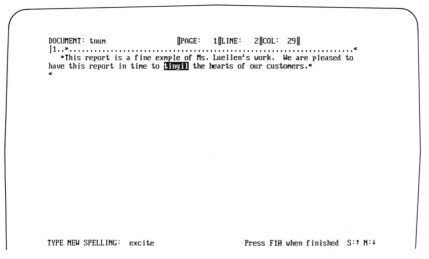

Fig. 14.4. Using MultiMate Advantage II to replace tingil with excite.

Deleting a Word from the Custom Dictionary

When any misspelled word is identified and the options in figure 14.2 appear, you may use the opportunity to delete a word from the custom dictionary. Selecting option 5 causes the screen illustrated in figure 14.5 to appear.

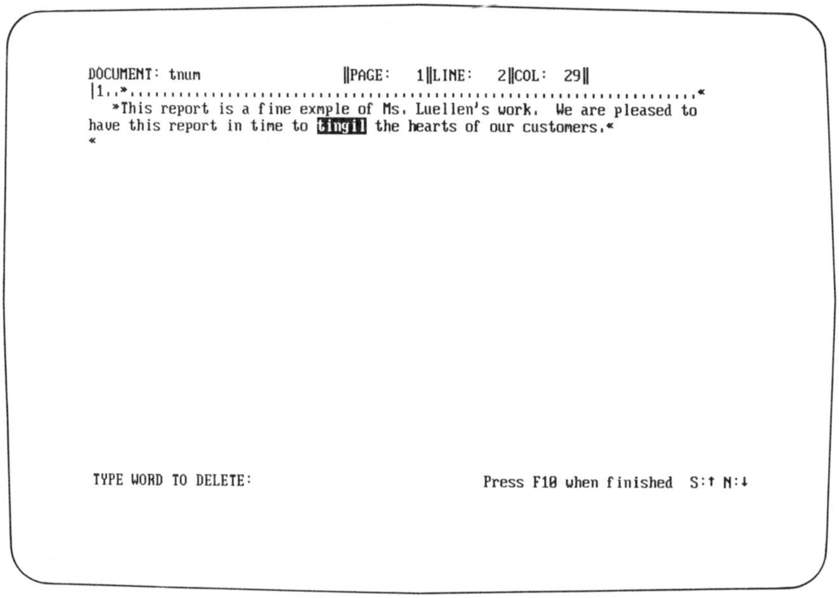

```
DOCUMENT: tnum                    ‖PAGE:   1‖LINE:   2‖COL:  29‖
|1..».................................................................«
        »This report is a fine exmple of Ms. Luellen's work.  We are pleased to
have this report in time to ████ the hearts of our customers.«
«




TYPE WORD TO DELETE:                    Press F10 when finished  S:↑ N:↓
```

Fig. 14.5. Deleting a word from the custom dictionary.

Type the word to be deleted and press *F10*.

Another way to delete words from the custom dictionary is through the Custom Dictionary utilities on the Utilities and Conversions Menu (see Chapter 19). If you find yourself adding and deleting custom dictionary words often, you may want to create several custom dictionaries for different activities and use the Edit System Defaults screen (described in Chapter 18) to change the custom dictionary name.

Ending the Spell-Edit

The last option available for handling a misspelling is to press *Esc* to return to the Document-Edit Mode.

If your system is a dual floppy disk drive system, replace the MultiMate Advantage II System disk with the Dictionary disk.

Spelling Tips

MultiMate Advantage II's Spell-Check feature is practically foolproof—but quirks do exist. If you are spell-checking a document, and the spell-checker "locks up," then spell-check a single page at a time until you find the characters that are causing the difficulty. Then strike over the characters and continue the spell-check.

Sometimes when you spell-check a document, you will find that your system has marked a frequently used, correctly spelled word. An example could be a company name that does not appear in the dictionaries. Once you have worked with the word, MultiMate Advantage II uses it that same way through-out the rest of the document.

The Thesaurus

NEW
With
MMA

Use the Thesaurus function to find definitions and to substitute words or phrases with up to as many as 50 characters (including spaces and hyphens).

1. Place the cursor on the word to be checked.

2. Press **Alt-T**.

This prompt appears:

    LOOK UP WHAT?

3. Move the cursor to highlight any additional words.

4. Press **F10**.

If you are using a dual floppy disk drive system, replace the System disk with the Thesaurus disk and press any key.

The screen shown in figure 14.6 appears. It contains the meaning of the word followed by a list of as many as nine synonyms.

In figure 14.6, the word *otherwise* brings up the definition *unlike in kind or character*, and nine possible synonyms are offered. The prompt in the lower left corner of the screen gives you these options:

5. Press the **space bar** to view additional synonyms.

Or

5. Type the number that appears next to the synonym you want to use.

```
DOCUMENT: tnum                    ||PAGE:   1||LINE:   4||COL:  44||
|1..».............................................................«
     »This report is a fine exmple of Ms. Luellen's work.  We are pleased to
have this report in time to excite the hearts of our customers.«
«
     »We need this type of exposure, otherwise, we will miss out on an
opportunity



                              THESAURUS
                              otherwise

     adj:  unlike in kind or character


     1) different        4) distant        7) other
     2) disparate        5) divergent      8) unequal
     3) dissimilar       6) diverse        9) unlike


     Enter Number for Replacement,  ESC - Exit Thesaurus,  ALT-T - Look Up New Word.
     SPACEBAR for More Synonyms  PGDN - Next Meaning    PGUP - Prior Meaning.  S:↑ N:↓
```

Fig. 14.6. Thesaurus options.

The screen prompts also explain that you can press *PgUp* or *PgDn* to view other meanings. Figure 14.7 displays the additional two meanings for *otherwise.*

```
DOCUMENT: tnum                    ||PAGE:   1||LINE:   4||COL:  44||
|1..».............................................................«
     »This report is a fine exmple of Ms. Luellen's work.  We are pleased to
have this report in time to excite the hearts of our customers.«
«
     »We need this type of exposure, otherwise, we will miss out on an
opportunity



                              THESAURUS
                              otherwise

     adv:  under different conditions


     1) else



     Enter Number for Replacement,  ESC - Exit Thesaurus,  ALT-T - Look Up New Word.
                     PGDN - Next Meaning    PGUP - Prior Meaning.  S:↑ N:↓
```

Fig. 14.7 (cont. on next page). PgUp and PgDn for other meanings.

```
DOCUMENT: tnum              ‖PAGE:  1‖LINE:  4‖COL:  44‖
|1..».................................................................«
    »This report is a fine exmple of Ms. Luellen's work.  We are pleased to
have this report in time to excite the hearts of our customers.«
«
    »We need this type of exposure, otherwise, we will miss out on an
opportunity



                              THESAURUS
                              otherwise

      adv:  in a different way or manner


    1) differently
    2) diversely
    3) variously


    Enter Number for Replacement,  ESC - Exit Thesaurus,  ALT-T - Look Up New Word.
                  PGDN - Next Meaning   PGUP - Prior Meaning,  S:↑ M:↓
```

Fig. 14.7 (cont.). PgUp and PgDn for other meanings.

If you find or think of a substitute for a word, and you would like to see information about it,

1. Press **Alt-T** from the Thesaurus options screen.

The screen in figure 14.8 appears.

2. Type the word that interests you.

3. Press **Alt-T**.

The new word and its synonyms appear.

You may press *Esc* to exit the thesaurus. If the thesaurus does not contain information about the word you have asked for, this prompt appears:

    NO INFORMATION FOUND, PRESS ANY KEY TO CONTINUE

4. Press **any key** to continue.

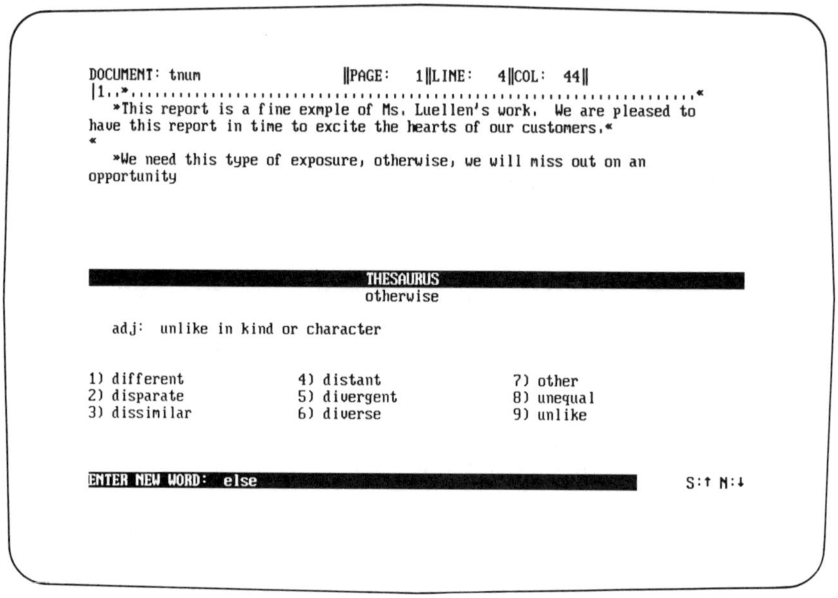

```
DOCUMENT: tnum              ||PAGE:   1||LINE:   4||COL:  44||
|1..»..............................................................«
     »This report is a fine exmple of Ms. Luellen's work.  We are pleased to
have this report in time to excite the hearts of our customers.«
«
     »We need this type of exposure, otherwise, we will miss out on an
opportunity




                            THESAURUS
                            otherwise

    adj: unlike in kind or character


    1) different        4) distant          7) other
    2) disparate        5) divergent        8) unequal
    3) dissimilar       6) diverse          9) unlike



ENTER NEW WORD:  else                                        S:↑ N:↓
```

Fig. 14.8. You may enter a new word.

15
Libraries

A library is a special kind of document in which you can store text that is routinely used in the documents you prepare. It is an independent document that can be inserted within a larger document. A library document can contain the following: names and addresses, forms, contracts, letters, invoices, expense sheets, reports, headers, footers, and even boilerplate document parts. Each page of a library document is called an *entry*.

As you work on your document, you don't have to type a particular block of text again and again. Simply place the cursor where you want to insert the library entry and press a few keys; MultiMate Advantage II will display the additional text in your document.

Libraries are particularly helpful if you regularly enter information on pre-printed forms, such as the expense report in figure 15.1.

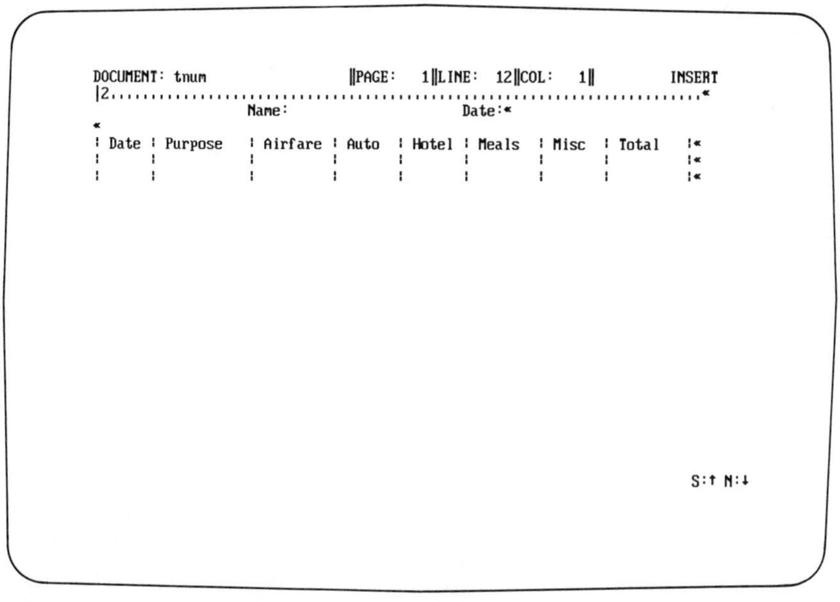

Fig. 15.1. An expense report.

Without the Library feature, you might have to choose between these two burdensome methods every time you created an expense report: You could use a positioning ruler to identify the horizontal and vertical position of each expense item and then place data on your screen accordingly. Or, you could edit an existing form; for example, you could take last month's expense report and change the amounts and the date. Reusing such a document, however, involves a lengthy process of inserting and deleting text.

Both of these methods are cumbersome, and the potential for error is great. By using the Library function, you can create a "master expense report," store it in a library, and then press a few keys to produce a ready-to-complete and perfectly positioned screenful of information. All that is left for you is typing in the data.

Libraries also are useful for storing standard headers and footers. You can type the same header and footer every time you create a new document, or you can use the External Copy feature to copy that header and footer from another document. A **much** faster alternative, however, is to type the header and footer into a library and insert the header and footer in your document with just two keystrokes.

Here's an example of how manageable the MultiMate Advantage II library is. Imagine that you are typing a letter to a client with whom you frequently correspond, and you need her address for the letter's inside address (heading). MultiMate Advantage II's Library feature permits you to simply press *F5* and name the entry (*H* for heading) to recall that heading text from the library and insert it at the cursor location in the letter (see fig. 15.2).

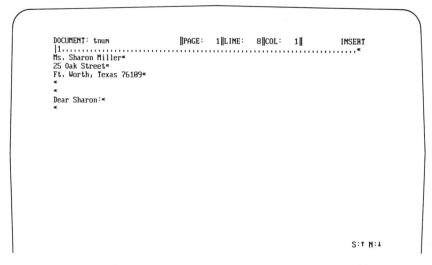

Fig. 15.2. Inserting a heading in a letter.

After you have recalled the heading from the library, you are ready to type the body of the letter; after that, you can type the address for the envelope. You could copy the heading to another page and edit the heading by deleting the salutation, but pressing *F5* and typing *E* (the entry name for envelope) is faster. Figure 15.3 shows the entry for an envelope.

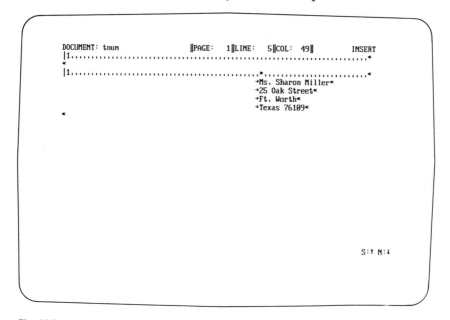

Fig. 15.3. Inserting an address for an envelope.

MultiMate Advantage II prints the envelope address using standard, business-envelope margin settings.

Three Steps

Here are the three major steps to create and use a library:

- Create a library document and its entry.
- Attach a library to your document.
- Recall a library entry.

Step One: Creating a Library

Libraries are separate MultiMate Advantage II documents. They are created and named in much the same way you create and name your working document.

Library entries can be no longer than one page in length. Each page, however, can contain as many as 150 lines of text.

Library entry names can be three characters (letters and/or numbers) long. MultiMate Advantage II is sensitive to uppercase and lowercase letters, so you must enter them correctly each time.

One library document can contain many entries, and those entries can be edited just like the text in any MultiMate Advantage II document.

It is wise to create a separate library for each distinct application. For example, you may create a *Contract* library that will contain the following:

- An entry that is the heading for the contract
- Several entries that contain boilerplate contract paragraphs
- One entry with the standard contract signature line

You may set up another library for *Internal Memos* that contains these items:

- Several entries that are individualized "To:" and "From:" text
- Several entries that are frequently used "cc:'s"

The Display Document Start-Up Screen option on the Edit System Defaults screen must be set at *Y* to create a library (see Chapter 18).

Creating the Library Document

You create a library document through the Main Menu:

    1. Press **2**

MultiMate Advantage II displays the Create a Document screen on which you type the name of the library.

    2. Type the name of your library.

Naming the Library

The rules for naming working documents apply to naming libraries as well. The library name can contain as many as 20 characters; only the first eight characters appear in the document directory, so those first eight letters should describe the library contents as specifically as possible. You can use letters, numbers, and hyphens, but you cannot use spaces or symbols other than hyphens. The name can be uppercase or lowercase; however, MultiMate Advantage II records and displays the name in uppercase.

Libraries appear in the document directory with your other documents. They appear in alphabetical order.

If you list the directory of a disk (with DOS) that holds libraries and working documents, you will see that all MultiMate Advantage II documents, including libraries, have the same file extension (*.DOC*). When you name a library, be certain that the name reminds you that the document is a library document.

An entry that contains the address of a customer, for example, should be stored in the same library document as other address-related entries. You could name such a library *ADDLIB*, a name that identifies contents (*ADD* for addresses) and the kind of document (*LIB* for library).

    3. Press **F10**.

Your system displays the Document Summary screen (which you use to create working documents but *not* to create libraries). The Document Summary screen has a highlighted prompt at the bottom:

    `F5 for Library (leave screen blank)`

    4. Press **F5**.

Filling in the entire screen is unnecessary because the name of the library document is the only library data you need or will be able to use.

This prompt is displayed on your screen:

    `Library Entry Name? [    ] -- Press F6 for a list of entries`

    5. Type the name of the entry you are creating.

Naming Library Entries

To review the names of existing entries, press *F6*; you can then make sure that the entry name you choose is unique. In this case, the entry is the first one, so no other entries will appear if you press *F6*.

Each entry in a library document must have a name unique to that library. When you attempt to enter an invalid entry name, MultiMate Advantage II will beep and refuse the entry. Do not use *999* because MultiMate Advantage II reserves this number to search libraries.

Table 15.1 illustrates both valid and invalid entry names.

Table 15.1
Valid and Invalid Entry Names

Valid Entry Names	*Invalid Entry Names*
A-G	1/7
K12	A,G
k1	*
000	D!
CUS	c.nms
top	[B]

Entry names should be easy to remember and quick to type. It is important to take a few moments and develop a logical scheme as you plan your libraries and name the entries.

For example, suppose that you will be putting several addresses in the *ADDLIB* library.

The first library entry you create may be an envelope address for *Sharon Miller*. A logical name for the entry would be *ASM*, which stands for *Address of Sharon Miller*. Remember, *ASM* and *asm* indicate two different entries to your system. You could then expand this convention to include the addresses of other people: *AGN* could stand for *Address of Glenn Nagel*, *ATT* could stand for *Address of Tom Towers*, and so on.

   6. Press **F10**.

A page appears that is similar to a page of a working document, and the words LIBRARY: and ENTRY: appear in the Status Line:

```
LIBRARY: ADDLIB I IENTRY: ASM I ILINE:1 I ICOL:1
```

The Status Line identifies the library you are working on, the entry, and the line and column location of your cursor.

On the entry page,

   7. Type the entry text.

You can use most of MultiMate Advantage II's regular editing features, such as Insert, Delete, Copy, and so forth. The Help function (Shift-F1) is available. Some of the editing features that you are accustomed to using between pages in a document (such as Copy and Move) or between documents (such as External Copy) cannot be used with library documents.

If you try to use a function that is not available, MultiMate Advantage II prompts INVALID KEY. Remember, each entry can be no longer than one page (a maximum of 150 lines).

Entry Format Lines

When you recall entries into your working documents, you **do not** recall the Format Line at Line 0 of the entry page. You can create an entry that consists of a Format Line only. You also could be using formatting symbols that depend on a specific Format Line (such as indent or tab), in which case you should insert the Format Line at a line other than 0 in the entry. Then, when you recall the entry, the Format Line and the text on the library entry page appear in your working document.

Consider the envelope address as a Format Line example. Because you will be printing the address on an envelope (rather than on a standard sheet of paper), and because the left margin normally used in printing is 10, this address should begin in column 35 in the entry. When you print the address, it begins in column 45 of the envelope. You can use tab marks and a Format Line outside of Line 0 to position the address in the entry, as shown in figure 15.4.

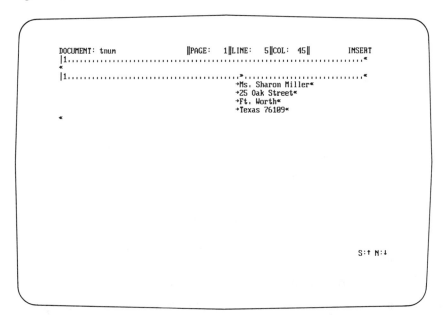

Fig. 15.4. Positioning the address in the library entry.

When you recall this entry for a working document, both the Format Line and the address appear.

When you recall an entry into your working document, you may not elect to insert a different Format Line—MultiMate Advantage II will reformat the text remaining on the page.

In such cases, you can use blank character spaces (rather than symbols that rely on recalling a different Format Line) to place the entry on the page. You also can protect the text by adding a Format Line to the text prior to recalling the entry. The Format Line in figure 15.5 protects the chart layout. Recalling a library entry above the Format Line does not affect the chart.

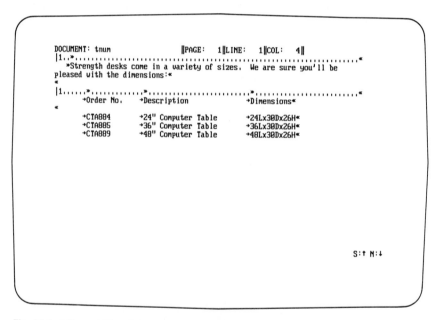

Fig. 15.5. A Format Line that protects the text following the cursor.

You do not need to insert a page break at the end of an entry in order to recall that entry. After you finish typing the entry,

    8. Press **F2** to create another entry.

    9. Repeat steps 5 through 8.

The system creates a page break automatically. (When you work on regular MultiMate Advantage II documents, pressing *F2* means *create a page break.*

When you work on libraries, pressing *F2* means *create another entry*. Adding entries to a library is covered a little later in this chapter.) After pressing *F2*, this prompt is displayed on your screen:

```
Library Entry Name? [      ] Press F6 for a list of entries
```

If you accidentally press *F2*, you **must** create another entry; you **cannot** undo the F2 keystroke by pressing *Esc*.

You can, however, create and get rid of the entry quickly by typing a new entry name and pressing *F10*. Then, with the entry page still blank, press *PgUp* to move to the previous entry page. Position the cursor at the end of this page and press *Shift-F2* to delete the following page (the undesirable entry).

   10. Press **F10** to save the library and the entries you have created.

Step Two: Attaching a Library to Your Document

After you create the library and its entries, you *attach* the library to the working document—a process that permits you to access the entries in that library and insert one or more into your working document. An important point to remember is that you can attach only **one** library to a document **at a time**, and the library remains attached to that document until you either leave the document or attach a new library to the document.

When you attach a library to a document, any library that was previously attached becomes "unattached." For instance, you can access and insert one or all of the standard contract clauses entries from your *CONLIB* library into your working document in one process; however, to add an address to that particular contract (your working document), you must "unattach" *CONLIB* and move to your address library (*ADDLIB*) to recall the client's address.

You can see now why it is important to consolidate all of the frequently used text for one type of document into one library. In this case, all of the standard contract clauses, headings, charts, and so forth, can be identified and inserted quickly and easily because they are incorporated in the *CONLIB* library. And, all of the addresses of your firm's clients are housed in the *ADDLIB* library. This arrangement permits you to create contract working documents efficiently.

After you create the library, you attach it to a working document from within that working document. Enter the text for your working document as you normally do. When you reach the point in your document where you want to insert the phrase or paragraph stored as a library entry,

1. Press **Shift-F5**.

This prompt appears at the bottom of the screen:

```
Drive:___ Library Document:_____
Path:_____
Press F10 when finished, Esc to cancel, F6 for directory
```

Identify the library you want to attach. To change the drive designation, use *PgDn*. (If you forget the name of the library, you can look at the file directory by pressing *F6*.)

2. Type the library name.

3. Press **F10**.

This prompt appears at the bottom of the screen:

```
LIBRARY ATTACHMENT SUCCESSFUL
```

When you move your cursor, the prompt disappears.

If you want to attach a different library to the document, press *Shift-F5* and type the name of a different library.

If you accidentally press *Shift-F5*, press *Esc*.

Step Three: Recalling a Library Entry

After you attach the library to your document, you can call up any (or all) of that library's entries and insert it (them) into the document:

1. Place the cursor where you want the entry to appear in your working document.

2. Press **F5**.

This prompt appears at the bottom of your screen:

```
Library Entry Name? [    ] -- Press F6 for a list of entries
```

3. Type the entry name. Or press **F6** to view the list of names and then type the entry name.

4. Press **F10**.

The contents of the entry page appear at your cursor location in your document. MultiMate Advantage II reformats the entry text to the document format.

Editing a Library Entry

From time to time you will want to update entries. Perhaps one or two of the address entries in your *ADDLIB* library have changed. You can make changes in your library entries in much the same way you edit working documents. Most of MultiMate Advantage II's editing features (Delete, Insert, Strikeover, Backspace, Copy, Move, Search and Replace, PgUp and PgDn) can be used as you edit library entries. To edit a library entry,

1. Press **1** on the Main Menu.

Your system displays the Edit a Document screen.

2. Type the name of the library document you want to edit.

3. Press **F10**.

The first page of the library document appears on your screen.

4. Press **F1**.

This prompt appears on your screen:

```
Library Entry Name? [    ] -- Press F6 for a list of entries
```

5. Type the entry name.

6. Press **F10**.

7. Edit the entry text.

8. Press **F10** to save your changes or repeat steps 4 through 7 to edit another entry.

Adding Library Entries

You may decide to expand a library by adding a new entry to it.

1. Perform steps 1 through 4 for editing a library entry.

2. Press **End** to display the last library entry.

3. Press **Ctrl-End**.

4. Press **F2**.

This prompt appears:

```
Library Entry Name? [    ] -- Press F6 for a list of entries
```

5. Type the new entry name.

If you cannot remember which entry names you have used in the library, press *F6*.

6. Press **F10**.

7. Type the entry text.

When you finish typing the entry, do not press F2 unless you want to add another entry.

8. Press **F10**.

Symbols that control printer functions (such as headers, hard spaces, and underlining) can be inserted in and recalled from library entries.

Deleting Library Entries

To delete a library entry, perform steps 1 through 6 in the Edit a Library Entry procedure. Then,

1. Press **Del** to delete the entry text.

MultiMate Advantage II deletes the entry name.

If you delete the first entry, use *Shift-F2* to combine the pages.

Renaming Library Entries

To rename a library entry, perform steps 1 through 6 for Editing a Library Entry. Then,

1. Press **F5**.

This prompt appears on your screen:

```
Library Entry Name? [    ] -- Press F6 for a list of entries
```

2. Type in the new entry name over the existing name.

3. Press **F10**.

Copying Document Text to a Library Entry

You can copy text from a document to a library as an entry. Attach to your working document the library you are copying to. Then,

1. Place the cursor under the first character of the text you want to copy to the library.

2. Press **Alt-J**.

The prompt LIBRARY COPY WHAT? appears on the screen.

3. Highlight the text to be copied.

4. Press **F10**.

This prompt appears on your screen:

    Library Entry Name?

5. Press **F6** to review your library entries.

6. Type in a name that describes the text you are copying.

If the entry name does not exist, the entry will be created. If the entry name already exists, the contents of the entry will be replaced with the highlighted text.

7. Press **F10**.

When you have completed the entry, MultiMate Advantage II prompts the following:

    -- Copy to library complete --

Footnotes **cannot** be copied to a library entry. If you copy text that contains footnotes to an entry, those footnotes will be removed during the entry copy process.

Printing a Library

You can print the contents of a library just as you print other documents. Two things, however, make library documents different from other documents:

- First, you must set the print parameters as printer defaults (see Chapter 10).

- Second, you cannot use some print parameters, including Start Print at Page Number and Stop Print After Page Number (entries have no page numbers, so all entries are printed) and Left Margin (a 0 margin is used).

16
Merging Documents

A very powerful feature is found in MultiMate Advantage II. That feature is the Merge Document.

MultiMate Advantage II's Merge feature permits you, with just a few keystrokes, to join two related documents into one final document. A common business application for Merge Document is creating form letters with personalized names.

One document (called the Merge Document) contains the body of the letter. The other document (called the Merge Data File) contains the mailing list and other data important to the Merge function.

Suppose that you develop a direct-mail, promotional campaign to introduce potential customers to a new product. First, you would type the letter describing the product in one document (the Merge Document). Then, you would type the mailing list in another document (the Merge Data File). Finally, you would merge the two related documents to produce a personalized sales letter (called the Result Document) for each person on the mailing list.

The Merge Data File can be from these sources:

- A MultiMate Advantage II List Document
- A keyboard merge
- An ASCII Sequential File
- An ASCII Random File
- A MultiMate Advantage II Information Handling data file
- A dBASE (.dbf) File

You can use the data in the Merge Data File for more than one purpose. For example, after you merge the mailing list with the sales letter, you can use the mailing list to generate a sales report that lists the names of all the individuals to whom a sales letter was sent. To create such a report, merge the text in the sales report (the new Merge Document) with the names in the List Document (your original mailing list).

The Merge and List Documents

How to merge a Merge Document with a MultiMate Advantage II List Document is covered first. Then, you will learn how to use the other types of Merge data files.

Remember, you use two documents in a merge: the Merge Document and the List Document. The *Merge Document* contains the main body of the text and does not vary from printed document to printed document. The *List Document* contains the list of variable information you insert into the Merge Document when you print it.

Each Merge variable is identified by a Merge Item name, and each Merge variable and Merge Item name make up a *Merge Item*.

To show MultiMate Advantage II where each Merge variable should be placed in the Merge Document, insert the Merge Item names in the Merge Document. A special symbol (⊦) called a *Merge Code* identifies the Merge items.

The Merge Code symbol is created when you press *Alt-M*. The Merge Code is not printed; it is a screen symbol. Do not underline it, or the merge will not work.

Figure 16.1 illustrates a Merge Document, and figure 16.2 illustrates a List Document ready for merging.

The Merge Document, shown first, contains the body of a direct-mail, promotional effort. Merge codes surround the Merge Item names; these codes indicate where MultiMate Advantage II should place each Merge variable in the List Document.

The List Document contains the mailing list, organized into Merge items; each Merge Item consists of a Merge Item name and the Merge variable set off with Merge codes. All the information about one customer is kept on one page, all the information about another customer is kept on another page, and so on. Each set of customer data makes up a *Merge Item Set*.

By comparing the Merge and List documents, you can see how MultiMate Advantage II matches each variable in the List Document with its position in the Merge Document; then, it prints a merged document like the one illustrated in figure 16.3.

```
DOCUMENT: tnum                  ||PAGE:   1||LINE:  14||COL:  22||
|1..>......................................................................«
|DEFINE|«
FILE TYPE MULTIMATE«
|END DEFINE|«
«
|name|«
|street|«
|citystate| |zip|«
«
Dear |first|,«
«
    >We trust that the |product| you purchased from Designers Unlimited
were well received.  Designers Unlimited is proud to announce a new
product in the same line.  Information about our glass window ornaments is
attached.  Our special price to you is |price|.«
    >We hope you'll order our glass window ornaments along with more
|product| soon.  |first|, we appreciate your business and look forward to
|close|.«
«
Sincerely,«
«
«
«
                                                           S:↑ N:↓
```

Fig. 16.1. Sample Merge Document.

```
DOCUMENT: client2               ||PAGE:  1||LINE:  1||COL:  1||
|1..>......................................................................«
|name|«
Ms. Judith Lundquist«
The Curiousity Shop|«
«
|position|«
Owner|«
«
|street|«
3 Park South|«
«
|citystate|«
New York, New York|«
«
|zip|«
10016|«
«
|first|«
Judith|«
«
|product|«
crystal snowflakes and wind chimes|«
«
                                                           S:↑ N:↓
```

Fig. 16.2 (cont. on next page). Sample List Document

```
DOCUMENT: client2              ‖PAGE:  1‖LINE:  29‖COL:  1‖
«
|product|«
crystal snowflakes and wind chimes|«
«
|price|«
$10.99|«
«
|close|«
a continuing relationship|«
«
```

Fig. 16.2 (cont.). Sample List Document.

Figure 16.3 shows the printed results of merging the Merge Document and the List Document. Notice the high degree of personalization that is achieved with MultiMate Advantage II's Merge feature. Notice also that the variable items in the body of the paragraph were inserted, and the paragraph reformed within the margins set in the Merge Document.

                                              June 10, 1989

Ms. Judith Lundquist
The Curiousity Shop
4 Park South
New York, New York 10016

Dear Judith,

     We trust that the crystal snowflakes and wind chimes you
purchased from Designers Unlimited were well received by your
customers. In response to the positive feedback we've gotten,
Designers Unlimited is proud to announce a new product in the
same line. Information about our glass window ornaments is
attached. Our special price to you is $10.99.
     We hope you'll order our glass window ornaments along with
more crystal snowflakes and wind chimes soon. Judith, we
appreciate your business and look forward to a continuing
relationship.

Sincerely,

Dean Muldare
Designers Unlimited

Fig. 16.3. The printed results of merging the two documents.

Creating the Merge Document

You create the Merge Document the same way you create other MultiMate Advantage II documents. To create the Merge Document,

   1. Press **2** on the Main Menu.

Your system displays the Create a Document screen.

2. Type the Merge Document name.

3. Press **F10**.

The Document Summary screen, on which you fill out any necessary information, is displayed. You probably will not search Document Summary screens used for merges; however, you may find the Comment field useful.

4. Press **F10**.

MultiMate Advantage II displays the Modify Document Defaults screen, on which you can change any default values.

5. Press **F10**.

In every Merge Document, you will want to enter a single Define Block before typing any other text. This provides the needed information to perform the merge. To enter the Define Block,

6. Press **Alt-M**.

7. Type **Define**

8. Press **Alt-M**.

9. Press **Return**.

10. Type **File Type** and follow it with the type of file that will be used as your Merge Data File:

MULTIMATE	For List or Information Handling files.
DBASE	For dBASE .dbf files.
RANDOM	For ASCII files in Random format.
SEQUENTIAL	For ASCII files in Sequential format.

11. Press **Return**.

12. Type any field name statements (described in the types of Merge data files).

13. Press **Alt-M**.

14. Type **End Define**

15. Press **Alt-M**.

16. Press **Return**.

17. Begin typing the text.

A Merge Document can consist of more than one page, with Merge Item names scattered throughout. You can use all the regular editing functions (such as Insert, Delete, and Copy) and all the regular MultiMate Advantage II features (such as headers and footers). Do not underline header and footer symbols, however, or the pages may not print in order (or at all).

When you reach a point in the text where you want to insert information from the Merge Data File (a Merge Item),

    18. Press **Alt-M**.

A Merge Code appears on the screen.

    19. Type the Merge Item name to indicate which Merge variable to insert.

A Merge Item name can have as many as 12 characters (letters, numbers, and symbols). The Merge Item name must match exactly the Merge Item name in the List Document.

    20. Press **Alt-M**.

You must insert Merge codes on *both* sides of each Merge Item name. If you forget to insert Merge codes, your system interprets the contents of the Merge Document as Merge variables, or it interprets Merge variables as Merge Document contents.

Check your Merge Document carefully to make sure all Merge Item names have beginning and ending codes.

Do not include spaces in Merge Item names. For example, if your Merge Item name consists of two words, do not include a space between the two words. You must enter Merge Item names consistently; otherwise, the system cannot match the Merge items in the Merge Document with the Merge items in the List Document.

You can use the same Merge Item name more than once in a Merge Document. MultiMate Advantage II matches the Merge Item names in the Merge and List documents, no matter how often the names appear in the Merge Document. (In figs. 16.1 and 16.3, the name *Judith* appears twice in the Merge Document and the Result Document.)

Make sure each Merge Item name in the Merge Document exists in the List Document. If a Merge Item appears in the Merge Document but not in the List Document, the system prints the document, but it omits the Merge variable and prints a blank space or blank line instead. (The only exception to this rule is when you use one of the special commands described later in this chapter.)

21. Repeat steps 17, 18, 19, and 20 as you complete the Merge Document.

22. Press **F10** to save your document.

Creating the MultiMate Advantage II List Document

To create a MultiMate Advantage II List Document,

1. Press **2** on the Main Menu.

MultiMate Advantage II displays the Create a Document screen.

2. Type the List Document name.

Remember that document names can be up to 20 characters long; however, only the first eight characters are recorded (in uppercase letters) in the document directory.

3. Press **F10**.

The Document Summary screen is displayed.

4. Type any comments you want to record.

5. Press **F10**.

The Modify Document Defaults screen is displayed.

6. Edit any default values necessary.

7. Press **F10** to move to the document page.

When you type Merge items, you can use all of MultiMate Advantage II's editing functions, such as Insert, Copy, and so forth.

Each time you type a Merge Item, begin at the left margin of a new line. Type the Merge Item name first and follow it with the Merge variable. The Merge Item name should be preceded by and followed by a Merge Code, and the Merge variable should be followed by a Merge Code. In figure 16.4, the Merge Item name is *name*, and the Merge variables are *Ms. Judith Lundquist* and *The Curiosity Shop*.

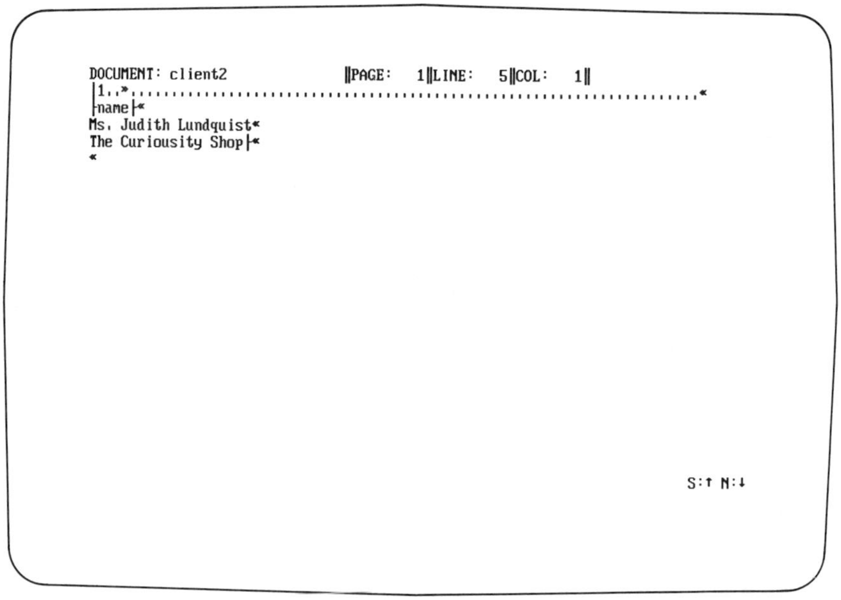

```
DOCUMENT: client2            ‖PAGE:   1‖LINE:   5‖COL:   1‖
|1..».....................................................................«
|name|«
Ms. Judith Lundquist«
The Curiousity Shop|«
 «




                                                            S:↑ N:↓
```

Fig. 16.4. Merge Item name with Merge codes.

    8. Press **Alt-M**.

The Merge Code symbol appears on the screen.

    9. Type the Merge Item name.

Do not leave a space between the Merge Code and the first letter of the Merge Item name. The Merge Item name must be identical to the name you select for the Merge Document. The Merge Item name can consist of as many as 12 characters.

    10. Press **Alt-M**.

    11. Press **Return**.

    12. Type the Merge variable text.

Note that a Merge Code is **not** used at the beginning of the Merge variable, but it is used at the end. Be certain to include any spaces that must appear before or after the Merge variable data. MultiMate Advantage II will respond to formatting symbols included in the Merge variable text.

    13. Press **Alt-M**.

    14. Press **Return**.

Your system matches the Merge Item names in both Merge documents without regard to their order. You can use a Merge Item more than once in the Merge Document. If a Merge Item is in the List Document but not in the Merge Document, MultiMate Advantage II ignores the Merge Item.

Individual pages should be set up in your List Document so that Merge items relating to one customer are typed on one page (sometimes referred to as a *record*) and Merge items relating to another customer appear on another page, and so forth.

During printing, MultiMate Advantage II first merges the Merge Document with the Merge items from the first customer page; then, it merges the Merge Document with the Merge items from the second customer page.

You can have as many records as you have pages in your document; if you need more room, you can create additional List documents to be merged with the same Merge Document. You can print an unlimited number of Result documents from a single Merge Document. And, only one thing limits the length of a variable data item: all variable data pertaining to a record must fit on one page (195 lines).

    15. Repeat steps 9 through 15 for each variable to be included in the Merge Item Set.

    16. Press **F2**.

Now you can type the Merge items for the next client page. After you type the last page, **do not** press *F2*; if you do, the system will look for a client record on the blank page that follows. Check each Merge Item visually to be sure that spaces and Merge codes are placed appropriately.

    17. Press **F10** to save your List Document.

Merge a Document

To merge the Merge Document and the List Document,

    1. Type **5** on the Main Menu or press **Alt-5** from within a document.

The Merge Print a Document screen is displayed.

As figure 16.5 illustrates, the Merge Document and the Merge Data File can reside on different drives.

```
                              MERGE PRINT A DOCUMENT
                    Drive:C              Merge Document:tnum
                    Path: \mm\

                    Drive:C              Merge Data File:client2
                    Path: \mm\
                    Approximately 00434176 characters [00173 Page(s)] available on C:
         CLIENT2   JLETTER  MEM01     MEM02    TNUM




                    Press F10 when finished, ESC to exit, PGDN to switch drives
                  Press CTRL-HOME to select default path, CTRL-END for next path
                         Press F6 to display document directory        S:↑ M:↓
```

Fig. 16.5. The Merge Print a Document screen.

2. Type the Merge Document name, the letter of the drive, and the path on which it resides.

3. Type the Merge Data File name, the letter of the drive, and the path on which it resides.

To switch drives, press *PgDn*. Press *Ctrl-End* or *Ctrl-Home* to change the path.

4. Press **F10**.

This prompt appears on the screen:

    SELECT DATA FILE RECORDS YOU WANT TO MERGE PRINT: [00001] to [99999]

(00001 to 99999 prints all records in the data file.)

5. Type the Merge Data File's range of record numbers.

The range of record numbers corresponds to the page numbers in your Merge Data File's Status Line. To merge each record (page) in your Merge Data File, leave the record numbers as *00001* to *99999*.

6. Press **F10**.

The Document Print Options screen appears.

7. Type the values.

8. Press **F10** to merge the documents.

Merge Print from Your Keyboard

You may enter data directly from your keyboard and merge it with a Merge Document. In effect, the Merge Data File is created as you enter data from the keyboard. From the Main Menu,

1. Press **5**.

2. Type the Merge Document name.

Leave the Merge Data File name blank.

3. Press **F10**.

Ignore the record numbers prompt.

4. Press **F10**.

5. Type the information on the Document Print Options screen.

6. Press **F10**.

This prompt appears on your screen:

        PLEASE WAIT...PRINTING A DOCUMENT

When MultiMate Advantage II comes to a Merge Item name, this prompt is displayed on your screen:

        REPLACE: <Merge Item Name> WITH:_____

7. Type the variable text that matches that Merge Item name.

8. Press **Return**.

9. Repeat steps 7, 8, and 9 for each Merge Item name and each record.

If your system finds a duplicate Merge Item name, it automatically replaces the name with the previously supplied variable information.

10. Press **Esc**.

The Result documents will print.

Document Organization

You can be flexible in the way you organize your documents. For example, you can organize mailing lists in alphabetical order, by the size of the customer account, by geographical location, and so forth.

If you use MultiMate Advantage II's External Copy feature with documents created for merging, you can maintain a "master" List Document to be used to create temporary and customized List documents.

Suppose that *Designers Unlimited* has a master List Document of 200 customers. The sales manager has decided to mail promotional letters to only the 22 customers who, together, purchase three-quarters of all of the crafts products sold. The sales department can create a new List Document, copy the contents of the master List Document to the new List Document, and then delete all but the 22 "best-customer" names in the new List Document.

Special Merge Commands

Five special Merge commands provide you with added flexibility in merging documents:

- REPEAT
- NEXT
- END REPEAT
- OB
- PRINTIF

By inserting these commands in the Merge Document, you can customize your merged documents even more *and* make use of other options during the merge.

REPEAT, NEXT, and END REPEAT Commands

The most common way to use MultiMate Advantage II's Merge feature is to merge one Merge Data File page at a time with the Merge Document. You merge the data on one page in the Merge Data File with the Merge Document; then, you merge the next page in the Merge Data File with the Merge Document, and so on. The result is as many copies of the Merge Document as there are Merge Data File pages.

You may want one copy of the Merge Document containing Merge items from all the pages in the Merge Data File. For such merges, you use the REPEAT, NEXT, and END REPEAT commands. For example, using the customer mailing list described previously, you could print a memo containing the list of 22 customer names and addresses. Figure 16.6 illustrates the first page of a multiple-page document.

```
To:          Jill
From:        Dean
Subject:     Window Ornament Promotion
Date:        June 15, 1985

     Jill, here are the clients to whom I sent window ornament
promotional materials:

Ms. Judith Lundquist
The Curiousity Shop
New York, New York

Mr. James Overhaut
Things and Things
Phoenix, Arizona

Mr. Ian Pearson
Pearson's Gifts
Atlanta, Georgia
```

Fig. 16.6. Document printed from a customer mailing list.

You would set up the Merge Document that creates the memo in figure 16.6 to look like figure 16.7. The commands are placed between the Merge codes.

```
DOCUMENT: tnum            ‖PAGE:  2‖LINE:  19‖COL:   1‖        INSERT
|1..►......►..............................................◄
|DEFINE|◄
FILE TYPE MULTIMATE◄
|END DEFINE|◄
◄
To:→      →Jill◄
From:     →Dan◄
Subject:  →Window Ornament Promotion◄
Date      →June 15, 1987◄
◄
     →Jill, here are the clients to whom I sent window ornament
promotional materials:◄
◄
|REPEAT:03|◄
|NEXT|◄
|name|◄
|citystate|◄
◄
|END REPEAT|◄
```

Fig. 16.7. Using the REPEAT, NEXT, and END REPEAT commands.

The REPEAT and NEXT commands tell MultiMate Advantage II to repeat the
Merge items that follow, choosing the Merge items from each page in the
List Document until all the records have been used. With the REPEAT value
set at 03, the system prints three name/city/state blocks on each page.

The system inserts the first Merge items; then, it repeats the process two more
times for a total of three Merge Item blocks per page. Note that a blank line
is inserted in the document after the Merge Item name ⊦city state⊦.
MultiMate Advantage II prints this space between each Merge Item block.

You may also repeat a single Merge Item by omitting the NEXT command.
This command sequence, shown in figure 16.8, will repeat the first name and
city state three times. It is useful in printing mailing labels for multiple
mailings.

```
DOCUMENT: tnum                    ‖PAGE:   1‖LINE:   9‖COL:   1‖
|1..».......».............................................................«
⊦DEFINE⊦«
FILE TYPE MULTIMATE«
⊦END DEFINE⊦«
«
⊦REPEAT:03⊦«
⊦name⊦«
⊦street⊦«
⊦citystate⊦ ⊦zip⊦«
«
⊦END REPEAT⊦«



                                                         S:↑ N:↓
```

Fig. 16.8. Using the REPEAT and END REPEAT commands.

OB Command

You use the OB command (for Omit if Blank) when you want to print Merge
items that appear on some pages of the Merge Data File but do not appear
on all the pages.

For example, suppose that you know the titles of only some of the *Designers
Unlimited* customers; you would include the title as a Merge Item on some
List Document pages but not on other pages (see fig. 16.9).

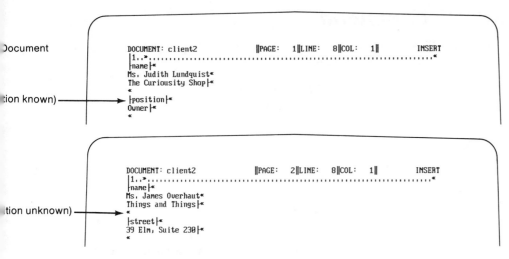

Document

tion known)

tion unknown)

```
DOCUMENT: client2        ‖PAGE:   1‖LINE:   8‖COL:   1‖      INSERT
|1..».....................................................................«
|name|«
Ms. Judith Lundquist«
The Curiousity Shop|«
«
|position|«
Owner|«
«
```

```
DOCUMENT: client2        ‖PAGE:   2‖LINE:   8‖COL:   1‖      INSERT
|1..».....................................................................«
|name|«
Ms. James Overhaut«
Things and Things|«
«
|street|«
39 Elm, Suite 230|«
«
```

Fig. 16.9. Using the OB command.

A Merge Item that appears in the Merge Document without a corresponding
Merge Item in the Merge Data File creates an undesirable blank line or space.

To avoid this problem, use the OB command. The command instructs the
system to look for the Merge Item in the Merge Data File. If the system finds
the Merge Item in the Merge Data File, the program prints that Merge Item.
If the system does not find the Merge Item, any blank line or space that would
otherwise result is omitted. The OB command is set between Merge codes
and follows the Merge Item name (see fig. 16.10).

```
DOCUMENT: tnum           ‖PAGE:   3‖LINE:  12‖COL:   1‖      INSERT
|1..».....................................................................«
|DEFINE|«
FILE TYPE MULTIMATE«
|END DEFINE|«
«
|name|«
|position| |OB|«
|street|«
|citystate| |zip|«
«
Dear |first|,«
«
```

Fig. 16.10. The OB command set in Merge codes.

When an OB command follows a Merge Item name in the Merge Document,
MultiMate Advantage II prints the variable only if it is available.

PRINTIF Command

Use the PRINTIF command to select the records in the Merge Data File you want to print. The criteria are shown in table 16.1.

Table 16.1
PRINTIF Selection Criteria

EQ	Equal to
NE	Not equal to
LT	Less than
LE	Less than or equal to
GT	Greater than
GE	Greater than or equal to

You may enter as many PRINTIF statements as you like. A statement includes the PRINTIF command, the Merge Item name, the selection criteria, and the Merge Item value in quote marks. If more than one statement is on a line, selected records must meet both criteria. If a statement is on a new line, selected records can meet either statement.

For example, here are two PRINTIF statements:

PRINTIF PAID LE "200" STATE EQ "TEXAS"
PRINTIF STATUS EQ "NEW"

Combined, the statements say this:

Print if the PAID Merge Item value is less than or equal to 200 *and* if the STATE Merge Item value is equal to TEXAS.

Or, print if the STATUS Merge Item value equals NEW.

Notice the use of *and* when the statement is on a line with another statement and notice the use of *or* when the statement is alone on a line.

Merging ASCII Data Management Files

You may combine a Merge Document with nearly any ASCII data management file. The data management file is used as the Merge Data File. There are two types of files:

- Sequential Data File Merge
- Random Data File Merge

Sequential Data File Merge

Be certain your database can create a Sequential Data File (Delimited File). For example, in dBASE III Plus®, this command is used:

COPY TO <newfile> DELIMITED

Special dBASE Merge Notes

To perform a dBASE Merge, enter the file type as *DBASE* in the Define Block. The Merge Item names should match the field names in the dBASE (.dbf) data file. You do not need to enter any field name statements.

Remember these points when merging dBASE fields with MultiMate Advantage II:

- dBASE memo fields cannot be included in the Merge Document.

- If decimal points do not align properly once the document is merged, use decimal tabs.

- If a dBASE date field is in a PRINTIF statement, the date must be in the same format as the Print Date Standard format on the Edit System Defaults screen.

If your database cannot create a Sequential Data File, go to the next section, *Random File Merge*.

Print the file using the DOS PRINT *newfile.txt* command. Identify the Field Delimiters (the characters surrounding each field), the Field Separators (the characters between each field), and the Record Separators (the characters between each record). The file may contain up to 255 field names.

In the example that follows, the Field Delimiters are quotation marks, the Field Separators are commas, and the Record Separators are Returns. When the print looks correct, save the file to disk.

"Jason","Holderness","Holderness Ltd.","$3,000.00" «

"Sally","Matherson","Wilson Sport","$8,000.00' «

1. At the beginning of your Merge Document, set up a Define Block to identify the fields that will be merged.

Line 1: Enter ⊢**DEFINE**⊢

Line 2: Enter **FILE TYPE SEQUENTIAL**

Line 3: Identify the Field Delimiter (if other than quotes).

Line 4: Identify the Field Separator (if other than a comma).

Line 5: Identify the Record Separator (if other than a Return).

For example, these lines show an exclamation point, a period, and a Return/ line feed as the marks:

FIELD DELIMITER '!'

FIELD SEPARATOR '.'

RECORD SEPARATOR <cr><lf>

2. Type in the name of the first field name by entering **FIELD NAME** <*name of field*>

The field names must match the Merge Item names you are using in the Merge Document.

3. Continue entering up to 225 individual field names in the same order as they are printed.

4. End the Define Block by typing ⊢**END DEFINE**⊢

Figure 16.11 illustrates a sample Merge Document with the Define Block that uses the MultiMate Advantage II defaults for Field Delimiter (" "), Field Separator (' '), and Record Separator (<cr><lf>).

```
DOCUMENT: tnum                    ‖PAGE:   1‖LINE:  12‖COL:   8‖
|1..»......»..................................................«
⊦DEFINE⊦«
FILE TYPE SEQUENTIAL«
FIELD NAME FIRST«
FIELD NAME LAST«
FIELD NAME COMPANY«
FIELD NAME CASH«
⊦END DEFINE⊦«
«
We are pleased that your company, ⊦COMPANY⊦ will be represented
by ⊦FIRST⊦ ⊦LAST⊦ at the annual awards banquet.  Thanks for your
generous donation of ⊦CASH⊦.  We look forward to presenting
⊦FIRST⊦ with our appreciation plaque.«
«
```

Fig. 16.11. Sample Merge Document with Define Block for Sequential Data File Merge.

Merge print the document:

5. Type **5** from the Main Menu.

6. Type the name of the Merge Document, drive, and path that contain the Define Block.

7. Press **Return**.

8. Type the name of the Merge Data File, drive, and path.

9. Type the number of the first record to print.

10. Press **Return**.

11. Type the number of the last record to print.

12. Press **F10**.

13. Type the values in the Document Print Options screen.

14. Press **F10**.

Random File Merge

To perform a merge of a Random Data File, you must know the maximum length of each field. It is a good rule to make those maximum field lengths a little longer than you anticipate is true, just in case you have overlooked the longest field. For example, the maximum field lengths that might be calculated for two records are illustrated in this example:

Records
    Jason Holderness, Holderness Ltd., $3,000.00
    Sally Matherson, Wilson Sport, $8,000.00
Maximum Field Lengths
    first: 10 characters
    last: 15 characters
    company: 20 characters
    cash: 15 characters

Print the file with a selected character (such as a period) filling in the maximum field length for each field. The following example shows the print generated using periods as the field fill-in characters. When the print looks correct, save the file to a disk.

    Jason ....Holderness.......Holderness Ltd ...$3,000.00 ....
    Sally ....Matherson ....Wilson Sport .....$8,000.00 ....

To identify the fields, you will need to set up a Define Block at the beginning of the Merge Document:

1. Type ⊢ **DEFINE** ⊢ on Line 1.

2. Type **FILE TYPE RANDOM** on Line 2.

3. Identify each field name and size (maximum characters plus additional characters):

   FIELDNAME *<name of field>* **SIZE** *<size of field>*

The field names must match the Merge Item names used in the Merge Document.

If you have a Return/line feed <cr><lf> in the database file, declare it as a separate field with *any name* and a length of *two*.

There may be a maximum of 254 field names, and they should be listed in the same order as they print.

4. Type ⊢**END DEFINE** ⊢

Merge print the document:

5. Type **5** from the Main Menu and press **Return**.

6. Type the name of the Merge Document, drive, and path containing the Define Block.

7. Press **Return**.

8. Type the name of the Merge Data File (your database file), the drive, and the path.

9. Type the number of the first record to print.

10. Press **Return**.

11. Type the number of the last record to print.

12. Press **F10**.

13. Type the values in the Document Print Options screen.

14. Press **F10**.

Figure 16.12 illustrates a sample Merge Document with a Define Block for Random File Merge.

```
DOCUMENT: tnum              ‖PAGE:  1‖LINE:  7‖COL:  13‖        INSERT
|1..>......>..................................................<
‖DEFINE‖<
FILE TYPE RANDOM<
FIELD NAME FIRST SIZE 18<
FIELD NAME LAST SIZE 20<
FIELD NAME COMPANY SIZE 15<
FIELD NAME CASH SIZE 8<
‖END DEFINE‖<
<
We are pleased that your company, ‖COMPANY‖ will be represented
by ‖FIRST‖ ‖LAST‖ at the annual awards banquet.  Thanks for your
generous donation of ‖CASH‖.  We look forward to presenting
‖FIRST‖ with our appreciation plaque.<
<
```

Fig. 16.12. Sample Merge Document with Define Block for Random Data File Merge.

Information Handling with MultiMate Advantage II

Instead of creating a List Document, you can create templates and records to make a data file that can be selected and sorted as well as merged. A *record* contains all the information related to a single person or item. A *template* shows how the information for a single record is arranged. Records are created by filling the template's data fields with information.

For example, you may want to maintain a record for every item inventoried in an office. Figure 16.13 is an example of an inventory template. Figure 16.14 illustrates the inventory record developed from the template.

```
DOCUMENT: template         ‖PAGE:  1‖LINE:  9‖COL:  1‖
|1..>....>....>...................................................<
Item:                    <
<
Date Purchased:              <
<
Cost of Purchase:              <
<
Location:              <
<
```

Fig. 16.13. A template to record inventory.

```
DOCUMENT: template         ‖REC#:  1‖TOT#:  1‖SELECTED‖

Item:Oak Desk

Date Purchased:18-1-87

Cost of Purchase:$328.88

Location:Mgr. Floor
```

Fig. 16.14. A single record developed from the template.

Using templates and records permits you to sort the data in ascending or descending order. MultiMate Advantage II's *Reference Manual* refers to these operations as *Information Handling*.

Data Files

The data file you create contains a template page and several records. Each record occupies its own page. The entire file may contain 255 records. The Display Document Start-Up screen on the System Defaults screen must be set to Y (see Chapter 18). To create a data file, you must create a new document. When the Document Summary screen is displayed, press *Shift-F10*.

You access a data file like any other document, through the Edit a Document option on the Main Menu.

Templates

You will create the template on the first page of the data file. The Format Line must be 80 columns. The page length for a template can be no more than 66 lines.

Figure 16.15 illustrates the parts of a template.

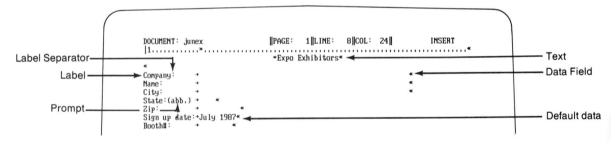

Fig. 16.15. A template with areas identified.

A template has *labels*, which are equivalent to the Merge Item names.

- Labels are used to identify a data field.

- Labels can consist of one or more words separated by hard spaces (Alt-S).

- Labels can contain as many as 79 characters; the first 12 characters must be different from the first 12 characters of any other label in the template.

- Labels are case-sensitive; Company and COMPANY are considered to be different labels.

- Labels are followed by colons—label separators.

- Labels may contain a maximum of 66 lines.

The *data field* is the space where you will enter information.

- Data fields are represented by an underline (created by pressing *Shift* and the *Underline* key).

- Data fields contain the information specific to the record. The information is entered in the data field as you create records.

- Data fields can be 255 characters long with up to 255 data fields on each template; however, the Merge feature can access only the first 64 fields.

- Data fields can contain information to fill a data field with information. The underlined text is the default data entered for all new records. This default data will be automatically entered on each record. Press *Alt* and the *Underline* key, enter the data, and then press *Alt* and the *Underline* key.

Information other than labels, data fields, and default data is assumed to be text or prompts. That information appears on each record and is used when viewing the template.

You may edit the template using the Insert, Delete, Strikeover, Move, or Copy features as they are used in any MultiMate Advantage II document. If your printer supports Line and Box Drawing, use this feature to graphically enhance the template.

The actual records reside on the pages following the template. When you leave the template page, the program verifies the template. If you have an error in your template, the system displays a message like one of those shown in table 16.2. If you receive an error message, return to the template and edit it.

When you reenter the document by choosing Edit a Document from the Main Menu, the template appears as the first page.

Table 16.2
Error Messages for Templates

Error Message/Response

ARE YOU SURE YOU WANT THE LABEL DELETED? (Y/N)

Press *Y* if you do want to delete the label.

FIELD SIZE EXCEEDS 225 CHARACTERS

Delete characters in the fields so that data fields are 225 columns or fewer.

FORMAT LINES MUST BE 80 COLUMNS

Change the Format Line to 80 columns.

LABEL NAME IS A DUPLICATE LABEL

The first 12 characters of two labels match; change one label to make it unique.

NUMBER OF FIELDS EXCEEDS 255

Reduce the number of data fields to 255 or fewer.

OLD LABEL NAME MISSING, HAS IT BEEN RENAMED? (Y/N)

Press *Y* if you renamed a label and then enter the label name at the prompt.

PAGE TOO LARGE, CANNOT EXCEED 66 LINES

Delete template lines to 66 or fewer.

SHORTENED FIELD LENGTH MAY CUT OFF DATA, DO YOU WISH TO CONTINUE? (Y/N)

You shortened the template data field. Check your data to make sure the field lengths are long enough. Then press *Y* or *N*.

TEMPLATE HAS NO DATA FIELDS

You must place at least one data field on the template.

Records

Records contain the data for the data fields of one template. The records begin on the page following the template, and each page contains the data for one record.

To begin typing records to the template,

1. Press **Ctrl-PgDn**.

This prompt appears on the screen:

ARE YOU SURE YOU WANT TO LEAVE THE TEMPLATE PAGE? (Y/N)

2. Type **Y**

The template appears on each record page so that you can enter the data for each data field.

3. Type the data for the first data field.

4. Press **Return** to move the cursor to the next data field or use the **arrow keys** to move the cursor within the data field or to a preceding data field.

The Tab, Home, End, PgUp, PgDn, and GoTo (F1) keys produce the same result as when editing any MultiMate Advantage II document.

When one record is complete,

5. Press **F2** to create a new page for a new record or press **F10** to save the template and records. Or, press **Ctrl-PgDn** to advance to the next existing record.

Editing Records

To edit records, use Insert, Delete, and Search/Replace. If you try to use an editing function that is not available, this message appears:

INVALID KEY

Table 16.3 shows the cursor-movement keys that you may want to use to speed the editing of records.

Adding Records

To add a record, press *F2* and enter the data for the record.

To move between records, press *F1* (Go to Page) or press *Ctrl-PgDn* to move to the next page with an existing record.

Table 16.3
Cursor Movement To Edit Data File Records

Within a Record,

Left-Arrow	Go one character left or to the beginning of the previous data field.
Right-Arrow	Go one character right or to the beginning of the next data field.
Up-Arrow	Go to the beginning of the data field above the cursor.
Down-Arrow	Go to the beginning of the data field below the cursor.
Shift-Tab	Go to the beginning of the previous data field.
Return	Go to the beginning of the next data field.
Tab	Go to the beginning of the next data field.
Home	Go to the beginning of the first data field on the screen.
End	Go to the beginning of the last data field on the screen.
PgUp	The screen moves up; the cursor moves to the beginning of the first data field on the screen.
PgDn	The screen moves down; the cursor moves to the beginning of the last data field on the screen.

Between Records,

PgUp	Go to the beginning of the last data field in the previous record.
Ctrl-PgUp	Go to the beginning of the same data field in the previous record.
PgDn	When on the last data field of a record, go to the beginning of the first data field of the next record.
Ctrl-PgDn	Go to the beginning of the same data field in the next record.
F1	Enter the page number of the record to display and press Return. Or, press End or Home.

Deleting Records

To delete a record, place the cursor anywhere on the record and press *Shift-F2*. This message appears:

ARE YOU SURE YOU WANT TO DELETE THIS RECORD?

Press *Y* to delete the record.

Sorting Records

Records may be sorted in ascending or descending order (alphabetically or numerically)—a single field at a time. Put the cursor on the field for sorting. Press *F5*. Select ascending (low to high) or descending (high to low) order by pressing *Alt-1*. Press *F10*. After sorting, the records appear on your screen in the order you specified.

Selecting Records

You can select records to be printed. When you create a record, it is automatically marked as SELECTED. With your cursor on a record marked SELECTED, press *Alt-F1*; the SELECTED message disappears from the top of the screen. Press *Alt-F1* to make the SELECTED message reappear.

To mark records to the end of the file, place the cursor on the first record, press *Alt-Y*, and press *Alt-1* to choose whether you want the records to be SELECTED or UNSELECTED. Press *F10*. Each record to the end of the file is marked. Only records marked as SELECTED will be printed. To print all the records, select all the records.

Print Data Files

To print a data file that has been created with a template, use Merge Print (see *Merge a Document* in this chapter). Merge Print a Document permits you to merge print your data files just as you merge print your List Document.

You may want to print the records without merging them with the Merge Document. At the Merge Print a Document screen, type the name of the data file in the Merge Document field and leave the Merge Data File field blank.

You print the template by printing page 1 of the data file and choosing option 3 on the Main Menu.

17
Key Procedures

The powerful Key Procedures feature permits you to customize your keyboard for the word-processing tasks you do with MultiMate Advantage II. You'll use the Key Procedures feature to save a particular sequence of keystrokes (that you use frequently) in a Key Procedure file. Then, when you would like to use that keystroke sequence, you will execute the key procedure simply by pressing two keys—MultiMate Advantage II plays back the keystroke sequence on your screen.

Any keystroke sequence you type on the keyboard can be saved and recalled, including letters, numbers, words, MultiMate Advantage II functions (such as Page Break and Indent), screen symbols (such as Shadow Print), and format information.

You can build a key procedure that tells MultiMate Advantage II to execute some of the keystrokes, to pause to allow you to type in information, and then to continue executing the stored keystrokes. You also can insert into a key procedure a prompt that permits you to choose whether to continue using the key procedure. Think of key procedures as MultiMate Advantage II *macros*; a macro is *one* instruction that represents a *sequence* of instructions.

Key procedures may seem similar to the Library and Merge features, but each MultiMate Advantage II feature has distinguishing characteristics that make it appropriate for specific circumstances. You use libraries to recall an entire block of text at once. You use the Merge feature to recall permanent data in the form of a Merge Document and to combine that data with the variable data in a List Document. You select the Key Procedures feature to save and replay any series of keystrokes.

Key Procedure Elements

Five elements are basic to the Key Procedures function:

- *Build*, which creates the key procedure
- *Execute*, which carries out the key procedure

- *Pause*, which temporarily stops the Key file from executing so that you may enter data

- *Prompt*, which allows you to continue executing the key procedure or stop to go on to something else

- *Replay*, which causes the key procedure to execute again

First, you must *build* key procedures; then, you can *execute* them. To build a key procedure, you use MultiMate Advantage II's keyboard options, as well as pauses and prompts designed specifically for building key procedures.

Although you can build a key procedure in any MultiMate Advantage II document, it is a good idea to build the key procedure in a separate file. By maintaining a separate file, you will have a clear record of the output of each key procedure.

You name the key procedure, and MultiMate Advantage II assigns the file the extension *.KEY*. The key procedures are then stored in a *.KEY* file rather than in the document. The relationship between documents and Key files is illustrated in this chart.

| The key procedure is named and built in any document. | → | The key procedure is stored in a file, such as *INV.KEY*. | → | The key procedure is recalled to any document by file name, such as *INV.KEY*. |

Building Key Procedures

Because building a key procedure in a separate document is preferred, you begin by creating a document file and naming it (using MultiMate Advantage II's naming conventions). A good way to identify your Key Procedure file is to begin each name with *KEY* or *K*. For example, *KEYINV* is an appropriate name for a key procedure that creates an invoice.

To begin building your Key Procedure file,

1. Type **2** on the Main Menu.

The Create a Document screen appears.

2. Type the name of the document.

Select a name that identifies what the key procedure is being used for or with. As an example, you might select *INVPROC* to identify the Key Procedure document for invoices.

   3. Press **F10**.

The Document Summary screen appears.

   4. Type any information you want to add.

   5. Press **F10**.

The Modify Document Defaults screen appears.

   6. Type any changes you want to make.

   7. Press **F10**.

The cursor now rests on page one of your document.

Naming a Key Procedure File

   8. Press **Ctrl-F5**.

This prompt appears on the screen:

```
KEY PROCEDURE FILE NAME: (F10 TO CONTINUE, ESCAPE TO ABORT)
```

   9. Type the Key Procedure file name with the drive and path. Press **F6** to see a directory of key procedures on the drive and path.

The name can have as many as eight characters (but no spaces or punctuation). The name should reflect its purpose. You can use uppercase or lowercase letters. In this case, *KEYINV* relates closely to the document name, *INVPROC*. The file extension *.KEY* will be added by MultiMate Advantage II.

   10. Press **F10**.

If you make a mistake, press *Esc* and start again.

When you press *F10*, a reverse video letter *B* appears between the Caps Lock and Num Lock prompt in the lower right corner of the screen. This letter indicates that you are building a Key Procedure file.

Typing the Keystrokes

At this point, you are ready to begin entering the keystrokes you want to save in the Key Procedure file. *All* the keystrokes that you enter become part of the key procedure. MultiMate Advantage II remembers your exact keystrokes;

if you make typographical errors and then backspace to correct the errors, MultiMate Advantage II replays the error-correction key sequences when your key procedure is executed.

You must type the keystrokes in one operation as you build your Key file. You *can* edit Key Procedure files; however, it is easier to get the keystrokes correct as you type them. *Plan your keystroke pattern carefully before you type it.*

If you want the system to recall the Format Line with the key procedure, insert the Format Line on the Key Procedure document page. MultiMate Advantage II does not execute the Format Line in Line 0 of the document page as part of the key procedure.

In addition to regular keystrokes, you can use two other options in building a Key Procedure file: pauses and prompts.

Pauses

A pause stops the execution of a key procedure to allow you to type characters from your keyboard. After you type the text to be included, MultiMate Advantage II resumes execution of the key procedure. You can insert as many pauses as you like in the Key Procedure file.

To insert a pause as you build your Key Procedure file,

    1. Press **Ctrl-F6**.

The word PAUSE appears in the lower left corner of your screen. After the PAUSE prompt disappears,

    2. Continue building the file.

After the Key Procedure file has been built, the key procedure has started executing, and the system has encountered the first pause, this prompt appears:

    PRESS (C) TO CONTINUE. PLEASE ENTER DATA, THEN CTRL-
    F6 TO RESUME

When the pause occurs, type the data. Then, press *Ctrl-F6* to resume the key procedure.

Prompts to Continue or Stop

At any point in the file, you can stop the execution of a key procedure by including a prompt in your keystroke sequence. To do so,

1. Press **Ctrl-F7**.

The word PROMPT appears in the lower left corner of your screen.

2. Continue building the file after the prompt has left the screen.

Then, during the execution of the key procedure, this prompt will appear as the prompt is encountered in the keystroke sequence:

DO YOU WISH TO CONTINUE OR STOP? (C/S)

If you press C (for continue) during a pause in a key procedure, the key procedure resumes execution; if you press S (for stop), the key procedure stops.

You can include the prompt anywhere in the Key Procedure file. You may elect to place it near the end of the key procedure, and you can use the prompt at logical stop points. For example, if you have the option of completing from one to three pages of a standard report, you may want the stop option to appear at the end of each page.

Completing the Key Procedures

1. Enter the keystrokes you want to save in the Key Procedure file.

   (Press **Ctrl-F6** to enter pauses.)
   (Press **Ctrl-F7** to enter prompts.)

2. Press **Ctrl-F5** to complete the building of your Key Procedure file, and the B in the bottom right corner of your screen disappears.

The B disappears as a signal that the building function has been completed.

3. Press **F10** to save the file.

Executing Key Procedures

You can execute the key procedure from inside any document. To do so,

1. Press **Ctrl-F8**.

This prompt appears on your screen:

```
Drive: C                    Key Procedure:.........................................

Path:\mm\.....................................................................................

Press F10 when finished, ESC to cancel, F6 for directory
```

2. Type the name of the Key Procedure file, the drive, and the path. Press **F6** to see a directory of key procedures.

3. Press **F10**.

The first key procedure entry appears on the screen.

An *E* appears in the bottom right corner of your screen indicating that a key procedure is being executed. MultiMate Advantage II plays back your keystrokes (in the exact order in which you typed them) until it reaches a pause, a prompt, or the end of the Key Procedure file.

If you happened to type the name of a nonexistent file, MultiMate Advantage II displays this message:

```
FILE NOT FOUND. HIT ANY KEY TO CONTINUE
```

Remember, when you encounter a pause, the pause prompt appears on the screen for a short time and then disappears. MultiMate Advantage II is waiting for you to type in text. To resume executing, insert the text and then press *Ctrl-F6*. After the first pause prompt (illustrated in the *Pauses* section of this chapter), all others look like this:

```
PLEASE ENTER DATA, THEN CTRL-F6 TO RESUME
```

Unlike a library, a key procedure that you call up from within a document is not inserted into the document; rather, the key procedure appears on the page following your cursor. If other text follows your cursor, MultiMate Advantage II writes over that text. To avoid writing over existing text, start executing a key procedure on either a blank page, the end of a page, or an insert.

During execution of a key procedure, this message will be displayed when the program encounters prompts entered while building the procedure:

```
DO YOU WISH TO CONTINUE OR STOP? (C/S)
```

Press *C* to continue execution or *S* to stop and return to the document. If you press *S*, the *E* in the lower right corner of the screen disappears. If you want to stop a Key Procedure file from executing, press *Esc* during execution, not during a prompt or pause.

This message appears if MultiMate Advantage II reads the Key Procedure file incorrectly:

```
EXECUTION ABORTED DUE TO READ ERROR. HIT ANY KEY TO CONTINUE
```

Press any key to continue. You may have to rebuild the Key Procedure file if the error persists.

Key Procedure Replacement (Writing Over)

You can edit key procedures, or you can write over a Key Procedure file—replacing the old key procedure with a new key procedure.

1. Press **Ctrl-F5**.

2. Type the name of the key procedure you want to write over.

This prompt appears:

```
FILE ALREADY EXISTS. DO YOU WISH TO REPLACE CONTENTS OF FILE?
(Y/N)
```

If you press *Y*, the *B* (for build) prompt appears in the lower right corner of your screen. The old keystrokes are "lost," and you are free to type new keystrokes.

4. Type the keystrokes.

5. Press **Ctrl-F5**.

To edit an existing key procedure, see Chapter 19.

Renaming and Deleting Key Procedures

Key procedures are files, not documents. For instance, if you delete the document containing the invoice (*INVPROC*), the Key Procedure file *KEYINV.KEY* still exists. You must use DOS commands to rename or delete key procedures; all key procedures have the file extension *.KEY*.

To see the Key Procedure files, make sure the DOS prompt (A>, B>, or C>) appears for the drive on which the file resides.

1. Type **dir *.key**

2. Press **Return**.

To rename a Key Procedure file, make sure the DOS prompt (A>, B>, or C>) appears.

1. Type **rename (old file name).key (new file name).key**

2. Press **Return**.

To delete a Key Procedure file, make sure the DOS prompt appears on your screen.

1. Type **erase filename.key**

2. Press **Return**.

Planning Key Procedures

As you work with key procedures, you will discover how important planning is. MultiMate Advantage II executes key procedures exactly the way you build them. You can use a special utility (see Chapter 19) to edit key procedures, but entering them correctly the first time is easier.

Before building complex key procedures, you should enter on the computer's screen exactly what you want to type and determine where you will use pauses, prompts, and special features. You can avoid retyping the entire key procedure because of a mistake, such as a forgotten prompt. Careful planning helps you create key procedures that execute smoothly.

One effective and efficient way to plan your key procedure is to type your key procedure in a MultiMate Advantage II document and then edit the screen, print it, and note prompts and pauses. This planning strategy provides you with a record of the key procedure (in case you want to change it later). Then, when you press *Ctrl-F5* to begin building the key procedure, you can simply type over the existing text, including all symbols, and enter pauses and prompts.

18
System and Document Defaults

This chapter focuses on how to customize MultiMate Advantage II system and document defaults. The chapter also describes how to return to DOS from the Main Menu.

The System and Document Defaults Menu

MultiMate Advantage II is designed with predetermined defaults that govern Format Lines, drive designations, and so forth. For example, the default drive designations are *A* and *B*. But, if your computer has a hard disk, you must change the drive designation to *C.* You can change default values any number of times. Simply select item 7 on the Main Menu (System and Document Defaults), and MultiMate Advantage II displays the System and Document Defaults Menu, shown in figure 18.1.

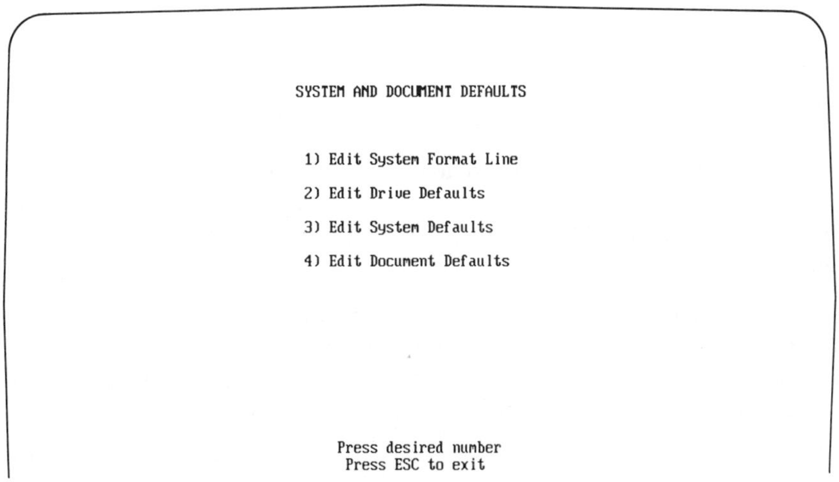

```
                      SYSTEM AND DOCUMENT DEFAULTS


                      1) Edit System Format Line

                      2) Edit Drive Defaults

                      3) Edit System Defaults

                      4) Edit Document Defaults








                         Press desired number
                         Press ESC to exit
```

Fig. 18.1. The System and Document Defaults Menu.

Edit System Format Line

If you select *1* on the System and Document Defaults Menu, MultiMate Advantage II displays the Edit System Format Line screen (see fig. 18.2).

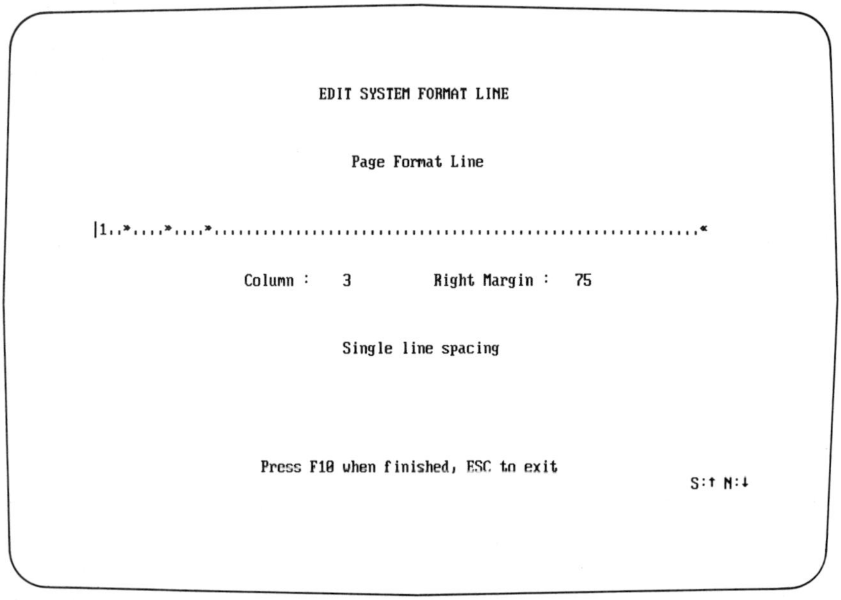

```
                    EDIT SYSTEM FORMAT LINE


                       Page Format Line


    |1..>....>....>...........................................<

             Column :   3        Right Margin :   75


                      Single line spacing




            Press F10 when finished, ESC to exit
                                                    S:↑ N:↓
```

Fig. 18.2. The Edit System Format Line screen.

The Edit System Format Line screen controls three system defaults:

- Line Spacing

- Tab Settings

- Right Margin

The line spacing system default is single line spacing. If you double-space most of your work, move the cursor under the number *1* in the System Format Line and type *2*. There are other line spacing options as well (see Chapter 6).

To delete tab settings in the default Format Line, use the space bar to strike over unwanted tabs. To set new tabs, move the cursor to the column where a new tab should appear and press the tab key. MultiMate Advantage II notes the cursor column position on the screen as you work.

The default Format Line has a right margin of 75; that is, 75 columns separate the left margin from the right margin when you print the document. To change this default, move the cursor to the desired column and press *Return*. You may lengthen or shorten the line length.

After you have made corrections to the System Format Line, press *F10* to save the revised defaults.

Edit Drive Defaults

To edit the drive defaults, select *2* to move to the Edit Drive Defaults screen (see fig. 18.3).

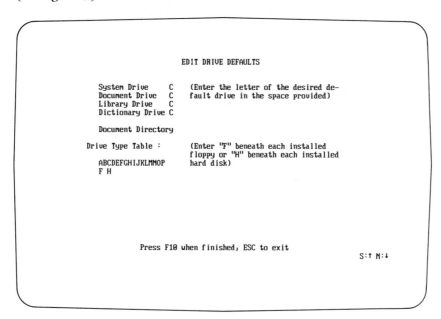

```
                      EDIT DRIVE DEFAULTS


         System Drive      C    (Enter the letter of the desired de-
         Document Drive    C    fault drive in the space provided)
         Library Drive     C
         Dictionary Drive C

         Document Directory

      Drive Type Table :      (Enter "F" beneath each installed
                              floppy or "H" beneath each installed
         ABCDEFGHIJKLMNOP     hard disk)
         F H




              Press F10 when finished, ESC to exit
                                                     S:↑ N:↓
```

Fig. 18.3. The Edit Drive Defaults screen.

Editing Drives on a Floppy Disk System

If you are using a dual floppy disk drive system, you will need to change the drive defaults. You insert the System/Boot and Dictionary disks into drive *A*, and you store your documents and libraries on disks in drive *B*. Type an *A* after System Drive. Type a *B* after Document, Library, and Dictionary Drive.

To indicate drive type, place *F*s under the appropriate letters in the Drive Type Table.

Editing Drives on a Hard Disk System

If you are using a hard disk system, you do not need to change the drive designation to *C* for System Drive, Document Drive, Library Drive, and Dictionary Drive.

In the Drive Type Table, an *F* under drive *A* and an *H* under drive *C* (with no designation under drive *B*) will appear.

Editing on Other Drive Configurations

If you have some other drive configuration, follow these general directions:

- In the System Drive field, type the letter of the drive on which you will store the MultiMate Advantage II System disk.

- For Document Drive, type the letter of the drive on which you will keep your working documents.

- In the Library Drive field, type the letter of the drive on which the Library Document will be stored.

- In the Dictionary Drive field, type the letter of the drive on which the dictionary will be stored.

- Finally, in the Drive Type Table field, enter either an *F* (for floppy disk) or an *H* (for hard disk) under the drive designation.

If you have created more than one subdirectory for your documents, type the name of the subdirectory to appear first when you begin using MultiMate. If the Document Directory field is left blank, the default directory will appear first.

After you edit the defaults, press *F10*. If you do not want to keep your edited changes, press *Esc*.

Edit System Defaults

Type *3* on the System and Document Defaults Menu, and the Edit System Defaults screen appears (see fig. 18.4).

Insert Mode

The first default lets you choose whether you want the text that appears after the cursor on an insert to be dropped to the bottom of the screen or pushed to the right.

```
                    EDIT SYSTEM DEFAULTS

   Insert Mode [(P)ush / (D)rop Down]? P   Acceptable Decimal Tab [. or ,]?     .
   Allow Widows And Orphans?           Y   Number Of Lines Per Page?           55
   Automatic Page Breaks?              Y   Display Spaces As Dots [·]?          N
   Destructive Backspace?              Y   Speed Up Movement Between Pages?     Y
   Backup Before Editing Document?     N   Strikeout Character?                 /
   Display Directory?                  Y   Display Document Startup Screens?    Y
   (D)ocument Mode or (P)age Mode ?    P
   (P)age Or (T)ext Associated Headers And Footers?                            P
   System Date Standard [(D)OS,(U)SA,(E)urope or (J)apan]?                     D
   Print Date Standard [(D)OS,(U)SA,(E)urope or (J)apan]?                      D
   Currency Symbol              $           (F)ootnotes Or (E)ndnotes?         F

   Section Numbering Style [(R)oman Or (N)umeric]?                             R

   Acceleration Rate [0-9]?            5   Acceleration Responsiveness [0-9]? 5
   Main Dictionary?              WEBSTER    Custom Dictionary?          CLAMFL



                 Press F10 when finished, ESC to exit            S:↑ N:↓
```

Fig. 18.4. The Edit System Defaults screen.

Decimal Tabs, Widows/Orphans, Lines Per Page, Automatic Page Breaks

Defaults for decimal tabs, widows/orphans, lines per page, and automatic page breaks appear on the Edit System Defaults screen when you create a document; these defaults were described in Chapter 3.

Display Spaces As Dots

The Display Spaces As Dots default controls the display of spaces as dots. When the space bar or right-arrow key is used to move the cursor, a default of *N* means no dots appear on the screen. If the default is *Y*, spaces are designated as dots that do not print.

Some users prefer the dots because the dots mark where the cursor has been and where it can go again on a horizontal move. (On a horizontal move, the cursor does not move into areas in which characters, including spaces, have not been typed.)

Other MultiMate Advantage II users prefer not to use the dots, because they find the document more difficult to proofread on the screen. Although the dots appear smaller and higher in the space than a period, some users find that dots and periods too closely resemble one another.

Destructive Backspace

The next document default involves setting a destructive backspace. When you press the backspace key, the cursor passes over existing characters, without changing them.

If you change the default value to *Y*, the backspace key deletes every character it encounters. Although most default values are tied to documents, this value is tied to the system. Changing the default affects the use of the backspace key in both new and existing documents.

Speed Up Movement Between Pages

If you press *N* to speed up movement between pages, MultiMate Advantage II saves your document pages each time you move from one page to another. This feature protects your work from a power interruption. If you press *Y*, MultiMate Advantage II saves the document only when you press either *Shift-F10* or *F10*.

Back Up Before Editing Document

If you press *Y* in the next field, MultiMate Advantage II automatically backs up your documents before you edit them. The copies of backed-up documents have *.DBK* extensions. Chapter 19 explains how to restore backed-up documents.

Strikeout Character

You can enter any character for use as a strikeout character. Strikeout characters are explained in Chapter 8.

Display Directory

If you do not want the document directories routinely displayed, press *N*. You may prefer to call up the Document Directory only when you need it. A screen prompt reminds you to press *F6* when you want to see the Document Directory. If you want MultiMate Advantage II to display the document directories, press *Y*.

Display Document Start-Up Screens

If you press *Y* in the field, MultiMate Advantage II displays the Document Summary screen whenever you enter a document for editing. When you create a document, you see the Document Summary screen and the Edit Document Defaults screen. You must use *Y* to create libraries or Information Handling files. If you press *N*, you will bypass the Document Summary screen and the Edit Document Defaults screen.

If you edit or create a document from DOS, the screens are always bypassed.

(D)ocument Mode or (P)age Mode

If you select *P* (for Page), one page is displayed on the screen at a time. If you select *D* (for Document), the pages are displayed "paper towel" style. That is, if the end of one page appears at the top of the screen, the top of the next page appears at the bottom.

(P)age or (T)ext Associated Headers and Footers, System Date Standard, Print Date Standard

You can change the default for page- or text-associated headers and footers (see Chapter 9) and the date standards (see Chapter 3).

The System Date Standard indicates how the date will appear on the screen. The Print Date Standard indicates how the date will be printed when you use the *&DATE&* command, which is described in Chapter 8.

Currency Symbol

The currency symbol is used with math functions. The default is $ and you may enter any symbol you like.

(F)ootnotes or (E)ndnotes

If *F* is entered, the footnotes are printed at the end of the page where the footnote reference is made in the text. If *E* is entered, all footnoted text is printed at the end of the document as endnotes.

Section Numbering

If you use automatic section numbering, you may set the section numbering style as Roman or Numeric. Numbering style is discussed in Chapter 3.

Acceleration Rate and Acceleration Responsiveness

The Acceleration Rate determines the rate at which your keystrokes are processed and displayed. You may set the value from zero to nine. Zero is the slowest rate of acceleration and nine is the fastest. Try several settings to determine which is the most appropriate for you.

Acceleration Responsiveness determines how long a key is held down before the key begins to repeat. Set the value from zero to nine. Zero is the slowest rate of responsiveness and nine is the quickest. Some users have trouble with the most responsive setting (9). Since *F10* is pressed to both enter and exit a document, a heavy key press results in returning to the Main Menu before stopping in the document itself!

Main Dictionary and Custom Dictionary

You also have the opportunity to install dictionaries. Unless you plan to install a dictionary of your own choosing, *WEBSTER* is the default for the main dictionary, and *CLAMFL* is the default for the custom dictionary.

After editing all defaults, press either *F10* to save the defaults or *Esc* to abandon the edited changes.

Edit Document Defaults

Type *4* and MultiMate Advantage II displays the Edit Document Defaults screen, on which you can edit the defaults (see fig. 18.5).

Use this screen to modify the drive designation. If you are using a hard disk, your documents are stored on drive *C*, and no editing is necessary.

If you are using floppy disks, change the drive designation to *B*; otherwise, make sure the drive default designation matches the letter of the drive on which you store documents.

Return to DOS

Type *9* on the Main Menu to return to DOS. You should return to DOS before you turn off your computer so that you can be sure MultiMate Advantage II has "closed" properly.

```
                           EDIT DOCUMENT DEFAULTS
                 Press F7 to Switch to the Edit Table of Contents Defaults Screen

             Drive:C                      Document:  junex
             Path: \mm\

             Approximately 00364544 characters [00145 Page(s)] available on C:
   CLIENT2   JLETTER   JUNEX      MEMO1      MEMO2      TEMPLATE  TNUM




                 Press F10 when finished, ESC to exit, PGDN to switch drives
                 Press CTRL-HOME to select default path, CTRL-END for next path
                       Press F6 to display document directory          S:↑ M:↓
```

Fig. 18.5. The Edit Document Defaults screen.

You may also access DOS from nearly anywhere within MultiMate Advantage II.

1. Press **Ctrl-2**.

2. This message appears along with the DOS prompt (you are in the subdirectory with the MultiMate Advantage II Wp.exe file):

   DOS Access requires returning to MultiMate Advantage II when done. Type EXIT when ready to return.

3. Use any DOS commands; do not delete or rename any MultiMate Advantage II file in use or any MultiMate Advantage II temporary or system file.

4. When you are done with DOS, type **EXIT**

5. Press **Return**.

Do not turn off or reboot your computer without returning to MultiMate Advantage II, or you may lose the page on which you were working.

19
Utilities and Conversions

MultiMate Advantage II offers utilities and conversions that you can call up from the Boot Menu or from the DOS prompt. The utilities and conversions can be used to edit PATs and key procedures. They can be used to convert files to work with other programs. And, the utilities and conversions can be used to change the color and intensity of the screen display, recover damaged documents, and work with custom dictionaries.

If you have a dual floppy disk system, the Utilities disk must reside in drive A, and the System disk must be in drive B. There are three ways to access the utilities and conversions. The first way is to press *3* on the Boot Menu.

The second way to access the utilities and conversions is from the DOS prompt. If you have a hard disk system, follow these steps (after the DOS prompt in the MultiMate Advantage II subdirectory):

1. Type **util**

2. Press **Return**.

The Utilities and Conversions Menu appears on your screen (see fig. 19.1).

If you have a floppy disk system, replace the System disk (in drive B) with your Document disk now.

MultiMate Advantage II provides several utilities and conversions menus. On each menu,

3. Press the **space bar** to highlight your selection.

4. Press **F10** to make your selection and continue.

To exit the utilities and conversions screens and return to DOS, press *Esc*.

The third way to access utilities and conversions is by using Utility Hot Start, which bypasses the menu screens. Use this option when you are familiar with the Utilities and Conversions options:

1. After the DOS prompt, type **util**, enter a space, and press the appropriate key for each menu you want to bypass.

```
         MultiMate Advantage II Utilities   Version 1.0


                    ┌─────────────────────┐
                    │ Printer Tables Editor│
                    └─────────────────────┘
                     Key Procedure Files Utility

                     File Conversion

                     Modify Console Defaults

                     Document Recovery

                     Custom Dictionary Utility




            Press SPACEBAR to select option, F10 when finished
                          Press ESC to exit
```

Fig. 19.1. MultiMate Advantage II Utilities and Conversions Menu.

    2. Press **Return**.

The italicized text in table 19.1 illustrates the keys to press and the information to enter for each option. Keys to press are indicated in uppercase letters, and information (such as a PAT file name) is shown in lowercase letters. The function is not case-sensitive; case conventions are used here for illustration purposes only. You may enter as many key presses as desired to travel as far through the menu options as you like.

For example, using a hard disk, this command line would take you into editing conversion defaults:

    C>**util f e**

The following command line would be entered to edit the PAT file *TTYCRLF*:

    C>**util p pat ttycrlf**

Using the Printer Tables Editor

If you select the first option on the Utilities and Conversions Menu, the Printer Tables Editor screen appears (see fig. 19.2).

Table 19.1
Hot Start Keys To Press

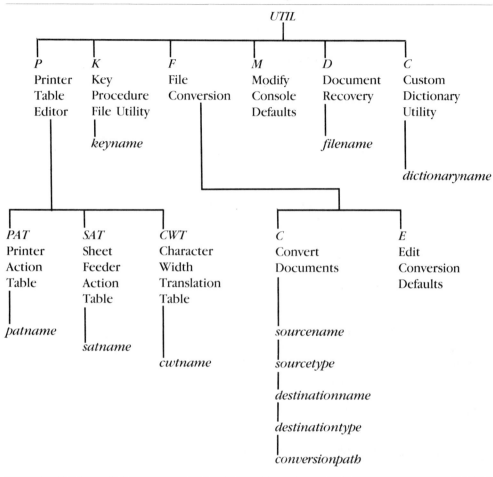

Three editing choices are available:

- Printer Action Tables

- Sheet Feeder Action Tables

- Character Width/Translation Tables

PATs and SATs contain the codes that permit printers and sheet feeders to work with MultiMate Advantage II. The Character Width/Translation Tables contain the codes to define character width and to redefine characters sent to the printer.

```
                    PRINTER TABLES EDITOR



                 Printer Action Tables
                 Sheet Feeder Action Tables
                 Character Width/Translation Tables






                Press SPACEBAR to select option, F10 when finished
       F1=turn display characters OFF                    Press ESC to exit
```

Fig. 19.2. Printer Tables Editor screen.

To edit printer tables, you must understand the hexadecimal coding system and the technical contents of your printer manual. You must also understand what hexadecimal information is required for each MultiMate Advantage II function and be able to translate the information in your printer manual to the corresponding MultiMate Advantage II function. The *MultiMate Advantage II Printer Guide* explains how to use these editing features.

Editing Key Procedures

In Chapter 17, you learned how to create and execute key procedures. To edit key procedures (the second option on the Utilities and Conversions Menu),

   1. Press **F10**.

You can choose to edit an old file, create a new file, or delete a file. The Key Procedure Files utility is cumbersome, so you should not use it to create new files (see *Building Key Procedures* in Chapter 17).

After selecting to edit or delete a file, a screen appears that lists all the Key Procedure files on your disk (see fig. 19.3).

2. Use the **space bar** to highlight the Key Procedure file you want to edit or delete.

3. Press **F10**.

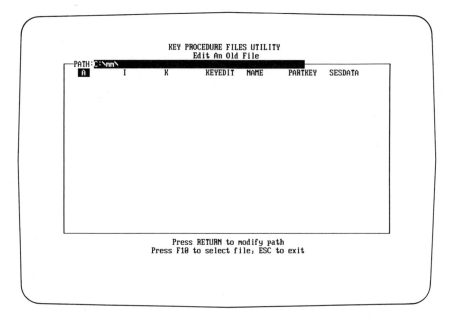

```
                        KEY PROCEDURE FILES UTILITY
                            Edit An Old File
   ┌PATH:C:\nn\
   │  A         I        K        KEYEDIT   NAME      PARTKEY   SESDATA




                         Press RETURN to modify path
                      Press F10 to select file, ESC to exit
```

Fig. 19.3. Key procedures on the disk.

If you are deleting a key procedure, respond to this prompt by selecting *YES*:

ARE YOU SURE YOU WANT TO DELETE FILE? YES NO

And MultiMate Advantage II deletes the key procedure.

If you are editing a key procedure, MultiMate Advantage II accesses the screen that displays the key procedures.

Figure 19.4 illustrates an executed key procedure. A pause occurred after *Name:* and *Address:*, which allowed the name and address to be typed in from the keyboard. A prompt appeared at the end of the key procedure, which allowed the key procedure to be executed again.

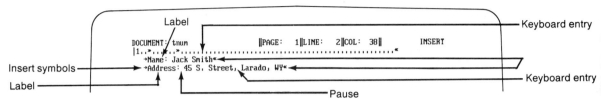

Fig. 19.4. The executed key procedure.

Figure 19.5 illustrates the key procedure ready to edit.

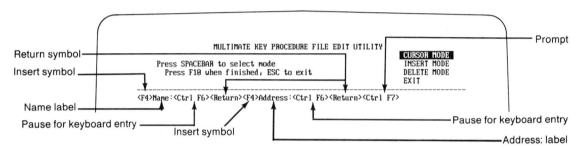

Fig. 19.5. The key procedure ready for editing.

Some keystrokes are automatically recorded in $<>$ symbols. Each alphabetic and numeric character appears as it was typed during the key procedure.

You edit the key procedure on the screen and then save it. Editing key procedures is not like editing MultiMate Advantage II documents; while editing key procedures, you can use each key on your keyboard to insert a particular keystroke into the key procedure.

For example, to insert a prompt into the key procedure, you press *Ctrl-F6*. The symbols $<$Ctrl F6$>$ appear. When editing, you will use the three modes shown in table 19.2.

Table 19.2
Three Modes for Editing Key Procedures

Mode	Function
Cursor	To move the cursor on the display, using the cursor control keys
Delete	To delete any keystroke from the Key Procedures file using the Del key
Insert	To add any keystroke to the Key Procedures file by typing the key to be added

4. Highlight **CURSOR MODE**.

5. Press **F10**.

You can now move the cursor to the position where you want to insert or delete characters.

6. Press **Ctrl-M** to select another edit mode.

If you select *DELETE MODE*, you will be able to press *Del* to delete the keystroke on which your cursor is positioned (as well as keystrokes that follow). Press *Ctrl-M* to leave *DELETE MODE*. If you select *INSERT MODE*, any key you press on your keyboard will be inserted where the cursor rests. Press *Ctrl-M* to leave *INSERT MODE* as well.

After you edit the key procedure,

7. Select **EXIT** to save the key procedure.

If you modify the key procedure and then decide not to save your edited changes, press *Esc* and respond *YES* to this prompt:

```
DO YOU WISH TO EXIT WITHOUT UPDATING THE KEY PROCEDURE FILE?
YES NO
```

Converting Files

The File Conversion option on the Utilities and Conversions Menu translates MultiMate Advantage II documents to (and from) the formats used by other programs. When you select File Conversion, a screen appears with two options:

- Convert Document(s)

- Edit Conversion Defaults

The Convert Document(s) option converts the document types shown in table 19.3. Conversion is provided to and from MultiMate Advantage II documents unless otherwise noted. (Contact technical support for other File Conversion formats that may be available.) The MultiMate Advantage II *Advanced Topics Guide* provides additional considerations about character and document handling for each File Conversion format.

Table 19.3
File Formats for MultiMate Advantage II Document Conversion

File Format	Definition
MM	MultiMate Advantage II documents with file extension *.DOC*
ASCII	Popular format with no common file extension; also dBASE
COMM	Telecommunications format with no common file extension; used modem to modem
DCA	IBM's Document Content Architecture, commonly using file extension *.RF*
DIF	Popular spreadsheet file format that often uses the *.DIF* file extension. Can be converted to MultiMate Advantage II but not from MultiMate Advantage II to *.DIF*.
VC DIF	Format used by VisiCalc™ spreadsheets with the *.DIF* extension. Conversion to MultiMate Advantage II but not from MultiMate Advantage II to *.DIF*
WPS	Wang Laboratories' dedicated word processors; Wang OIS/VS
WPC	Wang Professional Computer word processing format (The *.DOC* file extension is used for both MultiMate Advantage II and WPC files. Conversion is necessary.)
1-2-3	Lotus 1-2-3 WKS and WK1 worksheets. Can be converted to MultiMate Advantage II but not from MultiMate Advantage II.
HON	Honeywell L formatted documents
GSA	General Services Administration format (also called the Navy Document Interchange Format—Navy DIF)
JW	Just Write word processor
WST	WordStar word processor

After you highlight and select Convert Document(s), the Convert a Document screen appears (see fig. 19.6).

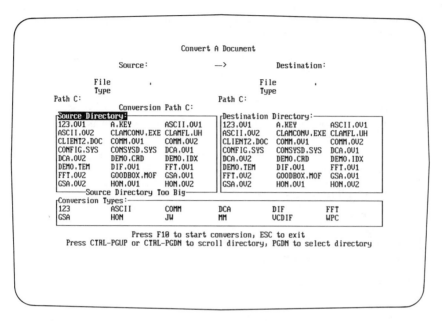

Fig. 19.6. Convert a Document screen.

To complete the Convert a Document screen,

1. Type the Source and Destination file names and extensions in
    the File fields.

The *Source:* Document is the one you want to convert. The *Destination:* Document is the new, converted document that is created.

If you cannot remember the file name (and if the File Directory contains more
names than appear), use the space bar to move the highlight to the directory
you want to display. Press *Ctrl-PgDn* or *Ctrl-PgUp* to view other file names.

The Source file name and the Destination file name may be the same. The
file extensions **must** be different.

2. Enter the file type for both the Source and Destination
    documents.

The file type will be MM (MultiMate Advantage II), ASCII, or some other type,
depending on what you are converting.

Be certain that the file type appears in the Conversion Types Directory on the lower portion of the screen.

3. Type in the path for both the Source and the Destination documents.

4. Type in the conversion path.

The path indicates the drive or subdirectory where the file is located. The conversion path indicates the drive or subdirectory where the conversion programs are stored. (In a dual floppy drive system, the conversion programs are stored on the Utilities disk.)

After you finish filling in the screen,

5. Press **F10**.

MultiMate Advantage II displays several messages as it executes the conversion. After the conversion is complete, this message appears:

```
CONVERSION COMPLETE
```

Converting TOC Files

When a MultiMate Advantage II file is converted to another format, the Footnote file (file extension .FNT) is converted and added to the last page of the Destination file. You must convert Table of Contents files (.TOC file extension) separately.

To convert the TOC file,

1. Convert the document file.

2. Enter the TOC file name as the Source Document.

Be certain to include the .TOC extension.

3. Enter a file name that differs from the converted document file as the Destination Document.

Complete the remainder of the screen as usual.

If you enter a Destination file using the name of an existing file, that existing file is erased.

Your MultiMate Advantage II *Advanced Topics Guide* has more information about file conversion.

Editing Conversion Defaults

You can edit conversion defaults, which you use to select default values such as page length, line length, and so on. On the File Conversion Menu,

1. Use the **space bar** to move the highlight to Edit Conversion Default(s).

2. Press **F10**.

The screen that appears is illustrated in figure 19.7.

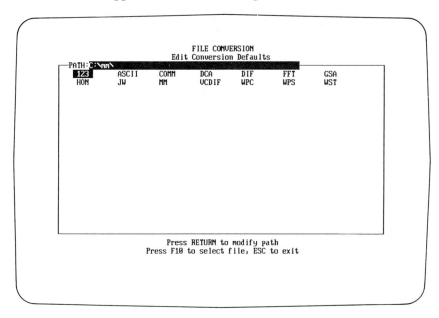

```
                            FILE CONVERSION
                       Edit Conversion Defaults
    ┌PATH:C:\mm\
      123       ASCII     COMM      DCA       DIF       FFT       GSA
      HON       JW        MM        VCDIF     WPC       WPS       WST




                       Press RETURN to modify path
                     Press F10 to select file, ESC to exit
```

Fig. 19.7. Edit Conversion Defaults screen.

3. Select *VCDIF, ASCII* or *DIF* file conversion type.

The others (*123, DCA, GSA, HON, JW, WPC, WPS, MM* and *COMM* files) involve no defaults, so if you select MM or COMM, the screen displays this message:

    No Defaults for Selected Conversion

Editing ASCII Defaults

If you choose to edit the *ASCII* defaults, MultiMate Advantage II displays the screen shown in figure 19.8. The defaults are highlighted.

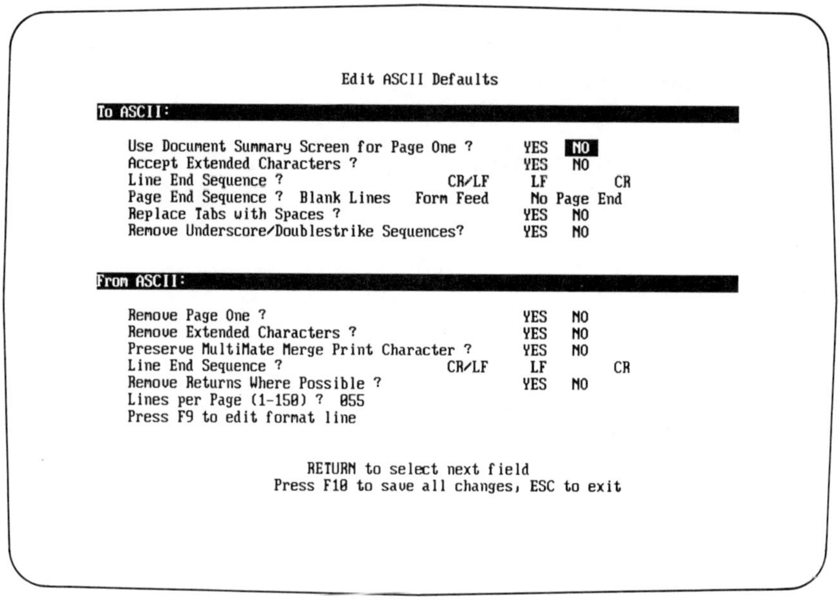

```
                          Edit ASCII Defaults
   To ASCII:

       Use Document Summary Screen for Page One ?     YES  NO
       Accept Extended Characters ?                   YES  NO
       Line End Sequence ?                    CR/LF   LF        CR
       Page End Sequence ?  Blank Lines    Form Feed  No Page End
       Replace Tabs with Spaces ?                     YES  NO
       Remove Underscore/Doublestrike Sequences?      YES  NO


   From ASCII:

       Remove Page One ?                              YES  NO
       Remove Extended Characters ?                   YES  NO
       Preserve MultiMate Merge Print Character ?     YES  NO
       Line End Sequence ?                    CR/LF   LF        CR
       Remove Returns Where Possible ?               YES  NO
       Lines per Page (1-150) ?  055
       Press F9 to edit format line


                      RETURN to select next field
                  Press F10 to save all changes, ESC to exit
```

Fig. 19.8. Edit File Conversion Type screen.

To change a default,

1. Use the **arrow keys** to highlight the default to be changed.

2. Press **Return** to move to the next field.

Pressing *tab* moves the cursor to the next line. To move the cursor to the previous line, press *Shift-Tab*.

Document Summary Screen for Page One

When you convert files to *ASCII*, you can specify whether the Document Summary screen should be converted as the first page of your ASCII file.

Extended Characters

You can also determine whether any special extended characters should be placed in the new file. These characters are symbols that do not appear on your keyboard. They are symbols you create by entering an *ASCII* value.

Line End Sequence

If you select *CR/LF*, MultiMate Advantage II places both carriage returns and line-feed commands at the end of each line in the document. Otherwise, select only carriage returns or line-feed commands.

Page End Sequence

You can choose whether to end the new document pages with a form feed (to eject the paper from the printer), blank lines (to place them between continuous pages), or no page end (to run the document pages together).

Tabs and Underlining

You may want to replace tabs with spaces rather than using the ASCII tab characters. Finally, you can also remove underline codes.

When you convert files **from** ASCII, you can remove the first page and extended characters and select carriage returns and/or line-feed commands at the end of each line. If you remove Returns, MultiMate Advantage II generates a Format Line for each page. You can determine the number of lines on a page.

Figure 19.9 shows the screen that appears if you press *F9*. You can use the screen to edit the Format Line that you want to place in your new document. You can edit the Format Line in the same way that you edit the MultiMate Advantage II system default Format Line.

```
                        Edit Format Line
 From ASCII:██████████████████████████████████████████████████████████████████




 |1..........................................................................


              Cursor at Column: █3█              Right Margin: █156█

                         Single Line Spacing



              INS to extend format line  DEL to compress format line
              TAB to insert tab stop  SPACEBAR to remove tab stop
              Use Left and Right Arrows to move within the format line

                  Press F10 to save all changes, ESC to exit
```

Fig. 19.9. Edit ASCII Format Line.

You can use this screen also to convert *DIF* and *VCDIF* files. Highlight and press *F10* to select *DIF* or *VCDIF* on the Edit Conversion Defaults screen. Figure 19.10 shows the screen that appears for either file type. Use this screen to select the number of lines per page you want in the converted document.

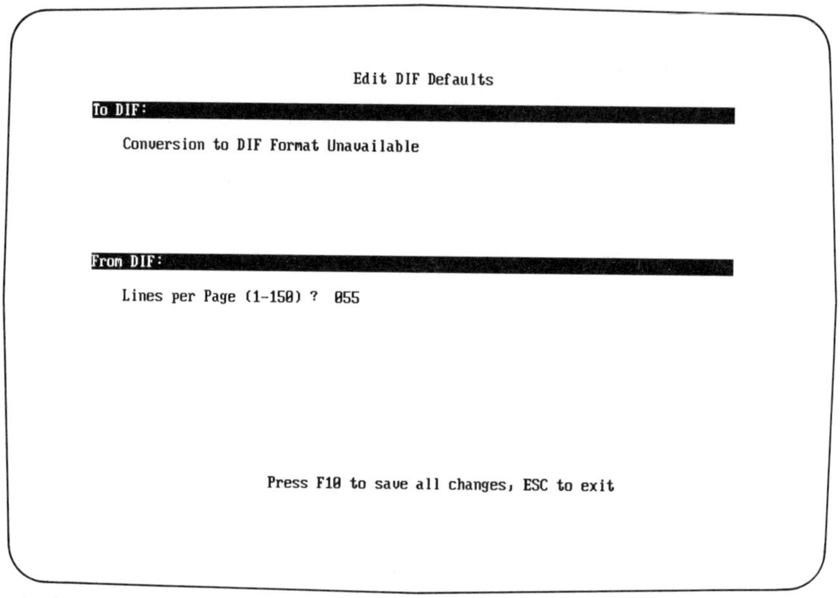

```
                          Edit DIF Defaults
To DIF:

       Conversion to DIF Format Unavailable




From DIF:

       Lines per Page (1-150) ?  055




               Press F10 to save all changes, ESC to exit
```

Fig. 19.10. Editing DIF or VCDIF defaults.

Modifying the Console Defaults

If you have a color graphics board and want to change the color or shading defaults, you can select the Modify Display Defaults option on the Utilities and Conversions Menu. Highlight and press *F10*. The screen shown in figure 19.11 appears.

Move the cursor arrow to identify the default to change. Then press the space bar to change options, colors, or shades. You may want to experiment with different colors and shades before selecting those you find most readable and pleasing.

With the *VSYNC Wait option (ON,OFF)*, you can make MultiMate Advantage II execute more quickly by selecting *OFF*. However, "snow" (white specks) appears on your screen. If you are satisfied with the speed, select *ON*.

```
                        MODIFY CONSOLE DEFAULTS


     VSYNC Wait (ON,OFF)........ ON        Keybd Acceleration (ON,OFF)   ON

     Background................ A B C  ←   Foreground..................   A B C

     Highlight................. A B C      Underline...................   A B C

     Background Reverse........ █A B C█    Foreground Reverse.........    █A B C█

          Highlight Underline.... A B C

     Character Colors    █AABB█CCDDEEFFGGHHIIJJKKLLMMNNOOPP
                         ████████████████████████████████


     Background Colors   AAAABBBBCCCCDDDDEEEEFFFFGGGGHHHH

                              ↑

                    Press SPACEBAR to modify field
              Press ARROW KEYS to select field to modify
                    Press F10 when finished, ESC to exit
```

Fig. 19.11. Modifying display defaults.

If you select *ON* after Keyboard Acceleration, the mode is activated. You may speed or slow your keyboard response through the Modify System Defaults screen or by pressing *Shift+* or *Shift-* (on the numeric/cursor keypad) from any MultiMate Advantage II screen.

Recovering Documents

Document Recovery, Option 5 on the Utilities and Conversions Menu, restores pages you have accidentally deleted (which could not be restored with the Undo Delete command) or pages that have been lost as the result of an accident (such as a power failure). You must use the Document Recovery utility immediately after the text has been damaged. If you edit the file first, you may not be able to recover the information. You may recover documents and Table of Contents files. You may not recover Information Handling files, libraries, and key procedures.

Figure 19.12 shows the screen that appears after you highlight and press *F10* to select the Document Recovery option.

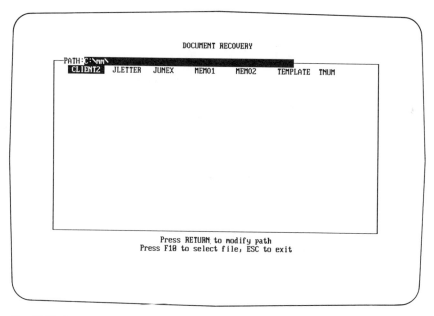

Fig. 19.12. Document Recovery screen.

For the path value, type the letter of the drive on which the document is stored. Highlight the name of the document you want to recover and press *F10*. If the process is successful, the following message appears:

    Document Recovered Press Any Key to Continue

If the process is unsuccessful, this message is displayed:

    Document Recovery Unsuccessful Press Any Key To Continue

Press *Esc* to return to the Main Menu and then to DOS.

Using the Custom Dictionary Utility

The final option on the Utilities and Conversions Menu is the Custom Dictionary utility. This utility permits you to edit an old custom dictionary, create a new custom dictionary, or delete a custom dictionary.

After selecting the Custom Dictionary utility,

  1. Press **F10**.

These options are now available: Edit an Old File, Create a New File, or Delete a File.

   2. Select **Edit an Old File**.

   3. Press **F10**.

The screen illustrated in figure 19.13 is displayed.

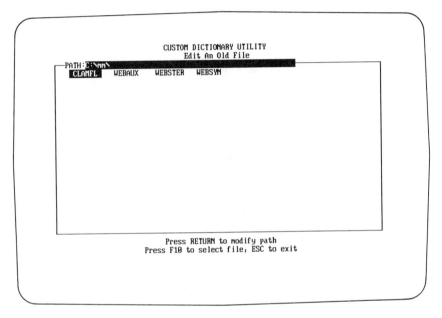

```
                    CUSTOM DICTIONARY UTILITY
                        Edit An Old File
 PATH:C:\mn\
    CLAMFL    WEBAUX    WEBSTER    WEBSYN




                     Press RETURN to modify path
                  Press F10 to select file, ESC to exit
```

Fig. 19.13. Edit an Old File screen.

   4. Move the cursor to highlight the file you want to edit.

   5. Press **F10**.

You may modify the custom dictionary to add, view, or delete words. Or you may reorganize the custom dictionary to optimize the speed with which you can access the dictionary.

   6. Highlight the option you want.

   7. Press **F10**.

If you choose to reorganize the dictionary, this message appears:

    PLEASE WAIT, REORGANIZING CUSTOM DICTIONARY

When the reorganization is complete, you are returned to the menu.

Add Words

If you choose to modify the custom dictionary, the options to add a word or view/delete a word appear.

   8. Select **Add a Word**.

   9. Press **F10**.

The screen illustrated in figure 19.14 is displayed.

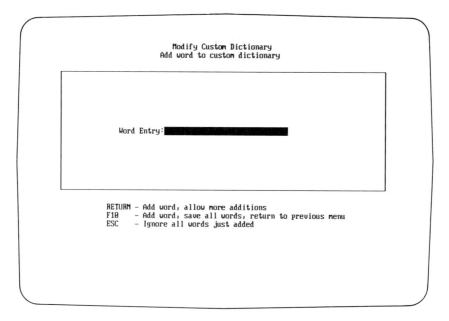

Fig. 19.14. Add a Word to a Custom Dictionary screen.

   10. Type the word to add.

   11. Press **Return** to add the word to the custom dictionary. Or press **F10** to add the word, save all words added, and return to the previous menu. Or press **Esc**.

If you press *Esc*, you will leave the screen, and the words added since entering the screen will be lost. When you press *Esc*, this message will appear on the screen:

   Do you really want to ignore all words just added? (Y/N)

Press *Y* to lose the words and press *N* to continue adding words.

View/Delete Words

If you choose to view/delete words from the custom dictionary, the screen shown in figure 19.15 appears.

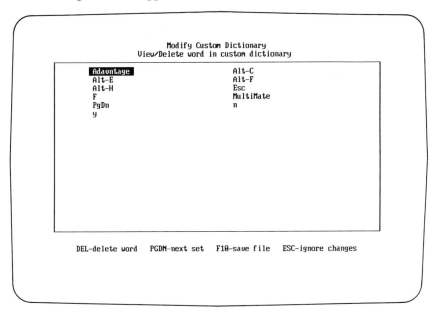

Fig. 19.15. View/Delete Words in a Custom Dictionary screen.

1. Highlight the word to be deleted.

2. Press **Del**.

You may press *PgDn* to view other words in the custom dictionary.

3. Press **F10** to save the changes.

A message appears displaying the name that the file will be saved under:

```
Save as C:FILENAME.UH RETURN--Save file with above name
```

4. Press **Return** to save the file with that name. Or you can type in a new file name.

5. Press **Return**.

You may press *Esc* to cancel the changes you've made since entering the screen. If you press *Esc*, this message appears:

```
Do you really want to ignore all deletions just made? (Y/N)
```

Press *Y* to keep the words and press *N* to delete the words.

Create a New File

Rather than work with an existing custom dictionary, select Create a New File from the Custom Dictionary Utility menu. The screen shown in figure 19.16 appears.

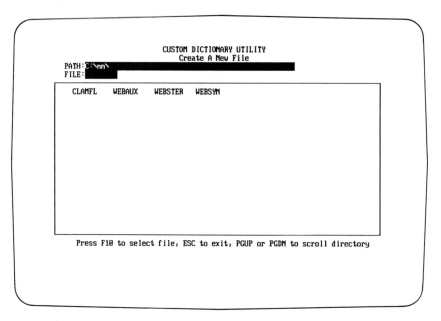

Fig. 19.16. Create a New Custom Dictionary screen.

The new custom dictionary name must differ from the existing dictionary names shown on the screen.

1. Type the name of the new custom dictionary.

2. Press **Return** if you want to change the path information.

3. Press **F10**.

The Add a Word to Custom Dictionary screen is displayed (see fig. 19.14).

4. Add the words you want in the new custom dictionary.

To use the new custom dictionary, enter the name on the Modify System Defaults screen.

Delete A File

From the Custom Dictionary Utility menu, you may choose to delete a custom dictionary.

1. Highlight that option.

2. Press **F10**.

The screen in figure 19.17 appears.

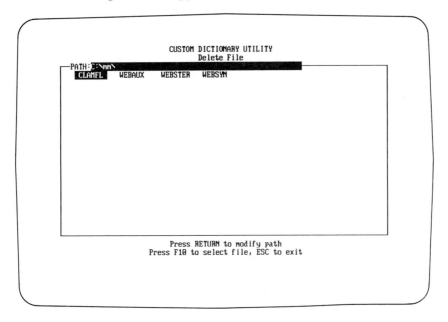

Fig. 19.17. Delete a Custom Dictionary screen.

If the dictionary you want to delete is on another subdirectory,

3. Press **Return** to change the path.

4. Highlight the dictionary you want to delete.

5. Press **F10**.

This prompt is displayed on the screen:

        ARE YOU SURE YOU WANT TO DELETE FILE? YES NO

6. Highlight **YES**.

7. Press **F10**.

The custom dictionary is deleted.

8. Press **Esc** to leave the screen.

20
On-File

On-File permits you to use your computer to create, sort, and print data. The On-File program is easy to effect because it is based on the simple concept of organizing information on 3-by-5 index cards. Using On-File, you create "boxes of cards," which can be sorted into "card decks" according to the criteria you select.

You use both sides of the "cards," and the information on each card is organized by means of card templates. Templates can be used to sort the data on cards and produce reports based on that data. You can create, sort, and print cards without templates; however, you will increase sorting and printing flexibility if you use templates.

A Few Words About Cards

You must first create a *card box* to store your cards. As you work with the card box, you select some cards for use; other cards remain filed. About 600 cards can fit in a card box on a floppy disk. On a hard disk, the number of cards that fit in your card box is about 7,500.

The cards in a card box may be divided into decks by searching for cards with specific characteristics. You can create a deck of up to 1,000 cards. Once a deck is created, you can perform additional searches of the deck to increase or decrease its size.

A card is made up of 12 lines divided into five areas:

- Subject Line
- Color
- Action Date
- Words and Phrases
- Index Line

The areas are arranged as illustrated in figure 20.1. You sort, select, and print cards according to these areas. This chapter describes how each area is used.

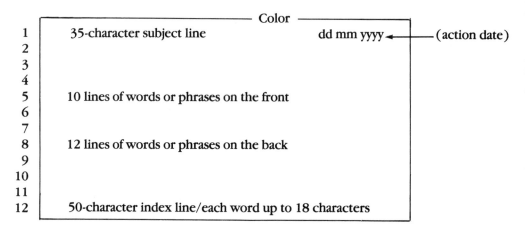

Fig. 20.1. The areas of a card.

A Few Words About Templates

A template looks like a card, but it contains area titles rather than the actual data. The template acts as a guide as you enter data on the card. Use the template to create, edit, view, sort, and print cards.

- A template area can be no more than 49 characters wide.

- One template can hold up to 20 areas.

- No template area can be longer than one line.

- A card box may house as many as 16 templates.

Figure 20.2 shows a template and a card that was created using the template.

The Keyboard

The keys used with On-File are assigned meanings that differ from their MultiMate Advantage II meanings. Table 20.1 lists the keys and how they are used in On-File.

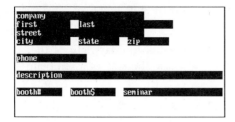

Fig. 20.2. A template and a card created with the template.

Table 20.1
Keys Used in On-File

Key	How the Key is Used
Ins (Insert)	Press Ins to turn Insert Mode on and off. When Insert is on, you can insert characters. When Insert is off, you can strike over characters.
Del (Delete)	Press Del to delete the character on which the cursor is resting.
Backspace	Press the backspace key (←) to delete the character to the left of the cursor.
Alt-I	Press and hold down Alt while you also press I to add a line on a card.
Alt-D	Press and hold down Alt while you also press D to delete a line on a card.
Cursor keys	Use the arrow keys to move your cursor. When you search a category, the arrow keys can be used to highlight the category.
Tab	Press Tab to move the cursor from one word to the next word.

Shift-Tab	Press and hold down Shift while you also press Tab to move the cursor to the preceding word.
- (minus)	Press the minus key on the far right of the keyboard to decrease the size of a template area.
+ (plus)	Press the plus key on the far right of the keyboard to increase the size of a template area.
Home	Use the Home key to resequence template areas. When you are editing, the Home key moves the cursor to the upper left corner of a card.
Return	The Return key may be used to signal that you have finished entering information. Return may also be used to move the cursor from one area to another when you are resequencing templates or sorting selected cards.
Esc (Escape)	The Esc key stops the activity you are performing and returns you to the Main Menu and then to the DOS prompt.
F6	Press F6 to flip cards from front to back and back to front.
F10	Press F10 to return to a previous function or finish an operation.
Other F keys	Other function keys are used for different purposes. Carefully read each screen to see the function key options.
PgUp and PgDn	Use these keys to move up or down one line on a card. You may also use them for drive changes and scrolling.

The Setup Screen

After you have copied On-File onto your disk (see Chapter 2), you must set up the program on your computer. You perform the setup only when you first install your system or when you use On-File on a computer with drives set up in a way that differs from your computer setup.

To set up On-File on either a hard disk or floppy disk system,

1. Type **setup** after the DOS prompt.

2. Press **Return**.

The Setup screen shown in figure 20.3 is displayed on your screen.

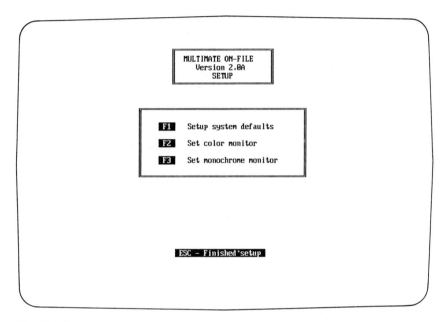

MULTIMATE ON-FILE
Version 2.0A
SETUP

F1   Setup system defaults
F2   Set color monitor
F3   Set monochrome monitor

ESC - Finished setup

Fig. 20.3. Setup screen.

3. Press **F1** to set the system defaults.

The system default screen is shown in figure 20.4.

4. Type the letter of the drive where your card box will be stored.

5. Type **Y** under the name of each drive you will use.

6. Type **Y** if you want sound or type **N** if you do not want sound.

7. Press **F1** to save your drive defaults and return to the Setup screen.

8. From the Setup screen, press **F2** if you have a color monitor or press **F3** to use a monochrome monitor.

The type of monitor is set, and you are not taken to another screen.

9. Press **Esc** when you have completed the setup.

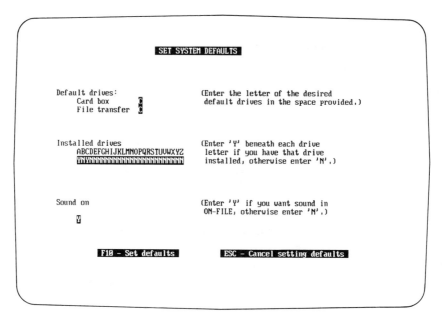

Fig. 20.4. Set System Defaults screen.

Starting On-File and Identifying a Card Box

You may access On-File through the Boot Menu (see Chapter 2). The On-File copyright screen appears, followed by the screen shown in figure 20.5.

You can press *PgUp* or *PgDn* to specify the drive for the card box. When you press *PgUp* or *PgDn*, the drive letter changes, and the boxes available on that drive appear. The drive that you specify becomes the drive where the card box will be created, stored, and later accessed.

After the correct drive is displayed,

1. Type the name of the box you want to create (or the name of the box you want to use); box names may not include spaces.

2. Press **Return**.

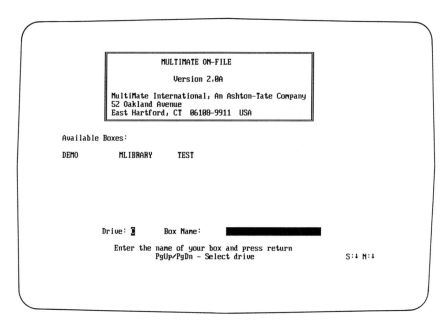

Fig. 20.5. Main Menu.

If you are creating a new box, this prompt appears:

Start a new box? (y/n)

3. Type **Y** for yes.

This prompt appears:

New box is being created

After selecting the box, the MultiMate On-File Main Menu is displayed (see fig. 20.6).

Menu and Screen Shortcuts

You may move from the DOS prompt to an On-File box. Table 20.2 shows the options you have from the DOS prompt. Enter the box name where you see <*boxname*>; do not enter the brackets shown here.

From within On-File, you may move to other menus by pressing the key combination shown in table 20.3. A Help menu with this information is available by pressing *Shift-F1*.

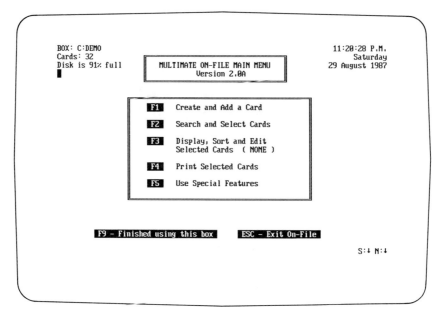

Fig. 20.6. On-File Main Menu.

Table 20.2
DOS Prompt Shortcut Commands

onfile <*boxname*>	To go to the On-File Main Menu
onfile <*boxname*> a	To go to the Create and Add a Card menu
onfile <*boxname*> s	To go to the Search and Select Cards menu

Table 20.3
Menu Shortcuts

Press:	*Menu Displayed*:
Alt-F1	Create and Add a Card
Alt-F2	Search and Select Cards
Alt-F3	Display of Current Card Selection
Alt-F4	Print Selected Cards
Alt-F5	Read and Write Cards
Alt-F6	Edit Card
Alt-F7	Write MultiMate Merge Data File
Alt-F8	Write MultiMate Document
Alt-F9	Sort Cards
Alt-F10	Return to Main Menu

Creating a Card Without a Template and Adding a Card

From the On-File Main Menu, you press *F1* to choose the Create and Add a Card option. The Create and Add a Card screen is displayed (see fig. 20.7). If the last card created was created with a template, that template appears. Press *F3* until the message No Template Selected appears. Then press *F10* to return to Create and Add a Card.

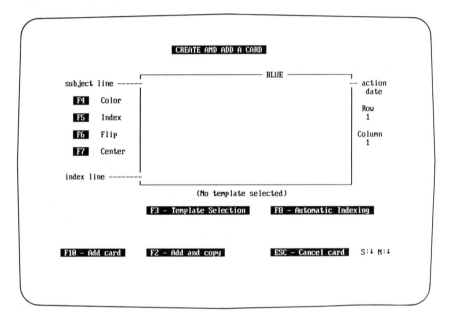

Fig. 20.7. Create and Add a Card screen.

Card Color

Cards may be one of eight colors: blue, green, brown, pink, purple, red, white, and yellow. If your computer screen does not show colors, you refer to the color by its name (**blue**, for instance).

The name of the color appears at the top right of the card. If a name is associated with the color, the name appears above the color.

Cards may be sorted by color, and the color of the card can be changed at any time. Press *F4* to change the color. By continuing to press *F4*, you can cycle through the colors and choose the color you want.

Subject Line

The subject line can contain as many as 35 characters. You may later sort cards by subject. When you view cards in the card box, the subject is visible for all cards on the screen.

Action Date

The action date is automatically entered when the card is created and may be changed at any time. The date appears as the numeric day, the first three letters of the month, and the numeric year (27 SEP 1990). You can group and select cards by the date.

Cursor Row and Column Location

The cursor row and column locations are displayed on the right side of the screen.

Card: Front and Back

The front of the card provides 10 lines for words and phrases, and the back contains 12 lines for words and phrases. These lines can hold up to 1,100 characters. Press *F6* to flip from the front to the back of cards and from the back to the front again. Pressing *F7* centers words and phrases on the card. On the front of the card, characters wrap around to a new line. On the back, words automatically wrap around.

Index Line

The index line is used to identify important words that can be used to select cards. The index line may contain 50 characters. Each index word can contain as many as 18 characters.

Index words are automatically converted to uppercase. You may store up to 1,000 index words in a box. Do not put spaces between words you want to join; instead, use a slash. For example, computer/class will be recognized as one index word. Index words are automatically alphabetized when the card is added to the box. You can enter an index word, press the space bar, and enter another index word. You can also place your cursor on a word in the card and press *F5*; that word is added to the index line.

Automatic indexing lets you add index words from an alphabetized list of index words already used in the card box. To use automatic indexing,

1. Press **F8**.

The index-word options appear.

   2. Use the **left-** and **right-arrow** keys to move through the list.

When the word you want lies between the arrows,

   3. Press **F5**.

The index word appears on the index line of your card. When you have added all the index words you want,

   4. Press **Esc**.

When you have finished filling out the card, you can review both sides:

   5. Press **F6**.

You then add the card to your card box (*F10*), add the card and keep it on the screen for continued work (*F2*), or cancel the card (*Esc*).

This section has presented how you can create a card without a template. But you can also create templates to specify where certain words or phrases are placed on the cards. You can then search for cards with specified words and phrases in particular locations.

Creating a Card with a Template: An Overview

If you want to use a template when entering the data areas on the card, press *F3* on the Create and Add a Card screen.

As you search through templates, you can use these options:

- Press *F3* to display another template.
- Press *F10* to select the template displayed.
- Press *Esc* to cancel the template-selection process.

After you have selected the template you want, you use the lower portion of the screen to enter the information for a template area. If you are entering numbers and later plan to sort by the numbers, enter leading zeros. For example, suppose that you enter *100* and then *50*; then you sort in ascending order (0-9,999). The 100 will appear before the 50. Instead, enter *100* and *050*.

When you press *Return*, the information is moved to the specified area on the card. If you want to skip an area, press *Return*. Pressing *F3* returns you to the Create and Add a Card screen, where you may fill in the template areas in any order you like. How to create and use templates is covered in greater detail later in this chapter.

Searching and Selecting Cards

After you have created cards in a box, you can search for and select (from the card box) those cards you want to view on the screen or print.

To choose the Search and Select Cards option, press *F2* from the Main Menu. This action takes you to the Search and Select Cards screen, shown in figure 20.8.

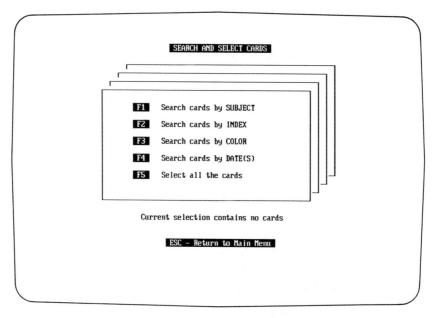

Fig. 20.8. Search and Select Cards screen.

A message indicating the number of cards from a previous selection appears at the bottom of the screen. If you have not selected any cards, this message appears:

    Current selection contains no cards

The number of cards selected tells you how large your card deck is; that number helps you verify whether you are increasing or decreasing your card deck through the selections.

You select a new group of cards by subject, index, color, or date(s). Or you can select all the cards.

F1: Search Cards by Subject

Press *F1* to choose the Search Cards by Subject option. (Remember that subjects are entered in the upper right corner of each card.) The Search Cards by Subject screen appears (see fig. 20.9).

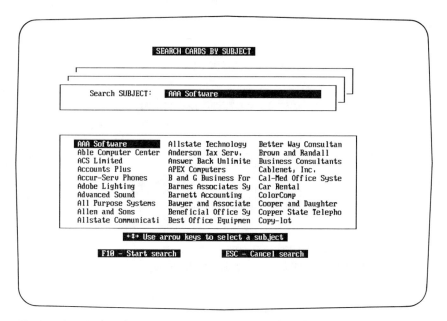

```
                 SEARCH CARDS BY SUBJECT

        Search SUBJECT:   AAA Software


        AAA Software        Allstate Technology  Better Way Consultan
        Able Computer Center Anderson Tax Serv.   Brown and Randall
        ACS Limited          Answer Back Unlimite Business Consultants
        Accounts Plus        APEX Computers       Cablenet, Inc.
        Accur-Serv Phones    B and G Business For Cal-Med Office Syste
        Adobe Lighting       Barnes Associates Sy Car Rental
        Advanced Sound       Barnett Accounting   ColorComp
        All Purpose Systems  Bawyer and Associate Cooper and Daughter
        Allen and Sons       Beneficial Office Sy Copper State Telepho
        Allstate Communicati Best Office Equipmen Copy-lot
              +‡+ Use arrow keys to select a subject
           F10 - Start search        ESC - Cancel search
```

Fig. 20.9. Search Cards by Subject screen.

All the subjects in the card box appear in alphabetical order on the lower part of the screen.

  1. Use the **arrow keys** to highlight the subject to use in the search or type in the first letter of the subject line until it is highlighted.

When the appropriate word is highlighted,

  2. Press **F10** to start the search.

Esc cancels the search.

During the search, each card with the subject is placed in your card deck, and the Build a Card Selection screen appears. This screen is discussed after the selection options are described.

F2: Search Cards by Index Words

When the Search and Select Cards screen is displayed,

> 1. Press **F2** to choose the Search Cards by Index option.

The Search Cards by Index screen is displayed (see fig. 20.10).

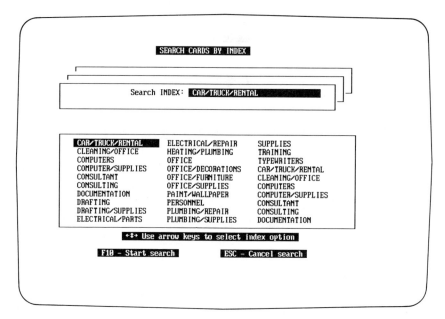

Fig. 20.10. Search Cards by Index screen.

The index words are shown in alphabetical order in the lower part of the screen. Thirty index words are shown at one time. If fewer than 30 words exist, the words are repeated.

If more than 30 words exist, you may use the right- and left-arrow keys to scroll through the index words. Use the arrow keys to select the index word to search for or type in the first letter of the index word until it is highlighted.

> 2. Press **F10** to start the search.

Esc cancels the search.

The search causes each card with the index word to be identified. The Build a Card Selection screen appears.

F3: *Search by Color*

From the Search and Select Cards screen, press *F3* to search cards by color.

This option takes you to the Search Cards by Color screen, shown in figure 20.11.

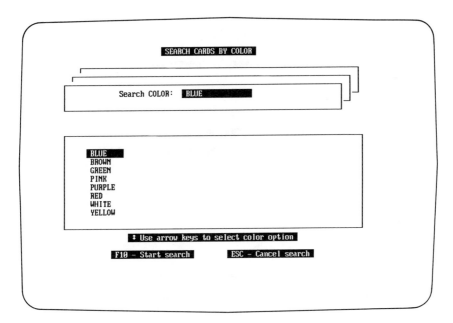

Fig. 20.11. Search Cards by Color screen.

You can choose any one of the eight card colors.

　　1. Use the **arrow keys** to select the color.

When the color you want is highlighted,

　　2. Press **F10** to start the search.

Esc cancels the search.

After cards are searched, the Build a Card Selection screen is displayed.

F4: *Search by Date(s)*

Press *F4* from the Search and Select Cards screen to select cards by a single date or all cards within a range of dates.

You move to the Search Cards by Date(s) screen, shown in figure 20.12.

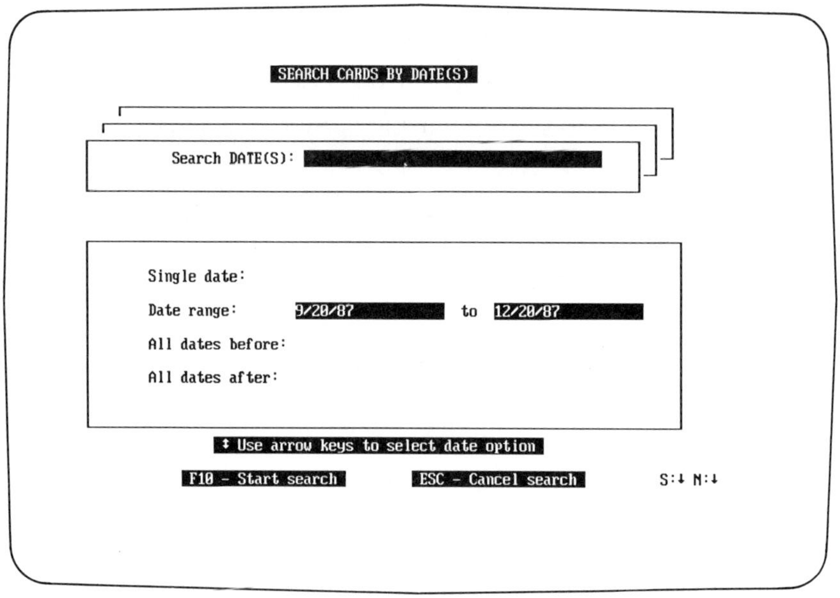

Fig. 20.12. Search Cards by Date(s) screen.

1. Use the **arrow keys** to highlight the date method for the search.

2. Type a single date, a date range (specify the beginning date and ending date), all dates before a specific date, or all dates after a given date.

Type dates as MM/DD/YY. If you type the date in another form, the date will be converted. After you have selected the method of the search and have entered the date,

3. Press **F10** to begin the search.

You can cancel the search before you press *F10* by pressing *Esc.*

After the cards are selected, you are taken to the Build a Card Selection screen.

F5: Select All Cards

You can use the Search and Select Cards screen to pick the Select All the Cards option: press *F5* when the Search and Select Cards screen is displayed.

This prompt appears on your screen:

```
Are you sure? (y/n)
```

Type *Y* to select all cards or type *N* to make another selection. You are returned to the Search and Select Cards screen.

F6: *Match by Word or Phrase*

After you have selected cards by subject, index, color, or date(s), or you have selected all cards, the option (*F6*) to match the selected cards by word or phrase is displayed on the Search and Select Cards screen (see fig. 20.13). You can search the card deck for matching words, phrases, or numbers.

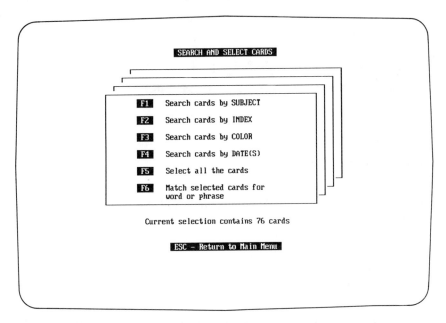

Fig. 20.13. Search and Select Cards screen.

1. From the Search and Select Cards screen, press **F6**.

The Match Selected Cards for Word or Phrase screen (see fig. 20.14) appears on your screen.

- You can enter any word or phrase on the card.

- Cards with identical characters are matched.

- If you enter brackets ([]) around the word or phrase, leading and trailing spaces in the brackets are included in the search.

- If you want to search for the word or phrase in the same row and column on all cards, use parentheses around the characters.

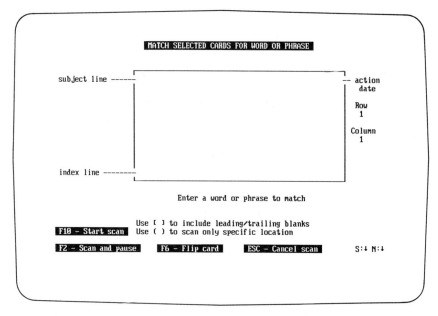

Fig. 20.14. Match Selected Cards for Word or Phrase screen.

- Uppercase and lowercase are not considered during the selection process.

Figure 20.15 illustrates how entering a word affects card selection.

Notice that the first entry results in the selection of cards A, B, and C. The word *Lincoln*, alone or as part of a larger word anywhere on the card, is selected.

The second entry results in the selection of cards B and C. The word *Lincoln*, alone or as part of a larger word, is selected as long as it is on line 3.

And, the third entry results in the selection of card C. The word *Lincoln*, with a space following it, will match when appearing anywhere on the card.

2. Type the word or phrase; press **F6** to flip the card.

3. Press **F10** or **F2** to begin the search.

If you press *F10*, the scan is performed and the cards that match are selected automatically. You may press *Esc* to cancel the search. If you press *F2*, On-File stops at each card. You may select the card (F10), skip the selection (F5), flip the card (F6), or cancel the search (Esc).

After the selection is done, the Build a Card Selection screen is displayed.

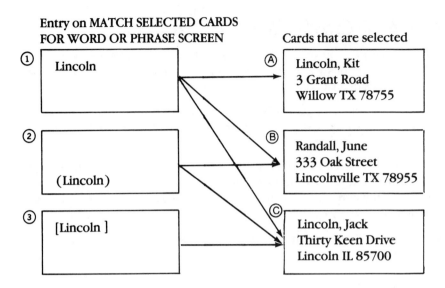

Fig. 20.15. Card selection example.

Building a Card Selection

After you have searched by subject, index, color, dates, or all cards (and optionally matched by word or phrase), the Build a Card Selection screen appears (see fig. 20.16).

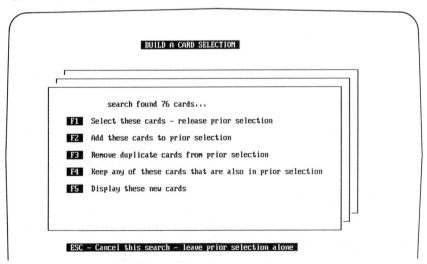

Fig. 20.16. Build a Card Selection screen.

F1: Select Cards/Release Cards

Pressing *F1* permits you to use the current selection of cards and to release any previous selections you have made. You may want to do this if your first selection was inadequate and you want to try again.

For example, if you selected cards with the index word *computer* and then selected cards with the index word *Iowa*, pressing *F1* causes only the cards with *Iowa* as an index word to remain.

The opposite effect can be achieved by pressing *Esc*. This cancels the search just performed and retains the previously selected cards. Refer back to the last example. If you pressed *Esc*, the cards with *computer* would remain, and the cards with *Iowa* would be lost.

You may want to press *Esc* if you realize the selection you just made is not what you want.

F2: Add Cards

F2 allows you to add cards just selected to the previously selected group of cards. This option lets you combine the results of several selections and increase the size of your card group.

For example, the first cards selected with the index word *computer* would be added to the cards in the next selection with the index word *Iowa*.

F3: Remove Duplicate Cards

If you press *F3*, cards from the current selection are removed from the cards already selected.

Using the same example, the cards with the word *Iowa* (the second selection) would be removed from the cards with the word *computer* (the first selection).

Only cards with the word *computer*, not the word *Iowa*, would be included in the resulting card group. This option makes the group of cards smaller by removing the cards that were just selected from the existing group of cards.

F4: Keep Cards

You may keep the cards in the current selection (that are also in the previous selection) by pressing *F4*.

For example, if you first select the cards with *computer* and then the cards with *Iowa*, pressing *F4* would select a group of cards with both the word *computer* and the word *Iowa*. This option decreases the size of the group of cards.

F5: Display Cards

Press *F5* to display the cards just selected.

Displaying, Sorting, and Editing Selected Cards

After the cards have been searched for and selected (*F2* from the Main Menu), you can display, sort, and edit the selected cards. This option is *F3* on the Main Menu.

The Display of Current Card Selection screen appears as shown in figure 20.17.

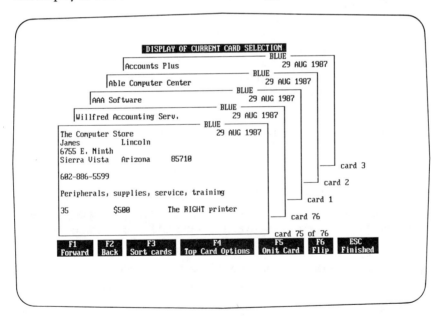

Fig. 20.17. *Display of Current Card Selection screen.*

From the Display of Current Card Selection screen, you have several options.

F1: Forward

Press *F1* to move forward through the cards.

F2: Backward

Press *F2* to move backward as you view the cards.

As you press *F1* and *F2*, the stack of cards shown rotates.

F3: Sort Cards

1. Press **F3** to sort cards with a template.

The Sort Cards screen appears.

2. Press **F3** to pick one of the templates in the box.

After you have selected the template you want,

3. Press **F10**.

The Define Sort Criteria screen appears.

4. Use **Return** to place your cursor over one template area.

5. Press **F3** to sort in ascending order (low to high, alphabetically or numerically) or press **F5** for descending order. Or press **F7** to sort by color in ascending order.

6. Perform steps 4 through 6 to select two other sort criteria, if desired.

You may choose two more template areas and corresponding types of sort before pressing *F10* to perform the sort.

For example, you first may want to sort the cards by state in ascending order. You would place your cursor over the template area marked *state* and press *F3*.

This action requests that the cards be in alphabetical order by state. You also may want the cards within each state ordered by ZIP code.

Place the cursor over *ZIP* and press *F3*.

Now the cards will be sorted from Alaska to Wyoming, and the cards within each state group will be ordered from 00000 to 99999 by ZIP code.

7. Press **F10** to begin the sort.

Press *Esc* at any time to cancel the sort. You are then returned to the Display of Current Card Selection screen, where you can see your cards.

If you allow the sort to be completed, your cards will have been reorganized when you are returned to the Display of Current Card Selection screen.

F4: *Top Card Options*

From the Display of Current Card Selection screen, *F6* can be used to flip the card called the *top card* into full view. Remember that *F1* and *F2* can be used to move forward and backward through the cards, which causes the top card to change. If you press *F4*, the Top Card Options screen is displayed with options for seven activities (see fig. 20.18).

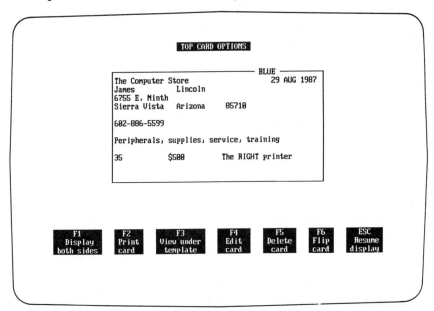

Fig. 20.18. Top Card Options screen.

From the Top Card Options screen, press *F1* to display both sides of the card on the screen at once. To uncover the overlapping corners as both cards are displayed, press *F10*. Press *Esc* to return to the Top Card Options screen.

Press *F2* to print the card.

Use *F3* to view the card under a template. Viewing the card under a template lets you compare other templates to the card layout.

Although the template areas appear, the names for each area do not appear. When you use this option, press *F3* to select the template, *F4* to move between the template and the card information, *F6* to flip the card, and *Esc* to return to the Top Card Options screen.

Press *F4* to edit the card. The options on the Edit Card screen are identical to the options used in creating the card. (Those options were described earlier in this chapter.)

- Use the *cursor keys* to move the cursor on the card.

- Press *Insert* to turn the Insert function on and off.

When the Insert function is on, any characters you type will be inserted.

- Press *Del* to delete a character.

- You may change the color of the card by pressing *F4* until the color you want appears.

- You may add new index words by placing the cursor over the word and pressing *F5*.

From the Edit Card screen, you may also select index words by pressing *F8*. Then, follow the directions on the screen to select an index word from all index words in the card box. You may flip the card from one side to the other by pressing *F6*.

Lines can be centered by pressing *F7*.

Templates can be called up by pressing *F3* and following the screen directions. Press *F9* to see the template area names or to make them disappear.

After editing the card, save the card by pressing *F10* or cancel your edits by pressing *Esc*.

Press *F5* to delete the card. Both sides of the card are displayed before deletion. Confirm that the card should be deleted by pressing *F10*.

If you decide not to delete the card, press *Esc* to save it.

Pressing *F6* flips the card. F6 is a toggle that allows you to move back and forth between the two sides of the card.

Esc returns to the display of the selected cards.

To return to the Main Menu from the Top Card Options screen, press *Alt-F10*.

F5: Omit Card

From the Display of Current Cards screen, you may press *F5* to omit the top card displayed. The card is removed from the screen display but not from the box.

F6: Flip

Press *F6* to flip the card from front to back and back to front.

Esc: Finish

From the Display of Current Cards screen, press *Esc* to return to the Main Menu.

The Use Special Features Screen

From the Main Menu, select *F5* to use special features. The Use Special Features screen appears (see fig. 20.19). Press *F9* to toggle the sound on or off or *Esc* to return to the Main Menu. The other options are described in this section.

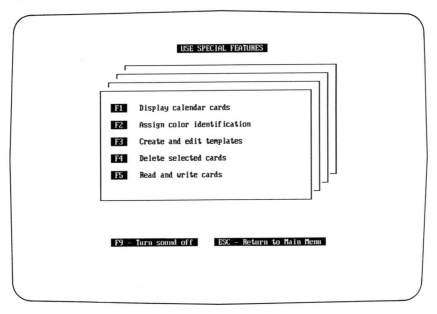

Fig. 20.19. Use Special Features screen.

F1: Display Calendar Cards

From the Use Special Features screen, press *F1* to display the current month's calendar. You press the function keys indicated to move ahead or back in time by month or year:

- *F1* shows you next month's calendar.

- *F2* shows you last month's calendar.

- *F3* moves you ahead one year.

- *F4* moves you back one year.

You may press these keys as often as you like to display future or past calendars. The screen always displays a single month.

F2: Assign Color Identification

From the Use Special Features screen, press *F2*; this takes you to the Assign Color Identification screen (see fig. 20.20). Use this screen to assign a name up to 40 characters long for each color.

1. Select the color with the **arrow keys**.

2. Type the name you want.

The name is displayed above the cards as you work with them.

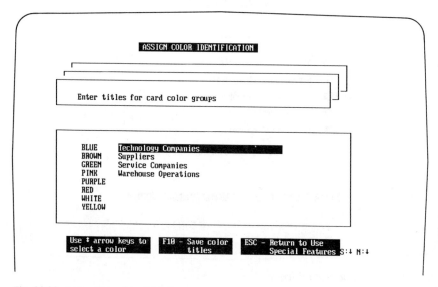

Fig. 20.20. Assign Color Identification screen.

F3: *Create and Edit Templates*

Press *F3* on the Use Special Features screen to create and edit templates. The Create and Edit Templates screen is displayed (see fig. 20.21).

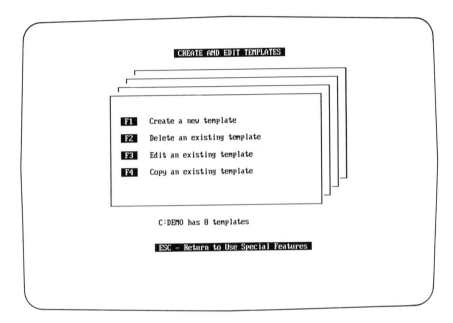

Fig. 20.21. Create and Edit Templates screen.

F1: Create a New Template

Pressing *F1* from the Create and Edit Templates screen allows you to create a template. You may have 16 templates in a box and 20 template areas in a template. The first field is the subject, and line 12 is the index.

1. Type the name for the template.

Press *Esc* to cancel the function. In figure 20.22, the template has been named *Inventory*.

2. Move your cursor to the desired location.

3. Type **any letter key** continuously to mark the area length.

A letter (A, B, C, and so on) is automatically assigned to the area.

4. Press **F10** when you have marked the area.

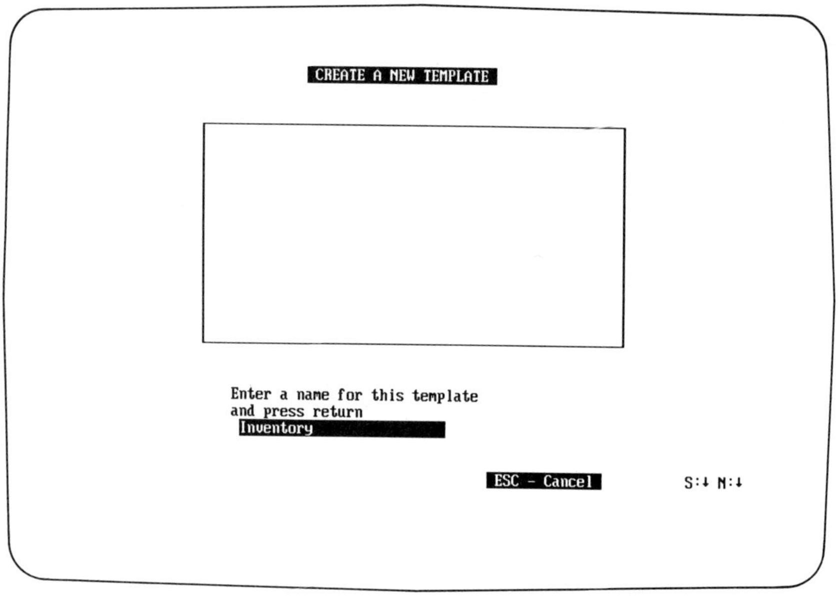

Fig. 20.22. Naming a template.

This prompt appears:

    Enter a title for the area designated A: and press Return

5. Type a title for the area.

6. Press **Return**.

Your cursor returns to the card, and you may mark a new area.

7. Repeat steps 2 through 6 until each template area has been identified and titled.

8. Press **F10** when you are finished identifying and naming template areas.

The order in which you enter areas determines the order in which areas are printed; however, you will learn later how to reorder the areas to print. Figure 20.23 shows the template just prior to entering the last area, which is named *Location*.

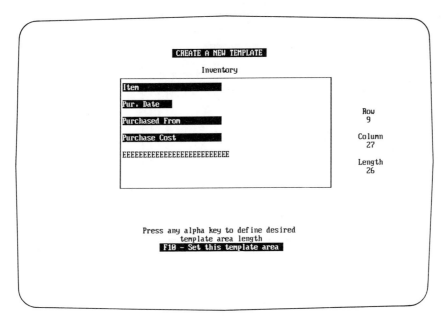

Fig. 20.23. Entering titles for template areas.

F2: Delete an Existing Template

Delete a template by pressing *F2* from the Create and Edit Templates screen. The Delete an Existing Template screen appears.

1. Press **F2** until the template to be deleted appears on the screen.

2. Press **F10**.

3. Type **Y**

Esc will cancel the deletion.

F3: Edit an Existing Template

You may edit a template by pressing *F3* from the Create and Edit Templates screen. Pressing *F3* accesses the Edit an Existing Template screen shown in figure 20.24. Press *F9* to find the name of the template you want to edit. As you press *F9*, different template names appear.

In figure 20.24, the template named *Inventory* is selected.

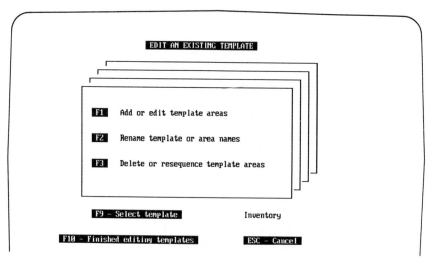

Fig. 20.24. Edit an Existing Template screen.

F1: Add or Edit Template Areas

From the Edit an Existing Template screen, press *F1* to add or edit the template areas. The Add or Edit Template Areas screen appears; this screen displays instructions about how to lengthen or shorten areas. You add areas in the same manner you created areas:

1. Move the cursor to the selected location.

2. Press **any letter key** to form the area.

3. Press **F10**.

4. Type the area name.

5. Press **Return**.

6. Press **F10** when you are finished adding or editing.

F2: Rename Template or Area Names

Press *F2* from the Edit an Existing Template screen to rename a template or template area. The Rename Template or Area Names screen appears.

1. Type the new name.

2. Press **F10**.

Press *Esc* to retain the same template name.

F3: Delete or Resequence Template Areas

From the Edit an Existing Template screen, press *F3* to delete or resequence template areas. The Delete or Resequence Area Names screen is displayed.

No matter how they appear on the screen, areas are printed on paper according to the A, B, C, etc., designation.

1. Press **Return** to place your cursor on the area title to be first in the sequence.
2. Press **Home**.

Continue pressing Return and Home in the print sequence that you want for the remaining template areas.

If you want to delete an area,

1. Move the cursor to the area to be deleted.
2. Press **Del**.

When you have specified the new sequence, this prompt appears:

```
Delete or resequence of template areas complete
Press any key to continue
```

3. Press **any key**.

F4: Copy an Existing Template

Copying a template makes modifying the template easy. You copy a template by pressing *F4* from the Create and Edit Templates screen. The Copy an Existing Template screen appears.

1. Press **F4** to determine the name of the template to copy.
2. Press **F10** to copy the template.
3. Confirm the copy by entering **Y**.
4. Type the name of the new template and press **Return**.

Copying and editing a template is an easy way to create new templates. For example, the *Inventory* template includes areas for the item, purchase date, purchase from, purchase cost, and location.

Suppose that you want to create a template called *Supplies* with these areas: supplies, purchase date, purchase from, purchase cost, and location. Rather than construct the template from scratch, you would save time by copying the *Inventory* template and then editing the first area name from *item* to *supplies.*

F4: Delete Selected Cards

Pressing *F4* from the Use Special Features screen allows you to delete all the cards most recently selected. After you press *F4*, this message appears:

```
# cards will be deleted Confirm by entering (y/n)
```

Type *Y* to delete the cards or type *N* to escape.

F5: Read and Write Cards

From the Use Special Features screen, choose *F5* to transfer cards to and from files. You use the Read and Write Cards screen shown in figure 20.25.

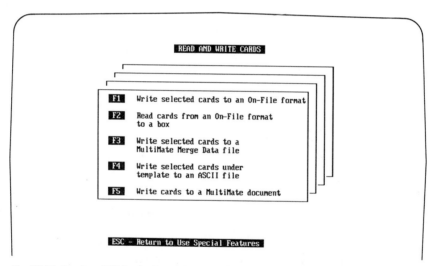

Fig. 20.25. Read and Write Cards screen.

F1/F2: Write and Read Selected Cards Using an On-File Format

Press *F1* so that the selected cards will be written to a file in On-File format. Press *F2* to put (read) data in an On-File format to a card box.

　　1. Press **PgUp** or **PgDn** to select another drive.

2. Type the file name.

3. Press **Return**.

If you are writing to a file, you may type the name of an existing file (erasing the existing contents), or you may type the name of a file to be created.

4. Press **Esc** if you decide against transferring the cards.

F3: Write Cards to a Merge Data File

You press *F3* from the Read and Write Cards screen to turn card data into a MultiMate Merge Data File to be used with the MultiMate Advantage II Merge feature (see Chapter 16 for more information).

1. Press **F3** until you see the name of the template you will use to identify the data to extract.

2. Press **F10**.

3. Press **PgUp** or **PgDn** to switch drives.

4. Type the name of the Merge Data File.

5. Press **Return**.

If you enter the name of an existing file, this message appears:

> There is already a file with that name. Replace? (y/n)

6. Type **Y** to replace the file contents or type **N** to retain the contents and begin again.

If you are creating a new file or if you select *Y*, the conversion begins. The resulting MultiMate Advantage II document lists each template area title as a Merge Item name, and each piece of data is listed as a Merge Item. Merge codes are automatically inserted.

F4: Write Cards Under a Template to an ASCII File

From the Read and Write Cards screen, press *F4* to create an ASCII file from your selected card data.

1. Press **F4** until you see the name of the template you want to use to extract data.

2. Press **F10**.

3. The letter of the drive on which the file resides appears.

4. Type the file name.

5. Press **Return**.

If the file exists, this prompt appears:

> There is already a file with that name. Replace? (y/n)

6. Press **Y** or press **N**.

The ASCII file that is created places the data on separate lines that wrap around. Each data item is placed in quotation marks, and the items are separated by commas.

F5: Write Cards to a MultiMate Document

From the Read and Write Cards screen, press *F5* to create a MultiMate Advantage II document from the selected cards.

1. Press **PgUp** or **PgDn** to select the drive if necessary.

2. Enter the name of the MultiMate Advantage II document file. Do not type in the *.DOC* extension; it is added automatically.

A file is created with one card on a page. The cards you want to transfer may be too numerous to fit into a MultiMate Advantage II document. If you anticipate this happening, use a numeric digit as the last character in the file name. On-File creates a new document and increases the last digit of the name of the new file. If you do not use a number as the last character in the file name, you will be prompted for a new file name before creating the additional document.

3. Press **Return**.

4. This prompt appears:

> Writing the file...

5. When the cards are written, this prompt appears:

> File transfer complete. Press any key to continue.

Printing Selected Cards

You must select cards before they can be printed. From the Main Menu, press *F4* to print the selected cards. The Print Selected Cards screen is displayed (see fig. 20.26).

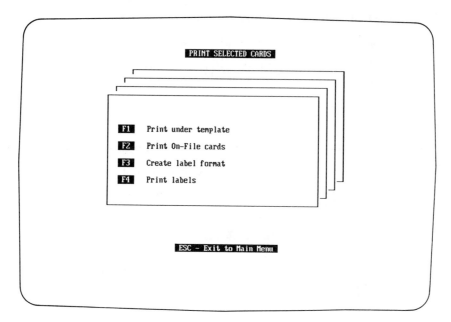

Fig. 20.26. Print Selected Cards screen.

Press *F1* to print using a template, *F2* to print cards, *F3* to create a label format, or *F4* to print labels. After selecting a print option, you are reminded to ready your printer. During printing, you can cancel a print by pressing *Esc.*

F1: Print Using Templates

The template you select determines the order in which the card information is printed.

The information is printed from left to right and up to 80 columns; then it wraps around to the next line.

If you want the printing compressed, you must send to your printer a MultiMate Advantage II word-processing document using an 8- or 9-pitch setting before you access On-File. The pitch setting is retained when you enter On-File. From the Print Using A Template screen,

1. Press **F4** to select the template that corresponds to the layout of your cards.

2. Press **F9** to select vertical spacing.

Select *1* for single spacing, *2* for double spacing, and so on.

3. Press **F10** to print the card or press **Esc** to cancel the print.

The date, time, and page number are printed on each page. Template area titles are used as column headings.

F2: Print Cards

To print the front and back of cards as they appear on your screen, press *F2*.

The Print On-File Cards screen appears, as shown in figure 20.27.

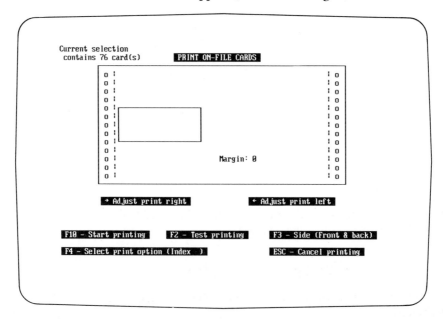

Fig. 20.27. Print On-File Cards screen.

From the Print On-File Cards screen,

1. Press the **right-** or **left-arrow** key to move the printed copy right or left without having to adjust the paper.

2. Press **F2** to print a test pattern, ready the printer, and press **any key**.

Printing a test pattern is especially useful if you are using perforated cards and are concerned with how the cards will line up.

3. Press **F3** to select the front of each card, the back of each card, or the front and back of each card for printing.

4. Press **F4** to toggle between 3-by-5 index cards or printing on 11-inch paper.

5. Press **F10** to start printing.

F3/F4: Create Label Format and Print Labels

You can create and print a label that contains data that is constant. First, you create the label format; then, you print the labels. A card box may have only one label format at a time, and the format must be associated with a single template.

From the Print Selected Cards screen, press *F3* to create a label format. The Create Label Format screen appears.

1. Press **F3** to select a template with data areas in the same order as your cards.

2. Press **F10** to create the label using the template displayed.

The Cut and Paste the Label Format screen appears.

The label area is shown at the top, and the template is shown at the bottom of the screen. To develop a label,

3. Move the cursor to the label where template areas should be copied.

4. Press **F3** to select an area of the template.

The blinking area of the template is the selected area. A new area is selected (indicated by blinking) each time you press *F3*.

5. Press **F4** to copy the template area to the label.

You can now copy another template area to the label.

6. Press the **space bar** to create shaded blocks where each blank space should appear.

You can type in characters that will appear on each label.

Pressing *F5* makes the word FLOAT appear in the upper right corner of your screen. *FLOAT* causes all data to be printed in the upper left part of the label, omitting any areas where data is not available. Pressing *F6* causes FIXED to appear in the upper right corner of your screen. *FIXED* causes the label to be spaced out.

Figure 20.28 shows a created label format and its appearance when printed
with *FLOAT* and *FIXED*.

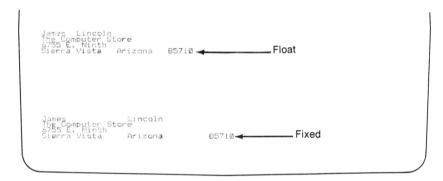

Fig. 20.28. A label format and the printed results in FLOAT and FIXED style.

You may want to experiment printing both ways. When the label is ready,

   7. Press **F10** to save it or press **Esc** to cancel it.

To print the label, press *F4* from the Print Selected Cards screen. Press *F4*
to go to the Print Labels screen (see fig. 20.29).

Fig. 20.29. Print Labels screen.

1. Use the **right-** and **left-arrow** keys to reposition the label on the screen; the margin setting changes.

The label actually moves on your screen. Use the plus (+) and minus (-) keys to adjust the spacing; the spacing setting changes.

2. Press **F5** to select continuous paper or sheet-feed paper.

This choice controls whether your printer pauses between labels. If you are using continuous-form paper, press *F6* to choose whether you want the printer to pause between labels.

3. Press **F10** to start the print.

If you press *F10* to start the print, you see options that allow you to start or resume printing (*F10*), readjust the print (*F9*), or cancel the print (*Esc*).

Using the Utilities

You use On-File Utilities to list the MultiMate Advantage II documents or On-File card boxes on a disk or hard drive. You can also convert MultiMate Advantage II Document Summary screens into a card box.

Existing Merge data files (see Chapter 16) can be converted to On-File card boxes. ASCII files may be created for use by On-File and vice versa. Templates may be transferred from one card box to another. Finally, you may recover damaged On-File boxes. If you have a dual floppy disk drive system, insert the On-File Utilities disk into drive A.

From either a floppy or hard disk system, select On-File Utilities. Press the space bar at the copyright screen to see the On-File Utilities Menu (see fig. 20.30).

MultiMate Advantage II Document Cataloging

You may catalog and list MultiMate Advantage II documents and On-File card boxes. MultiMate Advantage II documents are cataloged with the templates shown in figure 20.31.

The highlighted areas are the fields contained on the MultiMate Advantage II Document Summary screen. When documents are organized, the information for each document on your disk is copied onto a card. When card boxes are organized, each card box is represented by a card. This way, you can sort through the cards to see the documents.

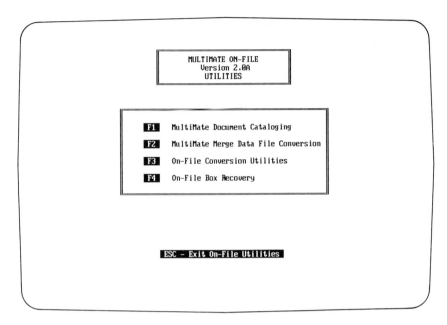

Fig. 20.30. On-File Utilities Menu.

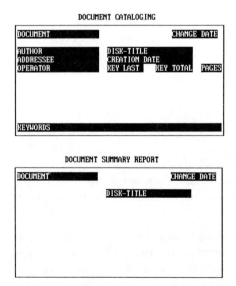

Fig. 20.31. Document Cataloging and Summary templates and area definitions.

Those MultiMate Advantage II documents that **cannot** have information copied to a card include the following:

- Library documents
- Documents containing key procedures
- Documents that have been renamed or copied to a different name with DOS commands
- Documents with zeros as the creation date

Document cataloging may handle up to 600 documents on floppy disk systems and 1,000 documents on hard disk systems.

Older MultiMate conversion utilities entered zeros for creation dates.

Before you can use the On-File Utilities to create a card box for data management, the box must contain the Document Cataloging template.

If you have a floppy disk system, make sure the Utilities disk is in drive A and the Document disk is in drive B. After the prompt A>,

    1. Type **copy a:mlibrary.* b:[cardbox].***

Insert the name of the card box for [*cardbox*].

    2. Press **Return**.

If you have a hard disk and want your card box on a floppy disk in drive A, after the C> prompt,

    1. Type **copy c:mlibrary.* a:[cardbox].***

Insert the name of the card box for [*cardbox*].

    2. Press **Return**.

If you have a hard disk and want your card box on drive C, after the C> prompt,

    1. Type **copy c:mlibrary.* [cardbox].***

Insert the name of the card box for [*cardbox*].

    2. Press **Return**.

Access the On-File Utilities from the Boot Menu.

At the copyright screen,

    3. Press the **space bar**.

From the Utilities Menu,

4. Press **F1**.

5. Remove the program disk from the default drive if necessary. Press **any key**.

The MultiMate Document Cataloging screen is displayed (see fig. 20.32).

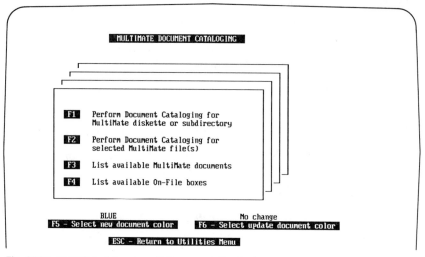

Fig. 20.32. MultiMate Advantage II Document Cataloging screen.

You may press *F5* to select the color for newly created cards or *F6* to assign a new color to an existing card box being updated. One of the options is "no change." Options *F1* to *F4* are described individually.

F1: Perform Document Cataloging for a MultiMate Diskette or Subdirectory

Press *F1* from the MultiMate Document Cataloging screen to create a new card box or update an existing card box. This selection takes you through a series of prompts.

1. Type the letter of the drive that contains the card box with the Document Cataloging templates. Press **Return**.

2. Type the name to give to the On-File box where you want to store the cards. Include the drive and path if necessary. (This is the box that was created when you copied *mlibrary*.) Press **Return**.

3. Enter the drive and path that contain the MultiMate Advantage II documents. Press **Return**.

4. Type the MultiMate Advantage II disk name (*disk 1*, for example) or subdirectory name. This name is used on the template area for organization. Press **Return**.

Note: If the error message Unable to Open File appears, you must install the *Files=15* command in your *CONFIG.SYS* file on your Boot disk (see Chapter 2). Or, you must copy the *mlibrary* files. (See the description earlier in this chapter.)

After you enter all the information (in steps 1 through 4), MultiMate Advantage II goes to work.

The system displays the following:

- The number of cards that match MultiMate Advantage II document names

- The number of On-File cards found in the box

- The number of MultiMate Advantage II documents found

- The number of cards to be removed (in cases where the documents have been deleted, moved, or renamed)

- The number of new documents to be added to the card box

After MultiMate Advantage II reports its findings, you have the option of pressing *F10* to update the card box or *Esc* to cancel the update. As the card box is updated, the names of documents that have been edited since the last card box update are displayed on the top of the screen, and the names of documents to be added appear on the bottom right of the screen.

If there are cards to be deleted, the Delete Extra On-File Cards screen appears. You may press *F10* to delete the cards, *F2* to review the cards before deletion, or *Esc* to keep the cards marked for deletion. If you choose to review the cards before deletion, you are shown each card with the option to flip the card, display template area names, delete the card, keep the card, or bypass reviewing and deleting any other cards.

A final summary of activity appears.

F2: Perform Document Cataloging for Selected Files

Press *F2* from the MultiMate Document Cataloging screen to update or add document cards one at a time.

1. Type the letter of the drive on which the card box resides; press **Return**.

2. Type the card box name. (The card box must exist.) Press **Return**.

3. Type the letter of the drive and the path on which the MultiMate Advantage II documents reside. Press **Return**.

4. Type the MultiMate Advantage II document file name. Press **Return**.

5. Type the MultiMate Advantage II disk or subdirectory name. Press **Return**.

When the process is complete, summary information about the cards found appears.

Press *F10* to update the box or press *Esc* to cancel the operation. If you update the box, a summary appears.

F3: List MultiMate Advantage II Documents

To list the MultiMate Advantage II documents on a drive, press *F3* from the MultiMate Document Cataloging screen.

1. Type the letter of the drive and directory on which the MultiMate Advantage II documents reside.

2. Press **Return**.

The directory of MultiMate Advantage II documents appears.

3. Press **F10** to list another directory or press **Esc** to return to the MultiMate Document Cataloging screen.

F4: List On-File Card Boxes

Press *F4* from the MultiMate Document Cataloging screen to list the On-File card boxes.

1. Type the letter of the drive and directory containing the boxes.

2. Press **Return**.

3. Press **F10** to list the card boxes on another drive or press **Esc** to return to the MultiMate Document Cataloging screen.

MultiMate Advantage II Merge Data File Conversion

By choosing *F2* on the On-File Utilities Menu, you can convert MultiMate Advantage II Merge data files into On-File cards. (Merge data files are described more fully in Chapter 16.) One card is created for each page in the Merge Data File.

As many as 250 cards may be transferred under one file name at a time. Be sure to have a template prepared in an existing card box to match exactly the item names in the Merge Data File. You may enter a template area name that is not an item name in the Merge Data File.

Before the files are converted, you may fill in the area with information that will be printed on each card. After pressing *F2*, a series of prompts is displayed to indicate that the On-File Utilities diskette may be removed from floppy drive systems. Press any key to go on.

1. Type the letter of the drive on which the card box holding the template resides. Press **Return**.

2. Type the name of the card box that holds the template. Press **Return**.

3. Type the letter of the drive on which the MultiMate Advantage II Merge Data File resides. Press **Return**.

4. Type the name of the MultiMate Advantage II Merge Data File. Do not include the *.DOC* extension. Press **Return**.

5. Type the letter of the drive on which the output file (the new card box) will reside. Press **Return**.

6. Type the name of the output file. Press **Return**.

Then the MultiMate On-File Merge Document Conversion screen appears (see fig. 20.33).

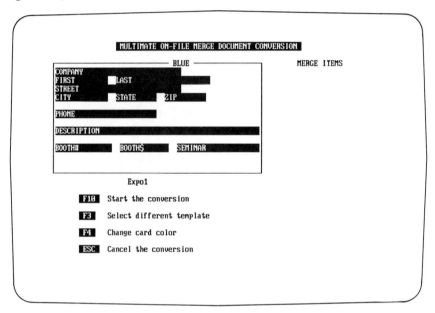

Fig. 20.33. MultiMate Advantage II On-File Merge Document Conversion screen.

The MultiMate On-File Merge Document Conversion screen shows you the template that will be used when the document file is converted.

- You may press *F3* to select a different template.

- *F4* allows you to change the color of the card.

- The Merge items are listed in order.

When you are ready to convert, press *F10*. Use *Esc* to cancel the conversion. After you press *F10*, the template areas are listed one by one.

Type the constant information to be printed on each card; this data will be entered when no data is available in the Merge Data File. Press Return if you do not have constant data to put in that template area; constant data is optional. Press *F9* to bypass the remaining template areas.

When you have moved through each template area, each card appears on the screen as the card is converted. The screen also lists the number of cards converted.

Press any key to return to the On-File Utilities screen. Use Read Cards from an On-File format to copy the data to your card box.

On-File Conversion Utilities

The third option on the On-File Utilities screen is *F3*. It allows you to convert a file from On-File format to ASCII or from ASCII to On-File format and to copy templates between card boxes. After you press *F3*, the MultiMate On-File Conversion Utilities screen is displayed (fig. 20.34).

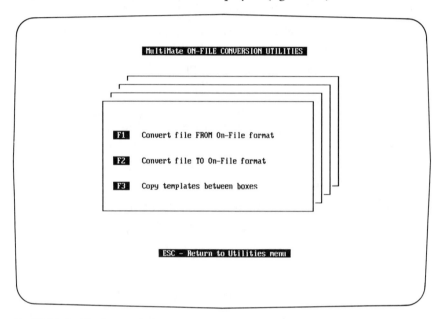

Fig. 20.34. On-File Conversion Utilities screen.

Press *F1* to convert an On-File card box (the file with a *.MOF* extension) to ASCII format. A sequential ASCII file is created. You are prompted to enter the On-File drive, the On-File file name, the drive where you want the ASCII file, and the name for the ASCII file. After you enter the data, the conversion begins.

During the conversion, you may press *Esc* to cancel the rest of the conversion. When the conversion is completed, you see this message, which lists the number of cards converted: Finished converting # card(s). Press any key to return to the On-File Conversion Utilities screen. Inserted Format Lines are counted as characters and are not recommended.

By pressing *F2* from the On-File Conversion Utilities screen, you can convert a file from ASCII to On-File format. The format rules for the ASCII to On-File conversion follow:

- There must be 25 lines (including characters and blank spaces) in a record.

- There may be 12 lines and a total of 597 characters.

- Lines longer than 50 characters are cut off on the front of the card and wrapped around on the back of the card.

- One of the eight colors handled by On-File must be typed on line 1.

- Line 2 must have 1 to 35 characters for the subject, and it must contain a date of up to 11 characters (in the DD-MMM-YYYY format).

- Lines 3 to 12 are the index lines; when the lines exceed 50 characters, the additional data is omitted.

- Fields are identified as the areas between double quotes.

- If a subject line has more than one space and more than 35 characters, the words after the multiple spaces are omitted.

- Fields are separated with single-carriage line feeds.

- Records are separated with double-carriage line feeds.

After you press *F2* from the On-File Conversion Utilities screen,

1. Press the function key to assign color to cards without color.

2. Type the ASCII file drive (the source drive); press **Return**.

3. Type the ASCII file name and extension; press **Return**.

4. Type the On-File drive (the target drive); press **Return**.

5. Type the On-File card box name; do not include an extension. Press **Return** to start the conversion.

Esc will stop the conversion.

When the conversion is completed, the following prompt (which lists the number of cards converted) appears:

```
Finished converting # card(s). Press any key to continue.
```

Press *F3* from the On-File Conversion Utilities screen to copy one or more templates from one or more card boxes to a single card box.

Remember, the existing templates in the card box you are copying to are erased.

1. Type the letter of the drive to receive the template (target drive). Press **Return**.

2. Type the name of the box to receive the template (target file name). Press **Return**.

If a box exists, you select whether to overwrite it. If you overwrite the box, the contents are replaced.

3. Type the letter of the drive containing the box with the template (first template drive). Press **Return**.

4. Type the name of the card box containing the template (first template file name). Press **Return**.

5. Press **F7** to display each template on the screen to choose the template you want.

6. Press **F8** to copy (transfer) the template to the card box.

7. Press **F7** to display the next template; continue to copy the templates you want from this card box.

After pressing *F10*, the following prompt appears:

    Would you like to transfer another template file? (y/n)

If you want to transfer another template to the card box,

9. Press **Y** and the process will begin again. Otherwise, press **N**.

Press *F4* from the On-File Conversion Utilities screen to recover damaged or problematic card boxes. Once the card box has been recovered, the cards can be read into a newly created box.

1. Enter the drive, path, and name of the box to be recovered; press **Return**.

2. Enter the drive, path, and name of the box to which you will write the recovered cards; press **Return**.

3. On-File displays this prompt and counts the cards as they are written:

   `Writing the file . . . cards 14`

4. When the recovery is complete, this prompt appears:

   `18 card(s) written`

   `Press any key to continue`

5. Press **any key**.

A
Keyboard Diagram

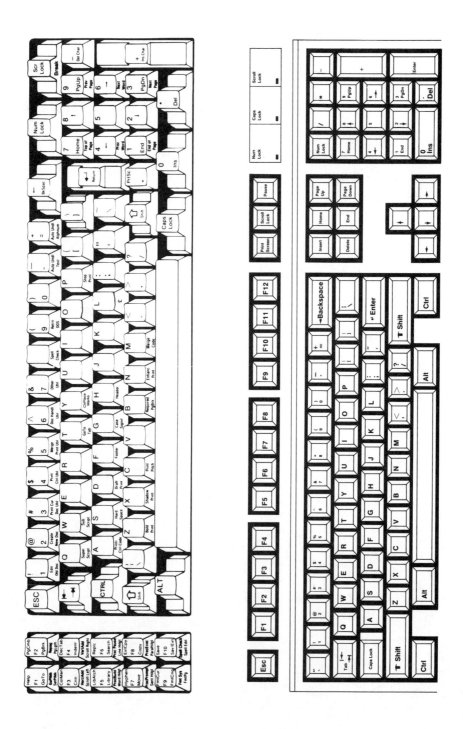

B
Menu Map

Following are the MultiMate menus referred to throughout this book. The Main Menu appears in the center.

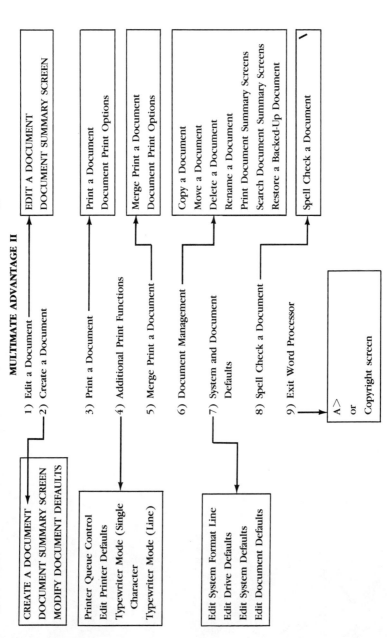

MULTIMATE ADVANTAGE II

CREATE A DOCUMENT
DOCUMENT SUMMARY SCREEN
MODIFY DOCUMENT DEFAULTS

1) Edit a Document
2) Create a Document

EDIT A DOCUMENT
DOCUMENT SUMMARY SCREEN

3) Print a Document

Print a Document
Document Print Options

4) Additional Print Functions

Printer Queue Control
Edit Printer Defaults
Typewriter Mode (Single
Character
Typewriter Mode (Line)

5) Merge Print a Document

Merge Print a Document
Document Print Options

6) Document Management

Copy a Document
Move a Document
Delete a Document
Rename a Document
Print Document Summary Screens
Search Document Summary Screens
Restore a Backed-Up Document

7) System and Document
Defaults

Edit System Format Line
Edit Drive Defaults
Edit System Defaults
Edit Document Defaults

8) Spell Check a Document

Spell Check a Document

9) Exit Word Processor

A>
or
Copyright screen

Index

C

More Computer Knowledge from Que

FOLD HERE

Place
Stamp
Here

———————————————
———————————————
———————————————

———————————————

Que Corporation
P.O. Box 90
Carmel, IN 46032

REGISTRATION CARD

Register your copy of *Using MultiMate Advantage,* 2nd Edition, and receive information about Que's newest products. Complete this registration card and return it to Que Corporation, P.O. Box 90, Carmel, IN 46032.

Name _____ Phone _____

Company _____ Title _____

Address _____

City _____ ST _____ ZIP _____

Please check the appropriate answers:

Where did you buy *Using MultiMate Advantage,* 2nd Edition?
- ☐ Bookstore (name: _____)
- ☐ Computer store (name: _____)
- ☐ Catalog (name: _____)
- ☐ Direct from Que
- ☐ Other: _____

How many computer books do you buy a year?
- ☐ 1 or less
- ☐ 2-5
- ☐ 6-10
- ☐ More than 10

How many Que books do you own?
- ☐ 1
- ☐ 2-5
- ☐ 6-10
- ☐ More than 10

How long have you been using MultiMate software?
- ☐ Less than 6 months
- ☐ 6 months to 1 year
- ☐ 1 to 3 years
- ☐ Over 3 years

What influenced your purchase of this book?
- ☐ Personal recommendation
- ☐ Advertisement
- ☐ In-store display
- ☐ Price
- ☐ Que catalog
- ☐ Que postcard
- ☐ Que's reputation
- ☐ Other: _____

How would you rate the overall content of *Using MultiMate Advantage,* 2nd Edition?
- ☐ Very good
- ☐ Good
- ☐ Not useful
- ☐ Poor

How would you rate the *Libraries chapter*?
- ☐ Very good
- ☐ Good
- ☐ Not useful
- ☐ Poor

How would you rate the *On-File chapter*?
- ☐ Very good
- ☐ Good
- ☐ Not useful
- ☐ Poor

How would you rate the *Advanced Utilities chapter*?
- ☐ Very good
- ☐ Good
- ☐ Not useful
- ☐ Poor

What do you like *best* about *Using MultiMate Advantage,* 2nd Edition?

What do you like *least* about *Using MultiMate Advantage,* 2nd Edition?

How do you use this book?

What other Que products do you own?

What other software do you own?

Please feel free to list any other comments you may have about *Using MultiMate Advantage,* 2nd Edition.

_____

_____

_____

_____

FOLD HERE

- -

_____

_____

_____

_____

Que Corporation
P.O. Box 90
Carmel, IN 46032

BOOK REGISTRATION

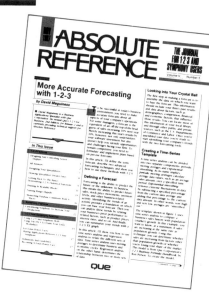

Here's a tiny sample of the kinds of articles you'll read in every issue of *Absolute Reference*:

Discover the incredible power of macros— shortcuts for hundreds of applications and subroutines.
- A macro for formatting text
- Monitoring preset database conditions with a macro
- Three ways to design macro menus
- Building macros with string formulas
- Having fun with the marching macro
- Using the ROWs macro
- Generating a macro for tracking elapsed time

New applications and new solutions—every issue gives you novel ways to harness 1-2-3 and Symphony.
- Creating customized menus for your spreadsheets
- How to use criteria to unlock your spreadsheet program's data management power
- Using spreadsheets to monitor investments
- Improving profits with more effective sales forecasts
- An easy way to calculate year-to-date performance
- Using /Data Fill to streamline counting and range filling

Extend your uses—and your command— of spreadsheets.
- Printing spreadsheets sideways can help sell your ideas
- How to add goal-seeking capabilities to your spreadsheet

- Hiding columns to create custom worksheet printouts
- Lay out your spreadsheet for optimum memory management
- Toward an "intelligent" spreadsheet
- A quick way to erase extraneous zeros

Techniques for avoiding pitfalls and repairing the damage when disaster occurs.
- Preventing and trapping errors in your worksheet
- How to create an auditable spreadsheet
- Pinpointing specific errors in your spreadsheets
- Ways to avoid failing formulas
- Catching common debugging and data-entry errors
- Detecting data-entry errors
- Protecting worksheets from accidental (or deliberate) destruction
- Avoiding disaster with the /System command

Objective product reviews—we accept *no advertising*, so you can trust our editors' outspoken opinions.
- Metro Desktop Manager
- Freelance Plus
- Informix
- 4Word, InWord, Write-in
- Spreadsheet Analyst
- 101 macros for 1-2-3

Mail this card today for your free evaluation copy or call 1-800-277-7999.

THE JOURNAL
FOR 1 2 3 AND
SYMPHONY USERS

Que Corporation
11711 N. College Avenue
Carmel, Indiana 46032-9903